EVALUATION OF JUVENILES' COMPETENCE TO STAND TRIAL

BEST PRACTICES IN FORENSIC MENTAL HEALTH ASSESSMENT

Series Editors

Thomas Grisso, Alan M. Goldstein, and Kirk Heilbrun

Series Advisory Board

Paul Appelbaum, Richard Bonnie, and John Monahan

Titles in the Series

Foundations of Forensic Mental Health Assessment, *Kirk Heilbrun, Thomas Grisso, and Alan M. Goldstein*

Criminal Titles

Evaluation of Competence to Stand Trial, *Patricia A. Zapf and Ronald Roesch*

Evaluation of Criminal Responsibility, *Ira K. Packer*

Evaluation of Capacity to Confess, *Alan M. Goldstein and Naomi Goldstein*

Evaluation of Sexually Violent Predators, *Philip H. Witt and Mary Alice Conroy*

Evaluation for Risk of Violence in Adults, *Kirk Heilbrun*

Jury Selection, *Margaret Bull Kovera and Brian L. Cutler*

Evaluation for Capital Sentencing, *Mark D. Cunningham*

Eyewitness Identification, *Brian L. Cutler and Margaret Bull Kovera*

Civil Titles

Evaluation of Capacity to Consent to Treatment, *Scott Y.H. Kim*

Evaluation for Substituted Judgment, *Eric Y. Drogin and Curtis L. Barrett*

Evaluation for Civil Commitment, *Debra Pinals and Douglas Mossman*

Evaluation for Harassment and Discrimination Claims, *William Foote and Jane Goodman-Delahunty*

Evaluation of Workplace Disability, *Lisa D. Piechowski*

Juvenile and Family Titles

Evaluation for Child Custody, *Geri S.W. Fuhrmann*

Evaluation of Juveniles' Competence to Stand Trial, *Ivan Kruh and Thomas Grisso*

Evaluation for Risk of Violence in Juveniles, *Robert Hoge and D.A. Andrews*

Evaluation for Child Protection, *Kathryn Kuehnle, Mary Connell, Karen S. Budd, and Jennifer Clark*

Evaluation for Disposition and Transfer of Juvenile Offenders, *Randall T. Salekin*

EVALUATION OF JUVENILES' COMPETENCE TO STAND TRIAL

IVAN KRUH

THOMAS GRISSO

2009

OXFORD
UNIVERSITY PRESS

Oxford University Press, Inc., publishes works that further
Oxford University's objective of excellence
in research, scholarship, and education.

Oxford New York
Auckland Cape Town Dar es Salaam Hong Kong Karachi
Kuala Lumpur Madrid Melbourne Mexico City Nairobi
New Delhi Shanghai Taipei Toronto

With offices in
Argentina Austria Brazil Chile Czech Republic France Greece
Guatemala Hungary Italy Japan Poland Portugal Singapore
South Korea Switzerland Thailand Turkey Ukraine Vietnam

Published by Oxford University Press, Inc.
198 Madison Avenue, New York, New York 10016
www.oup.com

Oxford is a registered trademark of Oxford University Press

Library of Congress Cataloging-in-Publication Data

Kruh, Ivan.
Evaluation of juveniles' competence to stand trial / Ivan Kruh, Thomas Grisso.
p. ; cm. — (Best practices in forensic mental health assessment)
Includes bibliographical references and index.
ISBN 978-0-19-532307-8
1. Forensic psychiatry. 2. Competency to stand trial. 3. Child psychiatry.
I. Grisso, Thomas. II. Title. III. Series.
[DNLM: 1. Forensic Psychiatry—Canada. 2. Forensic Psychiatry—United
States. 3. Adolescent—Canada. 4. Adolescent—United States. 5. Child—
Canada. 6. Child—United States. 7. Mental Competency—legislation &
jurisprudence— Canada. 8. Mental Competency—legislation & jurispru-
dence—United States. 9. Mental Competency—psychology—Canada.
10. Mental Competency— psychology—United States. W 740 K94e 2008]
RA1151.K8623 2008
614'.1—dc22

2008026675

9 8 7 6 5 4 3 2 1

Printed in the United States of America on acid-free paper

For you, Nana (1910–2008)
I.K.

About Best Practices in Forensic Mental Health Assessment

The recent growth of the fields of forensic psychology and forensic psychiatry has created a need for this book series describing best practices in forensic mental health assessment (FMHA). Currently, forensic evaluations are conducted by mental health professionals for a variety of criminal, civil, and juvenile legal questions. The research foundation supporting these assessments has become broader and deeper in recent decades. Consensus has become clearer on the recognition of essential requirements for ethical and professional conduct. In the larger context of the current emphasis on "empirically supported" assessment and intervention in psychiatry and psychology, the specialization of FMHA has advanced sufficiently to justify a series devoted to best practices. Although this series focuses mainly on evaluations conducted by psychologists and psychiatrists, the fundamentals and principles offered would also apply to evaluations conducted by clinical social workers, psychiatric nurses, and other mental health professionals.

This series describes "best practice" as empirically supported (when the relevant research is available), legally relevant, and consistent with applicable ethical and professional standards. Authors of the books in this series identify the approaches that seem best, while incorporating what is practical and acknowledging that best practice represents a goal to which the forensic clinician should aspire rather than a standard that can always be met. The American Academy of Forensic Psychology assisted the editors in enlisting the consultation of board-certified forensic psychologists specialized in each topic area. Board-certified forensic psychiatrists were also consultants on many of the volumes. Their comments on the manuscripts helped to ensure that the methods described in these volumes represent a generally accepted view of best practice.

The series' authors were selected for their specific expertise in a particular area. At the broadest level, however, certain general principles apply to all types of forensic evaluations. Rather than repeat those fundamental principles in every volume, the series offers them in the first volume, *Foundations of Forensic Mental Health Assessment*. Reading the first book followed by a specific topical book will provide the reader with both the general principles that the specific topic shares with all forensic evaluations and those that are particular to the specific assessment question.

The specific topics of the 19 books were selected by the series editors as the most important and oft-considered areas of forensic assessment conducted by mental health professionals and behavioral scientists. Each of the 19 topical books is organized according to a common template. The authors address the applicable legal context, forensic mental health concepts, and empirical foundations and limits in the "Foundation" part of the book. They then describe preparation for the evaluation, data collection, data interpretation, and report writing and testimony in the "Application" part of the book. This creates a fairly uniform approach to considering these areas across different topics. All authors in this series have attempted to be as concise as possible in addressing best practice in their area. In addition, topical volumes feature elements to make them user-friendly in actual practice. These elements include boxes that highlight especially important information, relevant case law, best-practice guidelines, and cautions against common pitfalls. A glossary of key terms is also provided in each volume.

We hope the series will be useful for different groups of individuals. Practicing forensic clinicians will find succinct, current information relevant to their practice. Those who are in training to specialize in forensic mental health assessment (whether in formal training or in the process of respecialization) should find helpful the combination of broadly applicable considerations presented in the first volume together with the more specific aspects of other volumes in the series. Those who teach and supervise trainees can offer these volumes as a guide for practices to which the trainee can aspire. Researchers and scholars interested in FMHA best practice may find researchable ideas, particularly topics that have received insufficient research attention to date. Judges and attorneys with questions about FMHA best practice will find these books relevant and concise. Clinical and forensic administrators who run agencies, court clinics, and hospitals in which litigants are assessed may also use some of the books in this series to establish expectancies for evaluations performed by professionals in their agencies.

We also anticipate that the 19 specific books in this series will serve as reference works that help courts and attorneys evaluate the quality of forensic mental health professionals' evaluations. A word of caution is in order, however. These volumes focus on best practice, not what is minimally acceptable legally or ethically. Courts involved in malpractice litigation, or ethics committees or licensure boards considering complaints, should not expect that materials describing best practice easily or necessarily translate into the minimally acceptable professional conduct that is typically at issue in such proceedings.

The present volume describes the "youngest" forensic evaluation in the series. For reasons described in Chapter 1, evaluations of youth's competence to stand trial in juvenile court were rarely performed until little more than a decade ago. In recent years, however, many juvenile courts order hundreds of these evaluations annually. This short history has had two consequences: (a) General information about models, methods, and practices for performing these evaluations is relatively scarce, and (b) development of the legal concept of competence to stand trial when applied to adolescents and juvenile delinquency proceedings is incomplete. This volume offers guidance for forensic mental health examiners based on the latest developments in evaluations for juveniles' competence to stand trial. It also provides a foundation on which greater certainty of methods can be built as new laws, research, and assessment practices in this area unfold in the coming years.

Thomas Grisso
Alan M. Goldstein
Kirk Heilbrun

Acknowledgments

This book reflects collective thinking within the field of forensic mental health regarding juvenile competence to stand trial (CST). It is really no more than a synthesis, summary, and application of the work of the many scholars, researchers, and clinicians cited within the book. It is a testament to each of them that the field of juvenile CST has progressed to the point where such a manual could be offered.

In preparation of the book, Randy Otto and Alan Goldstein carefully scrutinized an earlier draft of the manuscript, asked probing questions, and identified gaps, yielding a more accurate and usable guide. Anne Graffam Walker also kindly provided permission to include her work on forensic interviews of youth.

Ivan Kruh would also like to acknowledge that this book is an outcome of the gifts of many past mentors who cultivated his thinking on development, psychopathology, assessment, and forensic work. Most especially helpful have been Paul Frick, Jean Spruill, Carl Clements, and Stan Brodsky (University of Alabama); Gregg Gagliardi, Bruce Gage, Carl Redick, and Murray Hart (Western State Hospital in Tacoma); and Holly Galbreath and Jack McClellan (Child Study & Treatment Center in Tacoma). Much of the thought offered here reflects years of discussions with I.K.'s colleague at CSTC Forensic Services, Fran Lexcen, their assistant Jake Holeman, and the talented trainees with whom they have had the honor to collaborate.

Contents

FOUNDATION

The Legal Context | 1

Juvenile defendants' *competence to stand trial* (CST) has only recently become a concern for criminal and juvenile courts, but is now increasingly common. Understanding *juvenile CST* as a legal issue requires a grasp of the traditional concept of CST and of its differences when applied to juveniles. First, it is important to understand the original rationale of CST in criminal law, as well as the standards and procedures that govern its application. An introduction to the relevant issues is provided here; interested readers might also wish to consult the criminal competence volume in this series, *Evaluation of Competence to Stand Trial* (Zapf & Roesch, 2009), for more information. Second, clinicians must become familiar with the more recent specific application of CST to juveniles being adjudicated by the criminal and juvenile courts. This application of CST to adolescent defendants has not been carried out through a simple extension of its use in criminal court with adults, as a number of problems and unresolved issues have become apparent with juvenile CST. These issues, discussed in this chapter, must be understood by clinicians who assess juvenile CST.

Competence to stand trial (CST) is the legal and, therefore, traditional term of reference for the competence issue addressed in this volume (Mossman et al., 2007). Several newer terms, such as *adjudicative competence* and *competence to proceed to adjudication*, have appeared in the literature in recent years. Such terms can be seen as more appropriate in this context, as many juvenile courts do not use the term *trial* but rather use terms like *adjudication hearing*. These newer terms are also favored because, as discussed later in this chapter, the law is concerned with the ability of the defendant to participate in all stages of the adjudication process, including pretrial hearings, consultations with defense counsel to consider defenses, and plea agreements, not just at trial (Grisso, 2005; Mossman et al., 2007). Clinicians must conceptualize the target construct in this broader way. To be consistent with most statutory references and because of the familiarity of the term CST among legal parties, however, CST is used throughout this volume.

Concerns about CST may arise regarding juvenile defendants in either criminal or juvenile court. Some of the issues discussed in this volume are relevant to both contexts and others are specific to one or the other context. Therefore, simple reference to "juvenile CST" can become confusing and more explicit use of terms is necessary. *Juvenile CST* will be used as a general reference to the CST of juvenile defendants regardless of the court jurisdiction. *Juvenile court CST* will refer specifically to the CST of juvenile defendants being adjudicated in juvenile court. *Juvenile CST in criminal court* will refer to the CST of juvenile defendants being adjudicated in criminal court. *Criminal court CST* will be used as a general reference to CST in criminal court, whether referring to juvenile or adult defendants. Finally, *adult CST* will refer specifically to the CST of adult defendants being adjudicated in criminal court.

Sociolegal Purpose and History

The Rationale for CST in Criminal Court

Since at least the seventeeth century, English common law has appreciated the fundamental unfairness and threat to the integrity of the justice system posed by trying individuals who cannot meaningfully participate in the proceedings (Melton et al., 2007). Meaningful participation requires that defendants be able to comprehend the proceedings and punishments they face and mount a viable defense against the charges. The requirement for meaningful participation is intended to yield defense decisions that reflect the defendant's wishes, promote accurate and just adjudications, and retain the integrity and dignity of the court process (Grisso, 2003a).

INFO

Competence to stand trial requires meaningful participation of the individual in his defense at various stages of the proceedings.

The modern concept of CST addresses a variety of functional limitations typically caused by mental illness that threaten meaningful participation at various stages of the adjudication process (Bonnie & Grisso, 2000). By requiring this meaningful participation of defendants, both the defendant being tried and the state's pursuit of fair and reliable adjudications are protected (Zapf & Roesch, in press). In the United States, CST in criminal proceedings has Constitutional implications, because a lack of adequate abilities threatens Sixth Amendment guarantees of rights to effective counsel, to confront one's accusers, and to present evidence on one's own behalf (Wulach, 1980). In fact, CST is considered "fundamental to an adversary system of justice" and the conviction of a defendant who is *Incompetent to Stand Trial* (IST) is a violation of due-process protections (*Drope v. Missouri*, 1975).

The Evolution of Juvenile CST in Criminal Court

Prior to the 1990s, application of CST to juveniles in criminal courts raised little special concern. Most juveniles who were adjudicated in U.S. criminal courts arrived there through *judicial transfers,* which required discretionary decisions through court hearings. Decisions were based on several specified criteria, such as the youth's maturity level (Kruh & Brodsky, 1997). As a consequence of this judicial oversight, most youth who were transferred were close to the upper age of juvenile court jurisdiction and had "mature" offense histories (Bonnie & Grisso, 2000).

The situation changed in the late 1980s and early 1990s, as juvenile arrests for violent crime increased and peaked in 1994 (Office of Juvenile Justice and Delinquency Prevention [OJJDP], 1998, 1999). In response to this trend, legislatures changed laws to allow for the criminal court adjudication of younger juveniles and for a wider array of allegations, resulting in increasing numbers of criminal court adjudications of juveniles (Grisso, 2003b). In recent years, more than 200,000 juveniles have been prosecuted annually in adult courts (Allard & Young, 2002). The reforms introduced at this time also expanded mechanisms for trying juveniles in criminal court that did not require case-by-case judicial scrutiny. These changes have probably led to a more developmentally and psychologically heterogeneous

INFO

Most jurisdictions do not require that a juvenile undergo CST evaluation before being transferred to criminal court.

group of juveniles being tried as adults (Bonnie & Grisso, 2000).

Given these legislative reforms, many forensic mental health scholars have called for universal consideration of CST prior to the criminal court adjudication of juveniles (Bonnie & Grisso, 2000; Grisso et al., 2003; Johnson, 2006; Kruh & Brodsky, 1997; MacArthur Foundation Research Network, 2006; Redding, 2000; but see American Prosecutors Research Institute [APRI], 2006, for a different opinion). Nonetheless, only a few jurisdictions require that juveniles be evaluated and found competent before they can be transferred from juvenile court to criminal court (e.g., Virginia) or have explicitly identified CST as a consideration in transfer decisions (e.g., Alabama). Additionally, most jurisdictions have no requirement that juveniles being tried in criminal court be screened for CST (Bonnie & Grisso, 2000). Consequently, there is concern that many juveniles being tried in criminal court may lack important capacities for participation in their trials without that problem being identified.

The Evolution of Juvenile CST in Juvenile Court

Consideration of juvenile court CST has also received attention only recently, but for different reasons than juvenile CST in criminal court. Initially, the juvenile court was distinguished from criminal court by a *parens patriae* philosophy. This approach afforded judges the discretion of a benevolent parent who, along with a staff of social workers and treatment providers, sought to meet the "best interests of the child." Proceedings tended to be informal and expeditious in an effort to meet individualized, rehabilitative goals. Formal evidentiary rules and adversarial fact-finding were largely absent, so that all relevant information could be considered by the court. Within this rehabilitative context the extent to which the juvenile could understand the proceedings or assist in defending oneself was generally considered irrelevant (Grisso, 1998; Platt, 1969).

1960s AND 1970s

During the 1960s, the U.S. Supreme Court recognized that the state was abusing its *parens patriae* powers by failing to actually provide youth the rehabilitative outcomes that were promised in exchange for their liberty. Decisions in *Kent v. United States* (1966) and *In re Gault* (1967) ushered in an era of due process requirements for juveniles. The court extended to juvenile defendants the rights to written notice of the charges, to be represented by counsel, to avoid self-incrimination, and to confront and cross-examine witnesses.

The initial practical response to *Kent* and *Gault* was limited, as many jurisdictions continued to see protections as unnecessary in a rehabilitative court system (Bonnie & Grisso, 2000). Juvenile court proceedings gradually took a bifurcated form. The adjudication stage was adversarial, with attorneys advocating for and zealously defending their clients, but the disposition stage remained case specific and therapeutically motivated (Grisso, 1998; 2003b; Tobey, Grisso, & Schwartz, 2000). Although CST is closely tied to the logic of an adversarial adjudication process, the U.S. Supreme Court never specified if CST should be extended to juvenile court, if the specific due process rights extended to juvenile court constitute an exhaustive list, or whether state courts could extend further protections (Johnson, 2006). Still, within 20 years of these decisions, about one-third of U.S. states recognized the right of juveniles to be competent in juvenile court (Grisso, Miller, & Sales, 1987). For reasons that are not completely clear, however, the issue continued to be raised rarely and few CST evaluations were conducted. When the issue was raised, it was sometimes because court personnel wanted to obtain mental health diagnoses or treatment, not out of actual concern for youth's capacities as defendants (Grisso, 1997).

1980s AND 1990s

Building upon the increased attention to due process protections during the 1960s and 1970s, the 1980s and 1990s yielded a further "criminalizing" of the juvenile court (Johnson, 2006). This process paralleled the criminal court changes discussed earlier in

INFO

The rise in the number of cases involving younger children has led to increased recognition of juvenile court CST.

this chapter. Many "purpose clauses" in juvenile court legislation were redrafted to elevate the importance of punishment, accountability, and community protection to levels on par with if not above rehabilitation (Bonnie & Grisso, 2000). Juvenile court dispositions began to increase in length and severity, and "secondary consequences" of juvenile court adjudications also increased, such as juvenile offenses being included when calculating the application of three-strikes laws.

In addition, the age restrictions for juvenile court were lowered in many jurisdictions, allowing younger children to be charged with offenses (Bonnie & Grisso, 2000). Arrests involving juveniles age 12 or younger grew 24% between 1980 and 1995, while those involving juveniles ages 13 and 14 increased 54% during that time (Butts & Snyder, 1997). By 2004, 57% of all juvenile court delinquency cases involved youth age 15 or younger at the time of referral (Stahl et al., 2007). Juvenile offenses became more common in response to minimally serious misdeeds such as "stealing a roll of quarters [or] writing one's name on the gymnasium wall with permanent marker" (Levitt & Trollinger, 2002, p. 63). Consequently, children as young as 7 are being adjudicated for behaviors that were once managed by parents, schools, mental health services, and informal police intervention (Oberlander, Goldstein, & Ho, 2001).

With younger children facing more adversarial proceedings and more serious sanctions, defense counsel increasingly raised the question of juvenile court CST (Grisso, 2003b). Legislators and courts also responded. By 2000, half of the states explicitly recognized CST as a requirement for delinquency adjudication (Bonnie & Grisso, 2000).

CURRENT STATUS AND FUTURE OUTLOOK OF EVALUATIONS OF JUVENILE COURT CST

Evaluations of juvenile court CST were substantial by the early 2000s and are still increasing annually in many jurisdictions (Grisso

& Quinlan, 2005). These numbers may continue to increase, especially as juvenile courts and attorneys move beyond gross sensitivity to marked dysfunction and become more sensitive to the more normative adolescent weaknesses that can threaten CST. These evaluations are complicated by a court system marked by a complex tension between rehabilitative and retributive ideals that varies from jurisdiction to jurisdiction (Johnson, 2006; Steinberg & Schwartz, 2000).

Legal Procedures and Standards

The Legal Procedure

Most basic aspects of criminal court CST evaluation procedures and standards are fairly uniform across U.S. jurisdictions and Canada. However, procedure details do differ. Also, a few states have developed procedures or standards in juvenile court that differ significantly from local procedures for criminal court (Grisso, 1998; Johnson, 2006).

REQUESTING A COMPETENCE DETERMINATION

Defendants are presumed to be competent (*Medina v. California,* 1992), and with only rare exceptions (e.g., very young defendants accused of first degree or capital murder in Arkansas), there is no requirement that all defendants be examined to determine competence. Although CST is typically first questioned by defense counsel, doubt may be raised by anyone involved in the case. CST can be questioned at any point in the proceedings, including at multiple points, although it is typically raised prior to the adjudication hearing or trial.

Based on *Pate v. Robinson* (1966), the court *must* hold a competence hearing when the court finds that there is probable cause to doubt that the defendant is competent. The prosecutor can present evidence challenging the existence of probable cause, but the *threshold for questioning competence* is not difficult to reach. Courts will rarely refuse a request for a CST evaluation because of the concern that without it the outcome of the case would consequently be reversed (Melton et al., 2007). The court is more likely to stay the proceedings and order an evaluation.

INFO

Local laws differ in specifying how CST evaluations are to be conducted. These laws may specify

- what types of professionals can conduct the evaluations,
- specialized training or credentialing needed by examiners,
- how many examiners are needed,
- where evaluations may occur (such as at an inpatient psychiatric facility or the detention center),
- who can and cannot be present during evaluation interviews,
- how much time is allotted for evaluations to be completed (ranging from about 10 to 90 days in various states),
- and/or broad requirements for the contents of evaluation reports.

THE COMPETENCE EVALUATION

Once the determination has been made that a CST evaluation is needed, mechanisms by which courts can obtain the evaluation or evaluations vary from jurisdiction to jurisdiction (see Grisso & Quinlan, 2005, and Grisso, Cocozza, Steadman, Fisher, & Greer, 1994, for full descriptions of various CST evaluation system models in juvenile and criminal courts, respectively). Typical means of evaluation include court-based assessment clinics, state-run evaluation services, appointed and contracted service providers, and/or clinicians in private practice.

JUDICIAL DETERMINATION OF THE COMPETENCE QUESTION

After the evaluations are completed, the parties may find themselves with one or more expert opinions about CST. The translation of the professional opinion(s) into a legal determination is the role of the court. A formal court hearing determining the matter of CST after the evaluation is not mandatory (Dawson & Kraus, 2005). When a single expert opinion has been sought or multiple experts offer consistent opinions, it is common for both parties to stipulate to the findings. However, when multiple expert opinions diverge, a contested hearing may be held, which will often require expert testimony from the clinicians to examine the evaluation results and allow challenges from each party. Occasionally, a juvenile CST hearing may be necessary even when only one examiner is involved if there is an issue of ambiguity (e.g., the threshold for competence) and both parties believe they can argue their respective positions from the information contained in the report.

Local laws govern the procedural rules for CST hearings and standards and burdens of proof. Typically, the burden of proof that a defendant is IST falls to the defendant by no higher standard than preponderance of the evidence (*Cooper v. Oklahoma*, 1996; *Medina v. California*, 1992).

DISPOSITION AND REMEDIATION

If the defendant is found competent by the court, the legal proceedings resume. If the defendant is found IST, adjudication by plea or by trial and any proceedings that could be adverse to the defendant's interests are barred. If the defendant is IST, the case may be dismissed if the charges are not serious or if the defendant is deemed unlikely to be made competent within a legally defined time frame (usually ranging from 90 days to 1 year). If the charges are dismissed, there may be other mechanisms for mandated psychiatric treatment, such as *civil commitment*. When charges are dismissed due to incompetence, they are typically dismissed *without prejudice,* meaning the charges could be reinstated at a later point.

In many cases, however, the incompetent defendant will be legally mandated to receive services aimed at establishing CST so that the adjudication process can go forward. The CST intervention is traditionally referred to as *competence restoration,* based on the adult model of restoring the stable functioning of psychotic defendants. Applying the term restoration to juveniles, however, is often a misnomer. As discussed later in this chapter, many youth found IST have not yet developed capacities sufficient to participate meaningfully in trials, so that the notion of "restoring" those capacities is inaccurate (Grisso, 2005; Levitt & Trollinger, 2002; Viljoen & Roesch, 2007). The term *competence remediation* is more appropriate (Grisso, 2005). Although many laws and systems continue to use the more traditional language, the term remediation is used throughout this volume.

It is not clear to what extent incompetent juveniles in criminal court are provided remediation services that differ from remediation services typically applied to adults. Given the immature status of juvenile CST law, it seems unlikely that many jurisdictions have formal mechanisms for providing unique services to juveniles. Criminal court remediation services are often provided by public mental health systems at a state mental hospital or a forensic treatment facility and usually involve inpatient hospitalization. Hospitalization often occurs without any specific holding that it is medically necessary, appropriate, or the least restrictive setting within which adequate services could be provided (Melton et al., 2007), but some jurisdictions with alternative remediation mechanisms do require that these issues be examined (Grisso, 2003a). Inpatient criminal court remediation programs are bound by restrictions against indefinite commitment (see *Jackson v. Indiana*, 1972).

CASE LAW

Jackson v. Indiana (1972)

● held that the state cannot commit an individual for purposes of competence restoration unless there is a "substantial probability" that competence can be restored and, even then, may do so for no more than a "reasonable period of time"

States vary in the procedures for remediation with incompetent juveniles to be tried in juvenile court (Johnson, 2006; Redding & Frost, 2001). As of 1987, all states that recognized juvenile CST included provisions for treatment of juveniles found IST (Grisso et al., 1987). About half of the states allowed the juvenile court to maintain jurisdiction over the case and to resume the adjudication if the juvenile was successfully treated and gained CST; the other half provided only for civil commitment and loss of juvenile court jurisdiction over the case. The length of time allowed for juvenile court CST remediation continues to vary across jurisdictions, and many states still do not have specific parameters (Grisso, 1998; Viljoen & Roesch, 2007).

REHEARINGS ON COMPETENCE

Once CST remediation services have been initiated, defendants are returned to court under one of three circumstances:

1. when it is opined that the intervention was successful;

2. when it is opined that the competence remediation is not likely to be successful; or

3. after a statutorily mandated period of remediation efforts.

At any of these points, formal post-remediation CST evaluations and/or hearings may be required. As in the pre-remediation hearings, the court can then find the defendant competent and proceed with adjudication, find the defendant IST and unremediable and dismiss the charges, or find the defendant IST and in need of continued competence remediation. If successful remediation cannot be accomplished within a statutorily defined time frame, the case must be dismissed and the defendant must be released or (if appropriate) civilly committed for treatment (*Jackson v. Indiana,* 1972).

The Legal Standard

In many states, the traditional legal standards for CST that evolved in criminal court are applied to juvenile defendants in criminal or juvenile court. The extent to which the same standards are applied identically can raise a number of difficult issues because of both the developmental status of children and adolescents and ways in which juvenile and criminal courts differ in their purposes. Such issues are discussed later in this chapter. First, however, it is necessary for examiners to be familiar with the traditional standards for CST that have long been employed in criminal court proceedings.

THE *DUSKY* STANDARD

The legal concept of CST refers to the individual defendant's abilities to understand, believe, or do those things necessary at a minimum for undertaking the role of defendant (Grisso, 2003a). Although earlier cases identified and addressed the need for defendants to be competent, the CST construct was classically defined for U.S. courts in *Dusky v. United States* (1960), where the Court held that it is not enough for a district judge to find that "the defendant is oriented to time and place and has some recollection of the events, but that the test must be whether he has sufficient present ability to consult with his lawyer with a reasonable degree of rational understanding—and whether he has a rational as well as factual understanding of the proceedings against him" (p. 402).

A closer analysis of some of the terms used in the *Dusky* test help clarify its meaning:

- *Sufficient* ability and *reasonable* understanding specify that CST does not require complete and fully unimpaired functioning. *Reasonable* also implies relativity in relation to the context. That is, abilities must be better developed for complex cases than for simple cases.

- *Present* ability specifies that CST is explicitly a "current mental state question." Therefore, by definition, CST is independent of retrospective forensic mental health questions, such as mental state at the time of the offense. However, *present* is generally accepted to include the immediate future, as the trial process will typically proceed for some brief period after a determination of competence.

- *Ability* connotes that the test seeks to identify individuals who are unable to function adequately, not those who are unfamiliar with appropriate functioning or those who choose not to participate adequately.

- The distinction between *factual* and *rational* understanding communicates that more than a concrete, rote understanding is required to possess CST. The distinction between these concepts will be discussed in greater detail in Chapter 2.

- The *and* linking the two prongs indicates that both components are necessary.

DEFINING CST BEYOND *DUSKY*

Some U.S. Supreme Court and federal court decisions have helped clarify what *Dusky* means and how to apply it. In *Drope v. Missouri* (1975), the Court held that a competent defendant must be able to "assist in preparing his defense" (420 U.S. 162, 171 [1975]). Further, in the Court's CST decision, the characterization of the defendant by defense counsel is not dispositive of CST, the defendant's court demeanor is relevant but does not outweigh expert testimony regarding CST, and the court must be alert to changes in the defendant during the proceedings that may suggest incompetence.

Several cases have held that a psychiatric diagnosis on its own is insufficient for concluding that a defendant is IST (*Rees v. Peyton,* 1966; *United States v. Villegas,* 1990; *Wilson v. United States,* 1968). Rather, a functional analysis of the *impact* of that diagnosis upon the defendant's abilities to understand the proceedings, consult and assist counsel, and testify is required. The two latter cases highlighted that the anticipated nature of the case and necessary preparation for it may be relevant to CST determinations. Also, disruptive behavior, in and of itself, is not an adequate foundation for a finding of incompetence (*United States v. Holmes,* 1987).

CASE LAW
Drope v. Missouri (1975)

- further clarified the *Dusky* standard
- required that the defendant be able to assist in preparing his defense

GODINEZ v. MORAN (1993)

For some time there were threads of inconsistent case law regarding the relationship between CST and decisional competence to waive rights. Some courts held that there is a single CST standard to be applied across all situations, while others held that certain case-specific situations (especially the waiver of rights) required a higher level of ability. In the landmark case of *Godinez v. Moran* (1993), the U.S. Supreme Court decided that the standard for CST is the same as that for pleading guilty or waiving right to counsel. The Court reasoned that defendants must make complicated decisions throughout the adjudication and that a separate, higher standard for waiving rights is not necessary. One can argue that *Godinez* broadened the *Dusky* standard (e.g., Melton et al., 2007; Stafford, 2003), or that it simply emphasized the importance of decision-making abilities that was already implicit within the standard (e.g., Grisso, 2003a; Rogers & Shuman, 2005). In either case, there is now general acceptance that CST includes a "defendant's capacities to participate in all aspects of the adjudicative process and to participate in whatever decisions might be required during that process" (Grisso, 2005, p. 10).

JURISDICTIONAL STATUTES AND CASE LAW

Every U.S. jurisdiction has adopted a statutory definition of CST that closely resembles the *Dusky* test (Favole, 1983). The *Dusky* test remains a "standard [that] establishes the minimum criteria to satisfy constitutional safeguards" (Rogers, Tillbrook, & Sewell, 2004, p. 4). Jurisdictions can elaborate upon these requirements (*Godinez v. Moran,* 1993) and several states have done so (Rogers & Shuman, 2005; Stafford, 2003). Florida, for example, requires examiners to consider *Dusky*-based abilities including the capacity to disclose to her attorney facts pertinent to the proceedings and the ability to testify relevantly. Whereas jurisdictional elaborations of the *Dusky* standard are not necessarily binding outside of that

chapter 1

INFO

Traditionally, incompetence to stand trial must be caused by a mental disorder.

jurisdiction, familiarity with such efforts can help examiners see how some courts may interpret the CST construct.

A common jurisdictional augmentation of the CST standard involves the predicate requirement that functional deficits must be caused by certain mental disorders to yield incompetence. The *Dusky* case described dysfunction without reference to type or severity of the cause, but the *Drope* court discussed a "mental condition" as a possible source of incompetence. The mere presence of a mental disorder, no matter how severe, is never itself a sufficient basis for a finding of incompetence. But many jurisdictions require that a "mental disease or defect" causes the relevant CST deficits. Despite the fact that these are legal terms, most jurisdictions have offered little definitional guidance. In practice, the term mental disease typically has referred to acute psychotic disorders, such as schizophrenia or bipolar disorder, and mental defect has referred to severe cognitive deficits, such as mental retardation. Even in jurisdictions that do not specify these predicate requirements, it has been general consensus that some type of mental disorder must cause incompetence. As will be explained later, this historical relation between mental disorder and incompetence to stand trial presents difficulties when applied to youth with incapacities related to their cognitive immaturity rather than mental disorder.

Interpretations of broad statutory definitions in each jurisdiction require examination of the jurisdiction's case law. There may be state supreme court decisions that are binding in a particular jurisdiction, as well as appellate decisions that may be binding within parts of a jurisdiction and informative in others. It is beyond the scope of this volume to discuss state-by-state decisions that have refined CST generally. Examiners need to review and learn the local case law that impacts

BEST PRACTICE

Become familiar with the statutes regarding CST and the relevant case law for the jurisdictions in which you practice.

definitions of CST where they practice. *West's Annotated* publishes guides to statutes and relevant case law in each jurisdiction, and examiners should have access to these or similar summaries for the jurisdictions in which they practice.

CST IN CANADA

In 1992 the *Criminal Code of Canada* encoded an earlier CST test by requiring that defendants "in particular" be able to 1) "understand the nature or object of the proceedings," 2) "understand the possible consequences of the proceedings," and 3) "communicate with counsel." The phrase *in particular* suggests that these three criteria are not exclusive to the determination and that other incapacities could be relevant (Roesch, Zapf, Eaves, & Webster, 1998). Nonetheless, CST is often seen narrower in scope in Canada than in the United States (Viljoen & Roesch, 2007). Consistent with that interpretation, the case of *Regina. v. Taylor* (1992) established that the test is one of "limited cognitive capacity" and does not require the independent ability to act in one's own best interests (Zapf, Viljoen, Whittemore, Poythress, & Roesch, 2002). The Canadian CST test includes a predicate requirement that any inability be "on account of mental disorder" to meet the test, and case law suggests that a wide variety of disorders can qualify as the required mental disorder (Roesch et al., 1998). Although the issue of juvenile CST has not received much attention in Canadian courts, recent legislative changes that allow for juvenile court adjudications to include sentences into adulthood could yield increased concern in the future.

Applying CST to Juvenile Cases

As was described earlier in this chapter, application of CST to juveniles is relatively new to the law. Courts have long considered functional capacities of juveniles in other contexts (e.g., ability to marry, drink alcohol, drive, consent to medical treatment, enter contracts, etc.), and the U.S. Supreme Court has repeatedly referenced the immaturity of adolescent judgment relative to that of adults (e.g., *Bellotti v. Baird,* 1979; *Haley v. Ohio,* 1948; *Parham v. J.R.,* 1979) in an effort to protect youth from their own limitations (Feld, 1999).

But juvenile and criminal courts are only now beginning to confront the fact that when CST is applied to juveniles, the immaturity of adolescents compared to that of adults raises questions that are not easily managed by CST definitions and procedures that have been established in criminal law and applied to adult defendants. Moreover, neither court system has made much progress in resolving these issues and many basic questions remain unanswered (Mossman et al., 2007). As Wynkoop (2003) expressed it:

> Essentially, in most jurisdictions, juvenile adjudicative competence is an issue that has been forced upon us before the rules have been clearly established. It is analogous to playing a game with few rules and no clear criteria for scoring, but for which a referee is expected to declare a winner. (p. 47)

Until the law has had enough time to resolve these questions, examiners must be aware of the ambiguities that arise when applying CST to juveniles and recognize the limitations that these questions place on forming juvenile CST opinions. The following discussion is intended to assist in that process. First, the unique questions that arise when CST is applied to juvenile defendants being tried in juvenile court will be examined. Next, the questions that arise when CST is applied to juvenile defendants in either juvenile or criminal court will be discussed. In addition to this discussion of the issues in general, examiners must be aware of any formal or informal resolutions to these questions specifically within their jurisdiction of practice. Consultation with local legal and forensic mental health experts may be needed to accomplish this.

Do Juveniles Need to Possess CST in Juvenile Court?

Not all states have visited the issue of a right to CST in juvenile court, and the U.S. Supreme Court has never ruled on the matter. Nonetheless, it is now a "virtually inescapable conclusion" that CST is required in juvenile court (Bonnie & Grisso, 2000, p. 94). Almost all state appellate courts that have addressed juvenile court CST have concluded that it is a requirement (Grisso, 2005). Some state courts have held that juvenile court CST is a constitutional requirement (e.g., *In re Causey,* 1978). Others have reasoned that the extension of due process rights to juvenile court defendants, such as the right to legal counsel, would be meaningless without the right to be competent (e.g., *In the Interest of S.H., A Child,* 1996). However, one state (Oklahoma; *G.J.I. v. State of Oklahoma,* 1989) continues to hold that a *parens patriae* philosophy yields no juvenile court CST requirement to be adjudicated delinquent.

Even where it is clear that juvenile court CST is required, the laws for applying it are not well defined (Redding & Frost, 2001). Statutes and case law regarding CST in criminal court have unfolded since the beginning of the U.S. court system. This evolution forms the foundation of the application of CST in juvenile court. But criminal law is typically considered informative but not binding in juvenile court. Further, the direct application of criminal court CST laws to juvenile court is problematic because the laws were not intended for the unique procedures and goals of the juvenile court nor the developmental issues of the youth adjudicated in juvenile court. Consequently, when states have extended criminal court CST laws to juvenile proceedings, they have often afforded juvenile court judges wider discretion than criminal court judges in the application of the laws (e.g., *State v. E.C.,* 1996; *In re K.G.,* 2004).

Ideally, juvenile court CST issues would be clarified in juvenile court statutes and case law. However, juvenile court CST is only beginning to attract the attention of state legislatures and appellate courts. As of 2004, 26 states addressed juvenile court CST in statutes of varying specificity, with most offering only vague legal standards (Johnson, 2006; Redding & Frost, 2001). Further, case law is limited because few juvenile court cases are appealed (American Bar Association Juvenile Justice Center, 1995a). The reason for this may be that juvenile dispositions typically elapse before cases can be heard at an appellate level (Cowden & McKee, 1995) and/or because few juveniles are aware of their right to appeal (Saunders, 1981). As of 2004,

INFO

In most jurisdictions, the necessity for juvenile court CST is an implicit requirement, if not an explicit requirement.

10 states had addressed the issue of juvenile court CST through case law alone (Johnson, 2006; Redding & Frost, 2001).

Many important questions about juvenile court CST remain either unanswered or inconsistently answered across jurisdictions. The following questions are among the most important ones that often remain unresolved by law.

Does Competence in Juvenile Court Require the Same Types and Degree of Capacities as Competence in Criminal Court?

Whenever the legal question has been raised, courts and legislatures have agreed that the standard set forth in *Dusky* (or the state's own version of the *Dusky* standard) is appropriate for deciding CST in juvenile court proceedings. Nonetheless, there has been disagreement on *how* the standard should be applied—for example, the issue of whether the same degree of ability is required in juvenile court as in criminal court or whether lesser capacity is sufficient for juvenile court adjudication is under dispute.

Several arguments have been offered for maintaining what has been called an *adult norms standard* (APRI, 2007; Kruh, Sullivan, Ellis, Lexcen, & McClellan, 2006). For example, the threshold for criminal court CST is already quite low in many jurisdictions, and a juvenile court CST threshold that is still lower might increase miscarriages of justice that the CST doctrine was developed to prevent. Others, though, have argued for differential application of *Dusky* in juvenile court using schemes that we will discuss in terms of an *adjusted bar,* a *lower bar,* and a *flexible bar* (see Table 1.1).

ADJUSTED BAR

The types of demands placed on juvenile court defendants may be different than those in criminal court proceedings, so different abilities may be needed for meaningful participation. Bonnie and Grisso (2000), for example, divided juvenile court adjudications into those involving "quasi-criminal" outcomes (e.g., transfer, or adjudications that might lead to dispositions that exceed the normal jurisdiction for juvenile courts), and "ordinary" juvenile court adjudications involving sanctions that are limited in their consequences from a

Table 1.1	Schemes for the Alternative Application of *Dusky* in Juvenile Court

ADJUSTED BAR

- Eliminates the need for decisional capacities
- Requires only rudimentary understanding and fundamental communication abilities (*basic understanding and communication standard*)

LOWER BAR

- Considers a lower level or degree of *Dusky* abilities
- Competence may be determined through comparison of the juvenile's abilities either to those of average adolescents (*adolescent norms standard*) OR to those of average youth the same age (*age-peer norms standard*)

FLEXIBLE BAR

- The CST standard matches the level of needed protection given the seriousness of sanctions being faced

criminal court perspective. For the latter "ordinary" juvenile court cases, Bonnie and Grisso (2000) suggested that CST requirements for rational understanding and decision-making abilities articulated in *Dusky* and *Godinez* might be less important as long as the the juvenile has a basic understanding of the purpose of the proceedings and is able to communicate rationally with counsel:

> The competence requirement in juvenile court serves the limited, though important, purpose of reducing the risk of an erroneous finding of guilt. An autonomous decision-making role by the minor is aspirational, not obligatory, and the youth's decisional competence therefore should not be regarded as a constitutional prerequisite to adjudication [in ordinary juvenile cases that do not threaten quasi-criminal sanctions]. (p. 98)

An adjusted standard that eliminates the need for deeper appreciation of legal concepts and decisional capacities might be called a *basic understanding and communication standard,* requiring only the most fundamental skills of juvenile court defendants. For example, defendants might need only to be aware that the defense attorney will provide advocacy without understanding how that advocacy applies in practice in the courtroom (Scott & Grisso, 2005). Some argue, in fact, that the standard for CST already used in many juvenile courtrooms requires little beyond these rudimentary abilities to understand and communicate (APRI, 2006; Redding, 2000; Redding & Frost, 2001). Further, there is some evidence that juvenile defense attorneys may tend to apply this type of standard when deciding which clients to refer for CST evaluations (Tobey et al., 2000).

LOWER BAR

Another way of looking at a different CST standard in juvenile court recognizes all of the same *Dusky* abilities as those required in criminal court, but proposes that a lower level or degree of those abilities might qualify for competence in juvenile court. Many competent defendants will manifest weaknesses in the relevant abilities considered in CST decisions. But how much weakness is acceptable? Even in criminal court, the weighting of various CST factors is not defined; it is only clear that each must be considered (Grisso, 2003a). And, it is not clear if juvenile court CST requires the same levels of relevant functions as those required in criminal court (Grisso, 2003a, 2005; Redding & Frost, 2001; Viljoen & Roesch, 2007).

Just as in the arguments that juvenile court need not require certain abilities, it has been argued that it may allow competence when *Dusky* abilities are at a lower level than is required in criminal court because of the different nature of juvenile court itself. The juvenile justice system is an agent of rehabilitation services that may benefit many youth, and the exclusion of youth from that system based on findings of incompetence would exclude them from those services. In addition, the reliance of youth upon adults, such as attorneys, could be seen as normative and less problematic than it is with adult defendants. Others would argue, however, that the rehabilitation services that juvenile justice claims to provide too often are not made available to youth. Also, some would contend that the mere fact that youth rely on adults does not reduce their need for protection from abuses by the state when restriction of liberties is at stake.

Even if the arguments for a lowered bar were accepted, the method for lowering the bar would require clarification. Several approaches to a lowered bar have been discussed (Grisso, 1997, 2005; Redding & Frost, 2001; Scott & Grisso, 2005). An *adolescent norms standard* would require that the competence of juvenile court defendants be determined through comparison of their abilities to those of average adolescents. On the other hand, an *age-peer norms standard* would require that the competence of juvenile court defendants be determined by comparison of their abilities with those of average youth their own age. The latter approach might be based on the fact that juvenile courts need to accommodate young defendants of varying developmental status such that certain abilities are more or less critical at different ages (Evans, 2003).

FLEXIBLE BAR

The arguments for an adjusted bar or a lower bar might be persuasive if juvenile courts endorsed and honored broad, rehabilitative goals consistently and adjudications had consequences that were less serious than those found in criminal court (Scott & Grisso, 2005). However, cases in juvenile court range from hearings on relatively minor charges to transfer hearings on very serious charges that may have severe consequences, such as life sentences in prison. Under these circumstances, it is difficult to claim that certain CST skills are unnecessary or that reduced abilities are adequate for hearings merely because they occur in juvenile court (Bonnie & Grisso, 2000; Scott & Grisso, 2005). Consequently, the adjusting or lowering of the juvenile court CST standard raises significant threats to due process protections (APRI, 2006; Barnum, 2000).

Some have suggested that a *flexible bar* for juvenile court CST could resolve this concern (Bonnie & Grisso, 2000; Scott & Grisso, 2005; Schwartz & Rosado, 2000). Using this approach, the CST standard could match the level of needed protection. That is, a lower threshold could be applied in juvenile court cases involving less serious offenses and sanctions, or when sanctions in juvenile court are clearly less severe and more rehabilitative than those for similar acts in criminal court. In cases where the juvenile faces possible consequences more similar to criminal court sanctions, the same CST bar used in criminal court could be maintained (Bonnie & Grisso, 2000; Grisso, 2005). The flexible bar may be a good match for the emerging hybrid juvenile court philosophy that uses a *parens patriae* philosophy in instances of relatively minor crime, but an instrumental, offense-based interpretation of responsibility in instances of greater harm (Warren, Aaron, Ryan, Chauhan, & DuVal, 2003).

Despite discussions in the professional literature regarding possible differences between juvenile and criminal courts in the types and levels of needed abilities, the matter has received minimal attention by appellate courts (Grisso, 2005; Redding & Frost, 2001; Ryba, Cooper, & Zapf, 2003b). Many of the cases that have addressed the issue are *unreported* (i.e., not generally recognized as having precedential value, but may have such value in certain jurisdictions under certain circumstances; see Gerken, 2004). Some of these decisions have specified that the juvenile court CST bar is the same as in criminal court (e.g., Minnesota: *In the Matter of the Welfare of D.D.N.*, 1998), while others have held that juveniles need not demonstrate the same level of abilities expected of adults (e.g., Ohio: *In re Michael Roger Johnson* 1983; Michigan: *People v. Carey*, 2000). In Ohio, for example, the court held, "We accept the juvenile court's adoption of the adult competence standard, provided that in applying it, the court assesses juveniles by juvenile norms rather than adult norms" (*In re Michael Roger Johnson*, 1983, p. 4). Several subsequent appellate decisions reached similar findings (*In the Matter of Robert Lloyd*, 1997; *In re Paula McWhorter*, 1994; *Ohio v. Settles*, 1998).

What Are the Legally Relevant Causes of Incompetence for Juvenile Defendants in Juvenile or Criminal Court?

Most jurisdictions either explicitly or implicitly require that a finding of incompetence be based on a mental disorder, such as psychosis or mental retardation (Rogers & Shuman, 2005). These are often called the *predicates* for IST. However, strict adherence to these traditional requirements places juveniles at risk for being considered competent despite significant functional deficits that are caused by mental disorders rarely associated with incompetence in adults or that are due to developmental immaturity.

MENTAL DISORDERS

Psychotic disorders and, to a lesser extent, cognitive disorders are the most common predicate foundations for adult incompetence findings in criminal court. However, it can be expected that a wider array of

INFO

Currently, there is little legal guidance on what, if any, changes to the CST standard should be applied to juvenile court defendants. This has at least three implications for practice.

1. The standard applied could have significant impact on the numbers of juveniles found IST (Viljoen, Zapf, & Roesch, 2007).

2. Until this issue is clarified, courts and clinicians must be aware that disagreements about whether a particular youth is or is not competent may sometimes be due to differences in the clinicians' and decision-makers' perceptions about what types or level of abilities are required to be competent in juvenile court proceedings.

3. Examiners practicing in jurisdictions without explicit guidance are in a particularly poor position to provide *ultimate issue opinions*; that is, they must often limit their opinions to functional descriptions that allow individual courts to apply CST standards as they will. (See Chapter 6 for further discussion.)

INFO

A broader range of disorders may affect competence in juveniles than in adults.

mental disorders could significantly impair a juvenile defendant's CST functioning. Childhood psychopathology interacts with developmental limitations (discussed below), requiring less deviation from "normal" to yield major impairment. For example, pervasive developmental disorders, learning disorders, or severe attentional disorders might rarely yield findings of incompetence among adults, but could contribute to severe impairment among younger defendants.

Further, some children with clear limitations will not fit neatly into current diagnostic categories. Consequently, tight adherence to typical predicate requirements may cause many juveniles to be erroneously identified as competent despite significant impairment in CST abilities (Bonnie & Grisso, 2000). For example, prodromal symptoms of schizophrenia, such as extreme social isolativeness, may not meet diagnostic criteria and might be difficult to correctly label; nonetheless, they may profoundly debilitate a juvenile, such as preventing functional communication with an attorney. With limited legal definitions of CST-relevant mental disorders in most jurisdictions and no explicit expansions of the definition for juveniles, it is not clear to what extent courts recognize a broader range of disorders with juveniles than would typically be accepted with adults.

DEVELOPMENTAL IMMATURITY

A definition for developmental immaturity will be offered in Chapter 2, including ways in which immaturity in specific cognitive and psychosocial characteristics is (a) typical of children and adolescents at various stages of development and (b) relevant for abilities typically associated with the *Dusky* standard. Thus, for some youth who have serious weaknesses in *Dusky*-related abilities, those weaknesses might be found to be related to the fact that they simply have not yet matured sufficiently

INFO

Normal developmental limitations may also affect competence in juveniles.

to have developed the capacities. The proportion of youth entering the justice system who manifest cognitive immaturity is
expected to increase as younger children charged with juvenile
offenses and more youth under age 16 are tried in criminal court
(Scott & Grisso, 2005).

Despite the fact that youth may sometimes have deficits in
competence abilities due to developmental immaturity, only a
small number of states explicitly allow for developmental immaturity as a predicate or foundational consideration in juvenile
court CST determinations (Grisso, 2003a; Redding & Frost,
2001; Scott & Grisso, 2005). Florida statute, for example, allows
"mental age" and "age or immaturity" to be considered (see
Florida Rule of Juvenile Procedure 8.095(d)(2)(A) and Florida
Statutes 985.223(2)]). Louisiana has done the same through case
law (*In re Causey*, 1978).

Despite the lack of legal clarity in most juvenile courts, a recent
survey found that two-thirds of juvenile court CST examiners have
been involved in cases in which a defendant was found IST due to
deficits in CST abilities related to developmental immaturity
(Grisso & Quinlan, 2005). Furthermore, Baerger, Griffin, Lyons,
and Simmons (2003) found that nearly one-quarter of the incompetent juvenile court defendants they studied had neither a mental
illness nor mental retardation, leading to the presumption that
many of these youth exhibited CST deficits related to immaturity
(Poythress, Lexcen, Grisso, & Steinberg, 2006). Apparently, many
juvenile courts have recognized incompetence based on deficits
associated with immaturity despite the absence of a formal legal
mandate to do so or legal guidance for applying it (Borum &
Grisso, 2007; Otto, Borum, & Epstein, 2006).

This recognition of immaturity by juvenile courts is not
universal, however. In an unreported case in Washington State,
for example, the appellate court upheld the finding by a trial
court that a juvenile defendant was competent, based on his
lack of a mental disorder, despite multiple experts giving the
unanimous opinion that the youth had severe CST deficits
stemming from the fact that he was 8 years old (*Washington v.
Swenson-Tucker*, 2006).

The appropriate application of developmental immaturity in CST in criminal court determinations is also unclear (Bonnie & Grisso, 2000). There have been some criminal appellate decisions pointing to the relevance of deficits due to age and development in criminal court CST (e.g., *W.S.L. v Florida,* 1985). But there has been too little discussion of the issue in criminal court even to offer the arguments for and against it.

Do "Interested Adults" Play a Role in Juvenile CST?

In most contexts, the law does not view adolescents as autonomous agents and assumes that caregivers will essentially act on the child's behalf using adult judgment and mature advocacy (Barnum, 2000). Consistent with that perspective, some jurisdictions specify limited roles for interested adults to assist juvenile defendants. For example, Arizona requires that a Guardian Ad Litem be assigned in every juvenile offense case (Levitt & Trollinger, 2002), although his or her role may not be clearly defined.

Currently, however, there are no commonly accepted procedures for the broad involvement of caregivers or other interested adults in a juvenile's defense, and the general expectation is that juveniles must possess CST autonomously (Barnum, 2000). The law is clear that parents, guardians, attorneys, and any other adult advocates are not authorized to be proxy decision makers for juvenile defendants. In other words, an incompetent juvenile defendant cannot be made legally competent by virtue of assistance from an adult (Grisso, 2005).

Even if adults cannot "make a young defendant competent," it is evident that adults can play subtle roles in the functioning of juvenile defendants in many cases. Adults may place persuasive pressures on youth to handle their case in certain ways, such as influencing decisions about the types of information they provide defense counsel, taking or avoiding the stand, and accepting or rejecting plea agreements. For example, in a much-publicized murder case in Florida (*Tate v. Florida,* 2003), the 14-year-old

INFO

Assistance from an adult is not a substitute for juvenile competence.

defendant followed his mother's advice to reject a plea offer because she felt certain that a jury would not convict her son. Young Tate was then found guilty at trial and sentenced to life without parole. Later the verdict was overturned precisely because the court was concerned that the defendant's CST had never been considered.

Should Juveniles Found IST Be Provided the Same Remediation Services as Criminal Defendants?

MENTAL DISORDER

When adults are found IST in criminal court, the underlying cause may be a mental defect, such as mental retardation, requiring habilitation. Much more often, however, a mental disorder is the underlying cause (Roesch & Golding, 1980). Therefore, to the extent that treatment will assist in restoring competence, typically these adults are placed in treatment settings—often forensic hospitals—that will target the symptoms causing the incompetence.

For youth who are IST due to mental disorder, this remedy is not a straightforward solution. For several reasons, juvenile CST remediation may require longer duration and fewer intensive psychiatric interventions than with adults. Adults who are IST due to mental disorder typically suffer from mental illnesses that are often highly impairing and relatively rapidly responsive to medication interventions, such as psychoses. Youth may be IST due to a wider array of mental disorders, some of which may have rapid response to medication (e.g., attention-deficit hyperactivity disorder [ADHD]), but others having a more questionable treatment response (e.g., post-traumatic stress disorder [PTSD]) or one of limited utility (e.g., communication disorders). Additionally, symptoms of these disorders less frequently cause the levels of impairment typically associated with inpatient psychiatric hospitalization. In addition to addressing this broad range of mental disorders, juvenile remediation programs must also address CST deficits caused by developmental delays and/or developmental immaturity (Bonnie & Grisso, 2000; Grisso, 1997; Viljoen & Grisso, 2007). Teaching of the necessary skills to be competent may be possible in some cases, but even when appropriate such educational interventions are rarely clear-cut.

CST restoration treatment programs for youth found IST in juvenile court are rare, largely because there was no need for them until CST recently began to be raised in juvenile courts. A few states, such as Florida and Virginia, have developed specialized programs (see Viljoen & Grisso, 2007, for descriptions). For example, Florida has developed an inpatient hospital facility designed to provide CST remediation services only to incompetent juveniles who meet civil commitment criteria, and a statewide intensive outpatient remediation system for juveniles who do not meet those criteria. The multimodal remediation program includes "psychoeducational treatment groups focused on the legal system and its operation, administration of psychoactive medications, case management services, and counseling" (McGaha, McClaren, Otto, & Petrila, 2001, p. 429).

DEVELOPMENTAL IMMATURITY

What very few juvenile CST remediation systems have done is to adequately meet the needs of youth who are IST entirely due to developmental immaturity. In many cases, there is little likelihood that the deficits these youth demonstrate can be successfully remediated because they simply require maturation of capacities (not medication or teaching), and they are unlikely to adequately mature within the limited time frames required for restoration. It is for this reason that some states, such as Florida, have explicitly prohibited remediation requirements for youth found IST when their CST deficits are based on immaturity.

Cases in which youth are IST due to deficits associated with developmental immaturity present a point of considerable frustration for lawmakers and courts. Simply remanding these cases to current remediation systems is likely to be unsuccessful. Courts might hold such cases for future adjudication after the youth "grows up," but such an approach is very likely to be unacceptable to legislators, courts, prosecutors, or defense attorneys (Buss, 2000; Grisso, 2005). Courts are more likely to see no other option but to dismiss the charges. This, however, is often seen as unacceptable when the youth is accused of a serious violent offense. The most appropriate remedies may be those that offer alternatives that provide for public protection and continued court control even if the charges are dismissed. For example, some courts have transferred such cases to the child welfare jurisdiction of the juvenile court, where they are provided residential services or special court monitoring. Other courts have provided for the transition of imminently dangerous incompetent youth to appropriate mental health interventions, such as psychiatric hospitalization (see Chapter 6 for further discussion, and Viljoen & Grisso, 2007).

Conclusion

This chapter has included an introduction to the traditional legal doctrine of CST, an explanation of why it has only recently begun to be applied to juveniles in significant numbers, and a presentation of some of the more pressing dilemmas and legal ambiguities that arise from that application. This complex legal context leaves juvenile CST examiners particularly vulnerable to difficulties in providing useful responses to court requests for juvenile CST opinions. The translation of psychological knowledge into information useful to the courts is quite challenging in this context and requires great care. The development of concepts that can help examiners make these translations is the focus of Chapter 2.

Forensic Mental Health Concepts | 2

E xaminers need useful concepts to guide their CST evaluations of juveniles. As shown in Chapter 1, the law generally defines the abilities that are legally relevant for making CST judgments. It also provides general guidance on mental conditions that are relevant for explaining deficits in defendants' CST abilities. But these general legal guidelines must be translated into more specific *psycholegal* concepts that can assist the examiner in deciding what data to obtain and how to interpret it so that evaluations are legally relevant. This chapter offers an overview of psychological and psycholegal concepts that can assist the examiner in this regard when evaluating juveniles in CST cases.

Conceptualizing the Relevant Capacities

The two-pronged *Dusky* standard and subsequent legal conceptualizations of CST discussed in Chapter 1 leave a great deal of ambiguity about the specific functional capacities required for competence to stand trial. To provide more specific guidance, legal scholars and mental health professionals have sought to clarify the relevant capacities, typically consulting legal precedent, empirical research, and conceptual theories.

The earliest efforts to clarify the relevant capacities resulted in lists of proposed functional abilities (see Ausness, 1978; Bukatman, Foy, & Degrazia, 1971; Group for the Advancement of Psychiatry, 1974; Laboratory of Community Psychiatry, 1973; McGarry et al., 1973; Robey, 1965). These lists were limited in important ways.

They were developed on intuitive, rather than empirical, bases (Grisso, 1986, 2003a). In addition, they focused on abilities and behaviors at trial itself, with little recognition of the need to be competent at pretrial stages or when cases are resolved through plea agreements. Finally, they provided little guidance on how various functions fit with one another, making conclusory opinions more difficult. Whereas most of the abilities identified in those lists continue to be considered in CST evaluations, the following review examines more recent, broader, and more structured CST conceptualizations that have superseded those earlier efforts.

Structured CST Models

Several ways to classify and organize CST capacities have been offered by scholars in recent years and have gained frequent use in the courts. Four models have been especially important. After describing these four models (see Table 2.1), a more "generic" model is offered that incorporates most of the concepts of the four models.

COMPETENCY DOMAINS MODEL (OR SEMANTIC ANALYSIS MODEL)

The *competency domains model* (e.g., Melton et al., 2007; Shuman, 1994) is taken directly from the sentence structure offered in the *Dusky* test, and most CST statutes are based on it. It distinguishes between the ability to appropriately engage the court process relationally and the ability to think about one's case. The two prongs include (a) the rational ability to consult with counsel, and (b) rational and factual understanding of the proceedings.

COGNITIVE COMPLEXITY MODEL

The *cognitive complexity model* (see Rogers, Tillbrook, and Sewell, 2004) involves a reorganization of the CST abilities specified in *Dusky* based upon the sophistication of cognitive abilities required. The two prongs include (a) factual understanding and (b) rational abilities (including both rational consultation abilities and rational understanding). The former involves semantic memory, whereas the latter requires more complex cognitive processes, such as working memory, abstraction abilities, and problem-solving skills.

Table 2.1 Structured CST Models

COMPETENCY-DOMAINS MODEL (OR SEMANTIC ANALYSIS MODEL)

a. Rational ability to consult with counsel

b. Rational and factual understanding of the proceedings

COGNITIVE COMPLEXITY MODEL

a. Factual understanding

b. Rational abilities (including both rational consultation abilities and rational understanding)

DISCRETE ABILITIES MODEL

a. Rational ability to consult with counsel

b. Factual understanding of the proceedings

c. Rational understanding of the proceedings

BONNIE'S MODEL

a. Capacity to understand the legal process

b. Capacity to appreciate the significance of legal circumstances for one's own situation

c. Capacity to communicate information

d. Capacity to use reasoning and judgment in making decisions

---

DISCRETE ABILITIES MODEL

The *discrete abilities model* (e.g., Grisso, 2003a; Cruise & Rogers, 1998) honors the distinction between the ability to think about court and the ability to appropriately engage the court process. It also distinguishes between varying levels of cognitive complexity. The model identifies three prongs: (a) rational ability to consult with counsel, (b) factual understanding of the proceedings, and (c) rational understanding of the proceedings. On the basis of this model, defendants must demonstrate

- abilities that allow them to consult with defense counsel and help with the case,
- abilities that demonstrate a basic understanding of the court process, and
- abilities that demonstrate an ability to apply that knowledge to their own legal predicament.

This model has demonstrated greater empirical support than the competency domains and cognitive complexity models (Rogers, Jackson, Sewell, Tillbrook, & Martin, 2003). It has also been described as particularly useful for conceptualizing clinical CST evaluations (Rogers, Grandjean, Tillbrook, Vitacco, & Sewell, 2001).

Rogers and Shuman (2005) offered a conceptualization of the discrete abilities model with operational definitions for each of the three prongs supported by prototypical analyses (Rogers, Tillbrook, & Sewell, 2004). Grisso (2003a) has also developed a very similar and commonly cited operational conceptualization of the discrete abilities model (see Table 2.2).

BONNIE'S MODEL

In a re-formulation of CST that has attracted much attention, Bonnie (1992) proposed that CST consists of two related constructs: *competence to assist counsel* and *decisional competence*. The former includes a basic understanding of matters pertaining to the trial process, as well as the ability to work with and assist one's attorney by relating facts relevant to the defense. In addition to that foundational element, Bonnie argued for a more contextualized capacity to engage in cognitive and psychosocial reasoning processes and to make independent decisions with input from counsel.

The decisional competence factor, it is argued, must be added to more traditional CST conceptualizations because defendants who are competent on the basis of those models may not be competent to make the specific decisions relevant to the instant case during the adjudication process (Bonnie & Grisso, 2000). This factor is viewed as

Table 2.2	Grisso's (2003a) Conceptualization of the Discrete Abilities Model

CONSULTING AND ASSISTING COUNSEL

- Understands that counsel works for defendant

- Understands counsel's inquiries

- Capable of responding to counsel's inquiries in a manner providing relevant information for defense

- Can manage the demands of trial process (stress, maintain demeanor)

FACTUAL UNDERSTANDING

- Understanding that the defendant is accused of a crime

- Understanding that the court will decide guilt and innocence

- Understanding that the trial could result in punishment

- Understanding the various ways defendants may plead

- Understanding that certain sentences are possible (their nature and seriousness)

- Understanding the roles of various participants in the trial process

- Understanding the general process of trials

RATIONAL UNDERSTANDING

- Beliefs about one's own trial that are not distorted by delusional ideas

- Appropriately motivated to further one's defense

- Reasoning ability sufficient to process relevant information during decision making conceptually and clinically distinct from the foundational elements (Bonnie, 1992), yet also is more controversial (Bonnie, 1993). Rogers and colleagues, for example, have criticized this model as reaching beyond the requirements of *Dusky* (Rogers et al., 2003), failing empirical validation efforts (Cruise & Rogers, 1998), and reflecting an overemphasis on decisional competence (Rogers et al., 2001).

Bonnie's model can be seen to identify four components relevant to CST, including the capacity to (a) understand the legal process, (b) appreciate the significance of legal circumstances for one's own situation, (c) communicate information, and (d) use reasoning and judgment in making decisions.

An elaboration of this model, integrating the "understanding," "appreciation," and "reasoning" abilities of the discrete abilities model, suggests that both the competence to assist counsel and the decisional competence relevant to CST consist of these three capacities with decisional competence also requiring an ability to express a choice (Bonnie & Grisso, 2000; see Table 2.3).

Four Capacities Model

As the models above suggest, there are several ways to organize the abilities required for CST, and no one way is dominant. Therefore, examiners should be familiar with these different models and be thoughtful about how they correspond to their own practices. Through a variety of mechanisms (e.g., the tools selected to assess CST), the model favored by an examiner can impact the CST data available to the court and, therefore, the ultimate CST determination.

Despite the organizational differences, these models demonstrate relative consistency in the requisite CST abilities identified. Four primary CST capacities emerge across the models: (a) factual understanding of the proceedings (*Understanding*), (b) rational understanding or appreciation of the proceedings (*Appreciation*), (c) ability to consult with and assist defense counsel (*Assisting*), and (d) decisional capacity (*Decision Making*) (see Fig. 2.1). Even the two models most strongly debated in the literature—the discrete abilities model and Bonnie's model—include these four capacities. Both recognize the importance of decision-making capacity, even though it is seen as one of the rational-understanding or the consult-with-counsel

Table 2.3	Bonnie and Grisso's (2000) Conceptualization of a Merger of Bonnie's and the Discrete Abilities Models

COMPETENCE TO ASSIST COUNSEL

Understanding	Understand the charges and basic elements of the adversary system
Appreciation	Appreciate one's situation as a defendant in a criminal prosecution
Reasoning	Relate pertinent information to counsel concerning facts of the case

DECISIONAL COMPETENCE

Understanding	Capacity to understand information relevant to the specific decision at issue
Appreciation	Capacity to appreciate one's situation as a defendant confronted with a specific legal decision
Reasoning	Capacity to think rationally about alternative courses of action
Choice	Capacity to express a choice among alternatives

abilities in the discrete abilities models, rather than separated into a discrete decisional competence factor, as in Bonnie's model.

States that recognize the CST requirement in juvenile court have applied the *Dusky* standard. Therefore, these same four capacities apply in juvenile and criminal court (Grisso, 2005). There are limitations to the four capacities model. These capacities have not been identified empirically and they probably overlap with one another (Grisso, 2003a; Zapf & Roesch, 2005; Zapf, Viljoen, Whittemore, Poythress, & Roesch, 2002). Further, explicit guidance about their relative importance or the extent of mastery

BEST PRACTICE

Be familiar with the different CST models and the various ways they each organize the four capacities relevant to juvenile CST evaluations: Understanding, Appreciation, Assisting, and Decision Making.

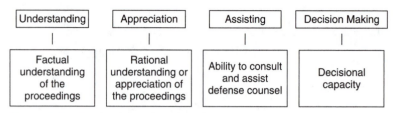

Figure 2.1 Four Capacities Model

required within each is unavailable, requiring examiners to be discretionary and case specific in applying them (Redding & Frost, 2001; Scott & Grisso, 2005).

Despite these limitations, the four capacities are very useful for a number of reasons. They help examiners to move beyond conceptualizing CST as a single construct and focus on the underlying abilities needed to be competent. The four capacities model also provides a type of shorthand for thinking about juvenile CST research and evaluations across various CST models. It is critical that examiners develop an understanding of these four capacities to guide their juvenile CST evaluations, and they will be referenced repeatedly in this volume as important organizing concepts.

UNDERSTANDING

It is necessary for the defendant to be able to possess, whether through prior knowledge or instruction, a basic factual understanding of the purpose and process of the proceedings in which they are participating (Bonnie, 1992; Rogers & Shuman, 2005). Rogers and Shuman (2005) suggest that the heart of Understanding is recall and recognition of the basic roles expected of the courtroom players, as well as understanding of the charges one is facing. Of particular import, an inability to understand defense counsel as a zealous advocate who will seek to translate the defendant's goals into effective trial strategy and argument may in and of itself negate a defendant's capacity to meaningfully participate in the proceedings (Buss, 2000; Rogers & Shuman, 2005). Possessing a factual understanding of the possible penalties being faced, the nature of available pleas, the overall adjudication process from arraignment to disposition, and one's rights as the proceedings unfold are also typically required for adequate Understanding.

APPRECIATION

The requirement for rational appreciation recognizes that factual understanding is a necessary but insufficient element of the knowledge about court proceedings needed for CST. Appreciation requires the abstraction abilities to manipulate what is factually understood, appropriately contemplate the implications and significance of what is understood, and apply that knowledge in actual case-related situations without distortion or irrationality (Bonnie, 1992; Grisso, 2005). A defendant who knows the roles of courtroom personnel but cannot adequately abstract the larger adversarial process that underlies the roles demonstrates a weakness in Appreciation (Rogers & Shuman, 2005). Likewise, a defendant who is unaware of his personal role in the proceedings or is not adequately motivated to achieve a self-serving outcome may be demonstrating abstraction weaknesses that threaten Appreciation (Rogers & Shuman, 2005).

In short, Appreciation references what the defendant "believes" about what is factually understood of the court process (Grisso, 1998, 2005). In adult defendants, the idiosyncratic and irrational beliefs that most commonly threaten Appreciation are the result of psychotic delusions. For example, a defendant who factually understands the role of the court personnel might nonetheless believe and act in court from the premise that "although defense attorneys are supposed to help the defendant, my defense attorney is a CIA agent and only the judge can save me from his plot to kidnap me." Thus he fails to appreciate (or to rationally apply) that which he understands about the role of the defense attorney and the judge.

Threats to adequate Appreciation from psychosis may occur in a small proportion of juvenile defendants with early-onset or substance-induced psychotic disorders. A threat to Appreciation that is likely more common in younger defendants (and adult defendants with limited cognitive abilities) comes from distorted beliefs rooted in concrete thinking, incomplete understanding of the process, and/or other factors (e.g., limited temporal perspective) that impair the ability to appropriately consider and apply information. These weaknesses increase the risk for overgeneralizations, undergeneralizations, confusion, immature presumptions, and frankly erroneous beliefs (Grisso, 2005). For example, a youth may be able to state that she is allowed

INFO

Common threats to
Appreciation in juveniles
include the following:

- Distorted beliefs rooted
  in concrete thinking
- Incomplete under-
  standing of the process
- Other factors that
  impair the ability to
  appropriately consider
  and apply information

to plead not guilty and may accurately define that term, but may believe that to plead not guilty when she knows that she committed the offense is not allowed "because it's lying, and you can never lie in court." Likewise, youth are at risk of having difficulty appreciating the role of defense counsel because it may be difficult for them to conceptualize why an adult would advocate for them against other adults, why an adult would put aside his own views to serve a principled purpose, and why their own authority eclipses that of an adult (Buss, 1996, 2000; Selman, 1980)—all of which are quite contrary to the usual social distinctions between children and adults that they face in most other aspects of everyday life.

ASSISTING

The Assisting capacity refers to the defendant's ability to participate with and meaningfully aid the defense attorney in developing and presenting the defense. Assisting requires the capacity to communicate with counsel, both receptively and expressively, about matters relevant to the case in a manner that counsel can understand (Bonnie, 1992; Rogers & Shuman, 2005). Defendants must be able to identify potential sources of relevant evidence and witnesses, identify reasons for confronting opposing witnesses, and provide information relevant for building a defense (Rogers & Shuman, 2005). Assisting applies to pretrial consultations, such as being able to communicate facts about the alleged incident to the attorney so that possible defenses can be contemplated. The defendant must then be able to engage in behaviors necessary to execute the agreed-upon defense. Assisting also applies to courtroom situations, such as being able to adequately follow and comprehend the testimony of other witnesses so that the defendant can alert counsel to any distortions of the facts. In addition, the defendant must be able to provide testimony with relevance, coherence, and independence of judgment.

INFO

Cognitive underdevelopment in juveniles may result in the following:

● Lack of engagement with proceedings

● Limited ability to offer basic assistance

● Withholding of information due to misunderstandings

Younger and/or cognitively limited defendants may be vulnerable to Assisting weaknesses due to general cognitive underdevelopment. They may believe that their primary role in court is simply to show up and avoid behaving inappropriately (Tobey, Grisso, & Schwartz, 2000). Furthermore, skill limitations in memory, attention, tracking, processing, verbal reception and expression, interpersonal perspective-taking, rapport development with strangers, and time perception may reduce Assisting abilities (Cauffman & Steinberg, 2000; Levin, et al., 1991; Levitt & Trollinger, 2002; Selman, 1980; Steinberg & Schwartz, 2000; Tobey et al., 2000; Walker, 1994). Younger defendants may also misunderstand the role of defense as advocate and withhold information from counsel for fear that counsel will use it against them (Grisso, 1983).

DECISION MAKING

Competent defendants must be able to consider alternatives and make legal choices, such as when pleading guilty, going to trial, accepting a plea agreement offer, testifying, calling certain witnesses, or considering certain defenses (Bonnie & Grisso, 2000; Rogers & Shuman, 2005). Juvenile court adjudications may present complex decision-making contexts not found in criminal court, such as whether to oppose transfer to criminal court or strategic decisions that can impact which justice system(s) provides punishment (Oberlander, Goldstein, & Ho, 2001). These decisions are appropriately based on the advice of counsel, but they cannot be made or altered by the defense attorney alone (Bonnie & Grisso, 2000). Defendants must be able to engage their case with autonomy, self-interest, and rational expectations so that case decisions are not merely capitulation to the attorney's ideas (Rogers & Shuman, 2005). Engaging in disruptive behavior in court might also be understood as a deficit in Decision

Making in some cases. Acting out despite knowledge of the possible consequences (e.g., ejection from the proceedings) can be seen as a decision to waive one's right to be present at the trial (Bonnie, 1992).

To make the connections between factors required for Decision Making, the defendant must have a capacity for transitive thinking. Abstraction abilities are required for imagining alternative courses of action, thinking of potential consequences of these hypothetical actions, estimating the probability of their occurrence, weighing the desirability of the consequences based on one's own preferences, and engaging in comparative deliberation about the alternatives and consequences to be used during legal decision making (Grisso, 2000). As discussed later in this chapter, these abilities are often still developing during adolescence.

Although not all CST models conceptualize Decision Making as a capacity that is distinct from Assisting (e.g., Cruise & Rogers, 1998), unique issues surround Decision Making in reference to juvenile CST that warrant independent discussion. First, the extent to which Decision Making is required in juvenile court CST is not fully clear. Some of the proposed approaches to applying CST in juvenile court that were discussed in Chapter 1 could reduce or eliminate the need to focus on autonomous decision-making abilities in juvenile court CST determinations (Scott & Grisso, 2005; Tobey et al., 2000). Second, there are developmental threats to adequate legal decision making that are more common among juveniles.

Predicate Requirements

Inadequate performance when a defendant's CST abilities are examined does not necessarily result in a finding of incompetence. The poor performance must be caused by underlying difficulties that are not easily or quickly remedied. These are called *predicates* for CST—that is, psychological conditions that the law recognizes as relevant potential causes for deficits in CST capacities. As noted earlier, the traditional predicates for incompetence have been serious mental disorders or mental retardation. The evaluation of CST in juveniles, however, has raised questions about predicates that do not have a history in the evolution of CST in criminal courts with adult defendants, such as a wider array of mental disorders and various types of immaturity.

Mental Disorders

Chapter 1 explained that many jurisdictions require, whether explicitly or implicitly, that impairments in CST capacities be due to a mental disorder for a defendant to be found IST, but the disorders that meet the requirement typically are not well defined. As with CST itself, forensic examiners must translate these legal standards into forensic concepts that they can assess. Again, severely debilitating conditions, such as psychotic disorders or mental retardation, are traditionally seen as the assessment targets in CST evaluations.

However, there is a broad array of problems that are considered mental disorders by clinicians (American Psychiatric Association, 2000), and diverse mental disorders are common among youth who are involved in the juvenile justice system. Epidemiological studies using rigorous diagnostic procedures, for example, estimate that between two-thirds and three-quarters of youth in juvenile justice facilities have one or more psychiatric disorders (Teplin, Abram, McClelland, Dulcan, & Mericle, 2002; Wasserman, McReynolds, Lucas, Fisher, & Santos, 2002). Many of the psychiatric problems that first emerge or markedly increase in severity during late childhood into adolescence can limit legal functional abilities (Kazdin, 2000).

NONTRADITIONAL MENTAL DISORDERS

Juvenile CST evaluations raise the possibility of impairments in CST abilities due to mental disorders that are not traditionally considered in adult CST cases (Barnum, 2000; Goldstein, Thomson, Osman, & Oberlander, 2002; Grisso, 2005). Symptoms arising from borderline intellectual functioning, learning disorders, behavior disorders, or anxiety disorders can impair cognitive functioning and social abilities

INFO

Any disorder that impacts cognitive functioning and/or interpersonal relatedness could sometimes yield functional impairments relevant to juvenile CST.

that may yield significant CST impairments (Grisso, 1997, 2005; Ryba et al., 2003b; Slobogin, et al., 1997). Affective disorders can limit a child's motivation to adequately engage with the attorney and/or the adjudication process (Slobogin et al., 1997). Attention-deficit/ hyperactivity disorder (ADHD) can impair a child's ability to communicate effectively with counsel (Slobogin, et al., 1997; Viljoen & Roesch, 2005). Prodromal symptoms of psychoses can cause social withdrawal and cognitive confusion (McClellan & Werry, 1999).

IMPACT OF DEVELOPMENT

A broader variety of mental disorders impair CST functioning in youth, in part because mental disorders in children occur within the context of normal stages of development (Kazdin, 2000). That is, all child and adolescent mental disorders interact with ongoing normative developmental processes that also place limits on functioning and coping resources. Most childhood disorders are actually exaggerated responses to normal developmental processes and experiences, and development is in turn impacted by the presence of mental disorders (Cicchetti, 1984, 1990). Childhood psychopathology and development are so intertwined that developmental psychopathologists have concluded that clear distinctions between the two cannot be drawn.

Developmental Immaturity

As discussed earlier, developmental factors can interact with mental disorders in youth and contribute to incompetence. In addition, some children lack the skills and abilities required of competent defendants because of developmental issues alone, even in the absence of mental illness. Although development occurs across the lifespan, changes are particularly striking between ages 11 and 18

INFO

The interaction of developmental processes and mental disorders often makes it difficult to distinguish between the two.

INFO

Developmental factors may be relevant to CST due to the following:

- Normative weaknesses in abilities due to young age
- Slower development of abilities than is typical of age-peers

(Borum & Grisso, 2007; Otto & Goldstein, 2005). During these years, there is progressive development in various domains—physical, cognitive, social, and emotional—until functioning reaches the "mature" level that is typical for young and middle adulthood (Grisso, 2005). Therefore, "immaturity," or functioning at a level that falls short of a mature level, is often relevant as adolescence unfolds.

There is substantial empirical evidence (reviewed later) that these maturing abilities can cause CST dysfunction similar to that of adults who are IST for reasons of mental disorder. At very young ages, it may be normative for youth to lack abilities that are relevant to CST. In other cases, relevant abilities may develop more slowly than is typical of age-peers. In these ways, youth without mental disorders may still demonstrate deficits relevant to CST. Therefore, examiners must be aware that developmental factors are increasingly recognized as a relevant predicate in CST evaluations (Borum & Grisso, 2007; Poythress, Lexcen, Grisso, & Steinberg, 2006).

Compounding these problems, maturity has not been clearly defined by mental health professionals themselves in clinical theory or practice (Reppucci, 1999). Juvenile CST examiners need a consistent forensic conceptualization of immaturity to understand its relationship to CST and to communicate effectively with courts (Grisso, 2005). Thus, it is important to define and conceptualize what is meant by "developmental immaturity" as it applies to CST among juveniles.

Defining Immaturity

Juvenile CST examiners must use the term *immature* with appropriate care. Youth are never simply "immature." Examiners who refer to them as such are engaging in substandard practice by not

INFO

Development is

- idiosyncratic,
- nonlinear, and
- to be understood relative to an identified comparison point.

offering the court adequately useful information. *Immature* should be applied to specific legal capacities and not used as a global descriptor of a youth (Grisso, 2005). A youth might be described as cognitively immature or emotionally immature, but should not simply be described as immature.

Appropriate descriptions of maturity and immaturity should reflect several critical features of child and adolescent development that must be understood by examiners and by courts. The following features of adolescent development are consistent with basic principles in developmental psychology, which can be reviewed in general texts on the subject (e.g., Flavell, Miller, & Miller, 2001; Steinberg, 2007).

DEVELOPMENT IS IDIOSYNCRATIC

First, *development is idiosyncratic.* Development in one domain (e.g., cognitive) does not directly translate to a similar level of development in other domains (e.g., emotional or social). Thus a youth at any given age may demonstrate quite different functioning within various developmental domains. This occurs because youth vary significantly in the rates and timing at which they develop various characteristics and abilities. A child who is developing normally emotionally may demonstrate cognitive delays, or vice versa.

DEVELOPMENT IS NONLINEAR

In addition, *development is nonlinear.* Development includes spurts, delays, and temporary regressions, is highly sensitive to environmental influences, and is sometimes context specific. Development at one point is influenced by the quality of development at earlier points, and the various domains of development are in constant interaction with one another (Wenar & Kerig, 2000). As a consequence, two children may reach different developmental destinations despite similarities in their developmental pathways, and similar developmental destinations may be reached by two children on quite different developmental pathways.

DEVELOPMENTAL PROGRESS IS TO BE ASSESSED RELATIVE TO AN IDENTIFIED COMPARISON POINT

BEWARE Aggregate estimates of typical development may not generalize to juvenile offender populations.

Also, *immaturity must always be understood relative to an identified comparison point.* Youth may possess immature abilities relative to "typical adult functioning" and/or "typical age-peer functioning." Thus it might be relevant to consider whether a 12-year-old is as cognitively mature as an adult, but it may also be relevant to consider whether the 12-year-old has developed the cognitive skills of most age-peers. Therefore, capacities may be described as immature because they have not reached adult levels and reflect *incomplete development,* or because they are not at the level that one would expect given the child's age and reflect *delayed development* (Grisso, 2005). So, one youth might be described as "cognitively immature relative to adults" or "demonstrating incomplete cognitive development," whereas another youth might be described as "emotionally immature relative to age-peers" or "demonstrating delayed emotional development."

When comparing youth to age-peers to discuss possible delayed development, examiners must carefully consider *typical development.* Whereas aggregate estimates of typical development are available for some capacities, they are often based on white, middle-class children and may not generalize to the disproportionately minority, low socioeconomic status, and developmentally delayed youth typical of juvenile offender populations.

Relevant Domains of Maturity and Immaturity

Three broad and interrelated domains of development have been identified as relevant to juvenile CST evaluations: biological, cognitive, and psychosocial development (Borum & Grisso, 2007), each of which has clear relevance to the development of CST skills. Development within each of these domains is summarized as follows (see Steinberg, 2007, for a more comprehensive discussion). Notably, delays in development in these domains are not uncommon among justice–involved youth (Grisso, 2005).

BIOLOGICAL DEVELOPMENT

In adolescence, increases and decreases in various hormones trigger the biological and physical changes of puberty. The biological processes underlying puberty are very gradual (Susman & Rogol, 2004). Furthemore, there are widely varying differences in the onset, progression, and completion of puberty across individuals (Brooks-Gunn & Reiter, 1990; Eveleth & Tanner, 1990; Tanner, 1972).

Puberty affects emotional and behavioral functioning. For example, sadness, anxiety, rebelliousness, and misbehavior increase among pubertal boys (Susman et al., 1987) and depression increases among pubertal girls (Angold, Costello, & Worthman, 1999). These changes are related to complex interactions between hormonal systems and structural brain development (Dahl, 2003; Nelson, Leibenluft, McClure, & Pine, 2005), the timing of puberty relative to peers (Aro & Taipale, 1987; Duncan, Ritter, Dornbusch, Gross, & Carlsmith, 1985; Ge et al., 2003; Graber, Lewinsohn, Seeley, & Brooks-Gunn, 1997; Stice, Presnell, & Bearman, 2001), and environmental factors such as family-level stress (Booth, Johnson, Granger, Crouter, & McHale, 2003; Susman, 1997). Puberty-related behaviors could have a significant effect on a juvenile's functioning in a legal context. Rebelliousness, for example, could lead a boy to sabotage the efforts of defense counsel, whereas depression could lead a girl to withdraw from counsel.

Significant neurological development also occurs throughout adolescence. Neural growth spurts occur between ages 6–8, 10–12, and 14–16 (Epstein, 1978, 1986). Further, through adolescence and into adulthood, myelination (growth of sheaths on neurons) and synaptic pruning (the elimination of unneeded synapses) continue in the prefrontal cortex (Paus et al., 1999; Sowell, Trauner, Gamst, & Jernigan, 2002; Strauch, 2003). Until these processes occur, communication within the prefrontal cortex is less efficient, yielding limitations in the executive cognitive functions (e.g., planning, organizing information) that

INFO

Changes in puberty affect emotional and behavioral functioning, which has implications for juvenile CST.

it controls (Giedd et al., 1999). Furthermore, communication with other brain regions is less efficient, yielding decreased ability to manage the brain centers that govern emotions (i.e., the limbic system) that are overactive in adolescence. Such weaknesses in the ability to regulate emotions could increase the risk that youth will base legal decisions on anger or sadness, or have difficulty modulating their behavior in court.

COGNITIVE DEVELOPMENT

During adolescence, individuals begin to acquire new knowledge, develop attention, organization, and memory abilities that improve information processing, and demonstrate verbal fluency, deductive reasoning, problem-solving, judgment, and abstract thinking (Flavell et al., 2001; Weider & Greenspan, 1992). As a result, adolescents grow into the abilities to consider hypothetical outcomes and abstract concepts, be more reflective and aware of thinking, consider multiple dimensions of an issue, and see the world in relative and dimensional terms (Steinberg, 2007). Even on average, many of these skills are still developing through mid-adolescence (e.g., hypothetical and abstract reasoning). Consequently, developing youth can demonstrate some of the same CST-related problems that are more typical of mentally retarded adults, including difficulty understanding more complex legal concepts such as plea agreements, remembering information presented by attorneys, or applying knowledge to unique or unanticipated circumstances.

These changes are linked to the neurological development discussed above, as well as to exposure to new experiences and new contexts within which youth work with their developing intellect (Scott & Grisso, 2005). Consequently, less well-rounded life experiences can limit cognitive development (Steinberg and Schwartz, 2000). However, even when youth are fully developed, they are less consistent than adults in applying these cognitive skills across situations.

INFO

Youth may not have fully developed cognitive skills, resulting in CST-related deficits.

PSYCHOSOCIAL DEVELOPMENT

Ways of socially relating also develop during adolescence (Steinberg, 2007). Identity is forming, affecting thoughts about self and others. Family relationships shift, with youth becoming more assertive and assuming more power. Peer relationships take on increased importance as they grow more intimate and more independent of adult supervision, expand to larger groups, and include members of the opposite sex. The progress of psychosocial development may be impacted by one's family's values, peer values, social relationships, spiritual influences, and/or popular culture.

The psychosocial development of adolescents includes changes in some factors that are particularly relevant to decision-making capacities (Cauffman, Woolard, & Reppucci, 1999; Scott, Reppucci, and Woolard, 1995; Steinberg & Cauffman, 1996). These factors can be seen as the theoretical sources of what is commonly described as "poor teenage judgment" (Grisso, 2000). Two primary models (the Scott-Reppucci-Woolard and the Steinberg-Cauffman frameworks) have collectively identified seven overlapping psychosocial factors that affect decision making during adolescent development (Cauffman et al., 1999). The two models have in common four psychosocial factors that are particularly relevant for CST: *autonomy (conformity and compliance), perceptions and attitudes about risk, temperance,* and *perspective taking.*

INFO

Psychosocial factors relevant to CST include the following:

● Autonomy (conformity and compliance)

● Perceptions and attitudes about risk

● Temperance

● Perspective taking

Autonomy (Conformity and Compliance) Decision makers require the abilities to think and behave in ways that are self-reliant, self-governing, independent, and autonomous so that they can make appropriate use of the perspectives of others without being overly or inadequately conforming or compliant (Cauffman & Steinberg, 2000; Steinberg & Schwartz, 2000). Underdeveloped perceptions of autonomy can yield instability in personal preferences and variable weighting of the opinions of others. Adolescence involves a gradual individuation and movement toward this autonomy, stable identity, and self-insight (Steinberg, 2007). This is why younger adolescents tend to be generally "suggestible" and susceptible to the influences and pressures of others (Bruck & Ceci, 2004; Owen-Kostelnik, Reppucci, & Meyer, 2006). So, for example, a youth might direct hostility at her adult defense attorney in an effort to appear "tough" and gain the acceptance of friends.

Children tend to be highly oriented toward caregivers and not toward peers. During preadolescence and early adolescence they tend to shift away from the influence of caregivers and to that of peers, and only in middle to late adolescence do they tend to demonstrate truly autonomous behavior (Steinberg, 2007; Steinberg and Schwartz, 2000). Even into adolescence, youth tend to be reliant upon caregivers in certain contexts, such as seeking guidance on issues involving values and beliefs, higher stakes, and longer-term planning (Brittain, 1963; Larson, 1972; Young & Ferguson, 1979). Adolescents also tend to be compliant with authority figures, particularly when they perceive such a person to be powerful (Bugental, Shennum, Frank, & Ekman, 2001).

Conformity to peers tends to be strongest in early to mid-adolescence (Berndt, 1979; Brown, 1990; Krosnick & Judd, 1982; Steinberg & Silverberg, 1986). This conformity includes a vulnerability to both direct pressure and an indirect desire for approval (Scott et al., 1995). Adolescents seem to be particularly responsive to the influence of peers in reference to short-term, day-to-day, and social matters (Brittain, 1963; Young & Ferguson, 1979). This sensitivity to peer pressure may be tied to changes in the processing of social information that result from changes in the functioning of the limbic system (Nelson et al., 2005). But sensitivity to peer pressure also seems to vary depending on family and parenting characteristics (Farrell & White, 1998; Wong, Crosnoe, Laird, & Dornbusch, 2003).

Perceptions and Attitudes About Risk   Adolescents tend to take greater risks than adults (Arnett, 1992; Centers for Disease Control and Prevention, 2006), with a spike in risk-taking behavior occurring between ages 16 and 19 (Steinberg & Cauffman, 1996). This risk-taking does not stem simply from an adolescent sense of invulnerability (see Quadrel, Fischhoff, & Davis, 1993, for an empirical review). Rather, the process of evaluating risk seems to be different for youth than for adults and is linked to the functioning of the prefrontal cortex (May et al., 2004).

Adolescents tend to foresee fewer possible outcomes of their risk-taking, underestimate the likelihood of negative outcomes, and overvalue the benefits of having fun and obtaining the approval of others (Furby & Beyth-Marom, 1992; Nurmi, 1991; Steinberg, 2002). Adolescents, especially those with lower intelligence, lower anxiety, and/or callous-unemotional traits, are also more likely than adults to place greater weight on expected positive gains than on possible losses or other negative outcomes (Benthin, Slovic, & Severson, 1993; Furby & Beyth-Marom, 1992; Gardner, 1993; Gardner & Herman, 1991; Grisso, 1981; O'Brien & Frick, 1996). Adolescents also place greater weight than adults on the perceived negative consequences of *not* engaging in risky behaviors (Beyth-Marom, Austin, Fischoff, Palmgren, & Quadrel, 1993). Therefore, a youthful defendant might decide to reject a plea agreement because he overvalues the attention he will be given during a trial and underappreciates the negative consequences of conviction, such as having a juvenile offense record.

Temperance   Temperance refers to the ability to maintain emotional and behavioral control and, in particular, modulate impulsivity (Cauffman & Steinberg, 2000; Steinberg & Schwartz, 2000). Immature temperance can yield impulsive decisions. For example, a youthful defendant might suddenly interrupt stressful proceedings by yelling out incriminating statements. The development of temperance is related to neurological development in the prefrontal cortex (Casey, Galvan, & Hare, 2005), but is also influenced by parental and societal feedback that helps youth identify "miscalculations" and integrate social limits on appropriate behavior (Scott & Grisso, 2005).

Perspective Taking   Perspective taking refers to the ability to understand the complexity of a situation and place it in a broader context (Cauffman & Woolard, 2005). Two types of perspective taking have been discussed: interpersonal and temporal. *Interpersonal perspective* refers to the ability to take the perspective of another person. As the capacities to imaginatively shift perspectives and think multidimensionally develop, youth begin to see that people influence one another, then become aware of the complexities of these influences, and finally become able to formulate arguments in ways that can be understood by others with different opinions (Selman, 1980). Before these abilities are mature, youth may be limited in their ability to respond to the perspectives of others, potentially yielding ineffective communications (Silverberg, 1986) and overly self-serving decisions. As a result, a youth might have difficuty, for example, appreciating that the prosecutor's pursuit of a conviction is not personal but a reflection of a more general professional pursuit.

Temporal perspective is the ability to appropriately consider both long- and short-term implications of decisions and actions. Relative to adults, adolescents tend to weigh more heavily the short-term consequences and discount the long-term consequences (Greene, 1986; Nurmi, 1991). This limited temporal perspective may occur because the capacities to project events into the future, consider future consequences, and plan for the future remain immature. These deficits may lead to less adaptive decisions (Cauffman & Steinberg, 2000; but see Alexander et al., 1990, as well as Beyth-Marom, Austin, Fischoff, Palmgren, & Quadrel, 1993, for different findings). For example, a youth might plead guilty in order to obtain immediate release from detention without adequately considering how an offense record could impact her ability to obtain jobs in later adolescence. Growing up in environments with limited hope for long-term success, as is common among juvenile offenders, yields particularly foreshortened time perspective (Gardner, 1993; Jessor, 1992a, 1992b).

With a traditional focus on the impairments of psychotic and mentally retarded defendants, the law has not tended to appreciate the role of cognitive and psychosocial factors when considering juveniles' functioning in relatation to CST (Bonnie & Grisso, 2000; Buss, 2000; Cauffman & Woolard, 2005; Grisso, 2000; Rogers & Shuman, 2005; Steinberg et al., 2003; Tobey et al., 2000). It is not yet clear whether lawmakers and courts will expand the predicates for CST in a manner that recognizes immaturity as a primary factor in CST decisions about juveniles.

Whether they will be recognized by the law or not, however, immaturity in these factors can lead youth to make choices about their cases based on values that they themselves may not hold when they are more mature (Grisso, 2005). For example, younger defendants may lack autonomy and overly rely on their attorney to reach important decisions in their case (Tobey et al., 2000). Or they may lack temperance and have difficulty managing the complex emotions that can arise in court, such as shame or humiliation, and engage in behavioral outbursts or disengagement from the process (Oberlander et al., 2001).

Conclusion

Having developed an understanding of the complex legal context of juvenile CST in Chapter 1, and having examined ways to translate between relevant legal and mental health perspectives in Chapter 2, juvenile CST examiners must also be knowledgeable about research findings that are relevant for these evaluations. That topic is addressed in Chapter 3.

Empirical Foundations and Limits | 3

The use of research data by examiners to inform their theories and practices increases the accuracy of evaluations and helps the courts to feel more confident about the opinions being offered. To meet practice standards, examiners must consider the empirical research when structuring their evaluations and when interpreting the results. This chapter reviews research findings on the practices of forensic examiners when conducting juvenile CST evaluations, youth whom they evaluate, methods they use, the conclusions they reach, and incompetence remediation issues that they must resolve.

Typical Practices in Juvenile CST Evaluations

Two studies have described examiners' practices in juvenile CST evaluations. One was a review of 1,357 evaluation reports of juveniles found IST in Florida (Christy, Douglas, Otto, & Petrila, 2004). The other was a national survey of 82 juvenile CST examiners (Ryba, Cooper, & Zapf, 2003a, 2003b). Because of the jurisdictional and outcome specificity of the former study and the small size of the latter, it is not clear that these studies describe actual practices nationally. Therefore, we know little about the actual nature and quality of juvenile CST evaluations in practice. Still, some findings from these studies warrant mention.

Assessment Methods

Ryba et al. (2003a) asked examiners about the abilities that they target in their judgments of maturity in CST evaluations. One-half identified cognitive abilities, more than one-third reported social skills, and about one-quarter said judgment and decision-making abilities. Most respondents said they assess capacities of a developmental nature using multiple strategies, especially interviews and psychological tests. Of the examiners who described the psychological tests they use for this purpose, one-half reported using intelligence tests or subtests. Between one-fourth and one-third reported using measures of adaptive functioning, personality and behavior tests, and/or projective assessment techniques. Overall, both Ryba et al. and Christy et al. found that IQ testing was the most commonly used test by juvenile CST examiners.

Both Ryba et al. and Christy et al. found the use of tools designed to specifically assess CST in less than half of their cases (46% and 29%, respectively). Most of those using these tools in the Christy et al. study used unpublished state-specific tools. Of the tools that will be discussed in Chapter 5, almost half of the respondents reported to Ryba et al. that they use the Competency Assessment Screening Test for persons with Mental Retardation (CAST*MR); about one-fifth reported using the MacArthur Competence Assessment Tool–Criminal Adjudication (MacCAT-CA).

Evaluating and Describing Competence and Remediation of Incompetence

An early study that included juvenile CST reports found that examiners more commonly addressed examinees' Understanding and Appreciation skills, but much less commonly described Assisting abilities (McKee, 1998). More recently, the findings of Ryba et al. and Christy et al. suggest much greater attention to each of the four capacities discussed in Chapter 2.

Ryba et al. found that most respondents recognized the importance of describing CST deficits, providing a rationale for identified predicates underlying the deficits (including immaturity), and drawing a connection between the observed deficits and court functioning. However, Christy et al. found that the rationale for examiners' opinions about CST deficits was omitted in about one-half of the cases, and the underlying cause of the functional deficits was omitted in more than one-third. The findings in both studies suggested that high rates of juvenile CST examiners offer ultimate issue CST opinions (a controversial issue that will be discussed in Chapter 6), but 10% of respondents to the Ryba et al. survey described that practice as contraindicated.

Nearly all of the reports reviewed by Christy et al. offered specific remediation recommendations for the court. Most reports provided opinions about the likelihood of successful intervention of relevant deficits, the estimated length of time successful remediation would require, and the recommended setting within which the remediation should occur.

Who Is Referred for Juvenile CST Evaluations

A number of studies have examined the demographic characteristics of juveniles referred for CST evaluations (Baerger, Griffin, Lyons, & Simmons, 2003; Cowden & McKee, 1995; Evans, 2003; Kruh, Sullivan, Ellis, Lexcen, & McClellan, 2006; McKee, 1998; McKee & Shea, 1999). They reported referral patterns that were consistent with general samples of juvenile justice–referred youth in terms of race and gender. But the average age of youth referred for CST evaluations in these studies ranged from 14.0 to 14.9 years, which is younger than the average age of general juvenile offender samples (about 15.5 years) in the United States.

History

Juveniles referred for CST evaluations tended to have a history of juvenile justice involvement, to be facing multiple charges, and to be facing felony charges (Cowden & McKee, 1995; Evans, 2003; McKee, 1998; McKee & Shea, 1999). Referred defendants also tended to have histories of special education services and mental health services (Cowden & McKee, 1995; Kruh et al., 2006; McKee, 1998; McKee & Shea, 1999).

Specific Diagnoses

Rates of specific diagnoses have been examined in two studies (Kruh et al., 2006; McKee & Shea, 1999), but with extreme differences between them in the percentages that they report (e.g., anxiety disorders, 22% and 1%; ADHD, 41% and 17%, respectively). The discrepancy suggests that there may be jurisdictional differences, thus it is difficult for examiners nationally to anticipate the proportions of youth with various mental disorders that are likely to be referred. A more consistent finding was the large proportion of youth referred for CST evaluations who had intellectual skills at or below borderline intellectual functioning (55% and 41%, respectively).

Correlates of Incompetence

As the studies reviewed below demonstrate, four main factors have been found to be related to CST functioning among youth. Age and intelligence have consistently been found to be associated with CST. Learning and academic functioning and mental health problems also seem to be associated with CST, but the patterns of those relationships are still being clarified. In the review below, attention is given to how these four correlates relate to CST and to each of the four fundamental CST capacities discussed in Chapter 2 (Understanding, Appreciation, Assisting, and Decision Making). These capacities were assessed in many of the studies using subtests from measures like the MacCAT-CA (e.g., assessing cognitive Decision Making with the Reasoning subtest) or the Fitness Interview Test–Revised (FIT-R) (e.g., assessing Assisting abilities with the Communication subtest), both of which will be discussed in more detail in this chapter and in Chapter 5. Examiners should think of their evaluations in terms of these four different abilities because significant impairment in any one capacity can yield a finding of IST.

INFO

Four main factors found to correlate with juvenile IST are the following:

● Age

● Intelligence

● Learning and academic functioning

● Mental health problems

Age

In controlled studies examining various community, psychiatric, and detention samples, older adolescents and adults have tended to perform better than younger adolescents on broad CST assessment tools (Burnett, Noblin, & Prosser, 2004; Ficke, Hart, & Deardorff, 2006; Grisso et al., 2003; Viljoen & Roesch, 2005; Viljoen, Zapf, & Roesch, 2007; and two of three CST measures by

Warren, Aaron, Ryan, Chauhan, & DuVal, 2003, but not Redlich, Silverman, & Steiner, 2003, when examined within the context of other variables). Studies of youth undergoing CST evaluations have also revealed that the likelihood of being

INFO

Juveniles of younger age are at higher risk for CST deficits.

found IST decreases with age (Baerger et al., 2003; Cowden & McKee, 1995; Kruh et al., 2006; McKee, 1998; McKee & Shea, 1999).

The most comprehensive study of age and juvenile CST to date examined 927 adolescents and 466 young adults in detention and community settings from four geographic locations (Grisso et al., 2003). About one-third of all youth ages 11 to 13 and one-fifth of all youth ages 14 to 15 showed CST deficits similar to those of adults who had been found IST in criminal court. Juveniles between 11 and 13 years of age were more than three times as likely as adults to show such severe deficits, and juveniles between 14 and 15 were more than twice as likely to show such weaknesses. However, juveniles ages 16 and 17 were about as likely to show these deficits as adults. These findings varied little by race, ethnicity, gender, socioeconomic status, or geographical region.

UNDERSTANDING

Younger adolescents have performed more poorly than older adolescents and adults on CST assessment tools and subtests that focus on factual understanding of legal concepts (Burnett et al., 2004; Cooper, 1997; Ficke et al., 2006; Grisso et al., 2003; McKee, 1998; Pierce & Brodsky, 2002; Savitsky and Karras, 1984; Viljoen & Roesch, 2005; Warren et al., 2003, but not Redlich et al., 2003, when examined within the context of other variables). In one large sample, 20% of 11- to 13-year-olds and 13% of 14- to 15-year-olds showed significant impairment in Understanding, with 60% of 11- to 13-year-olds and 53% of 14- to 15-year-olds showing mild to significant impairment (Grisso et al., 2003). The critical ability to understand the role of defense counsel is also weaker in younger juveniles than in older juveniles (Pierce & Brodsky, 2002).

3
chapter

Patterns in the development of CST Understanding are becoming clearer. On average, fundamental knowledge of trial processes and trial participants seems to be relatively undeveloped in the preadolescent years and is still being organized and integrated in early adolescence (Peterson-Badali & Abramovitch, 1992; Peterson-Badali, Abramovitch, & Duda, 1997). Substantial development in this knowledge occurs between ages 10 and 13, culminating with knowledge that is typically similar to that of older adolescents and adults (Cashmore & Bussey, 1990; Saywitz, 1989; Warren-Leubecker, Tate, Hinton, & Ozbek, 1989). Nonetheless, youth ages 14 to 16 may still demonstrate less well-developed Understanding ability than that of typical adults (Grisso, 2000). Certain important legal concepts may remain confusing well into adolescence, such as the presumption of innocence (Peterson-Badali, & Abramovich, 1992) and the process of plea agreements (McKee, 1998). Youth are also vulnerable to misunderstandings about the concept of rights as protective legal entitlements (Grisso, 2000). This is particularly the case with juvenile offenders and youth from lower socioeconomic status (Read, 1987; Grisso, 1981, 2000; Lawrence, 1983; Wall & Furlong, 1985).

Some studies have examined the ability of youth to learn basic legal information (i.e., to develop understanding where it was lacking) using simple interventions, such as basic verbal explanations (Viljoen, Odgers, Grisso, & Tillbrook, 2007), the use of simplified language (Ferguson & Douglas, 1970; Manoogian, 1978), or use of an educational videotape (Cooper, 1997). These studies have found that such methods do not significantly or adequately improve understanding. Further, younger juveniles benefit less from basic instruction than older adolescents (Viljoen et al., 2007).

APPRECIATION

Younger juveniles perform more poorly than older juveniles and adults on various CST subtests measuring rational understanding of legal concepts (Burnett, Noblin, & Prosser, 2004; Ficke, Hart, & Deardorff, 2006; Grisso, et al., 2003, Viljoen & Roesch, 2005, but not Ficke et al., 2006 or Redlich et al., 2003, when examined within the context of other variables). One study did not find an overall age trend, but still found that 40% of youth ages 10 to 13 demonstrated mild to major impairment on an Appreciation measure (Warren et al., 2003).

In particular, deficits in appreciation of the advocacy role of defense counsel and the attorney–client privilege are common among younger juveniles, and they even occur among a substantial proportion of older adolescents (Grisso, 1980, 1981; Grisso & Pomiceter, 1977; Peterson-Badali & Abramovitch, 1992). These weaknesses could limit juveniles' trust in their attorney. In fact, CST examiners perceive younger juveniles as less trusting of their attorneys than older juveniles (McKee, 1998), although younger juveniles do not report less trust in their attorneys (Pierce & Brodsky, 2002). Also, younger juveniles have shown deficits in their appreciation of the relation between the seriousness of an offense and the seriousness of possible punishments (Grisso, 1981).

ASSISTING AND DECISION MAKING

On measures that assess Assisting and Decision Making together, younger juveniles tend to earn lower scores than older juveniles and adults (Burnett et al., 2004; Ficke et al., 2006; Grisso et al., 2003; Viljoen & Roesch, 2005; Warren et al., 2003, but not Redlich et al., 2003, when examined within the context of other variables). For example, in one large sample of adolescents, 16% of 11- to 13-year-olds and 9% of 14- to 15-year-olds demonstrated significant impairment in their abilities to assist and make decisions, and about 36% of 11- to 13-year-olds and about 15% of 14- to 15-year-olds demonstrated mild to significant impairment, even when controlling for intelligence and the extent of past experience with the legal system (Grisso et al., 2003).

There may be a number of reasons for age-based weaknesses in Assisting. Adolescents have demonstrated difficulty understanding the lexical language that is common in legal contexts, which reduces their ability to communicate in that context (see Owen-Kostelnik, Reppucci, & Meyer, 2006). Also, younger adolescents are vulnerable to providing distorted information when they face pressures, such as negative feedback about their initial responses

(Grisso, 2000; Gudjonsson, 1992; 2003; Gudjonsson & Singh, 1984; Richardson, Gudjonsson, & Kelly, 1995). These factors may explain why CST examiners tend to view younger juveniles as evidencing weaker Assisting abilities, such as disclosing pertinent facts to counsel (McKee, 1998).

Age-related differences in Decision Making have been demonstrated for many types of legal decisions (Abramovitch, Higgins-Biss, & Biss, 1983; Abramovitch, Peterson-Badali, & Rohan, 1995; Cauffman & Steinberg, 2000; Ferguson & Douglas, 1970; Grisso, 1981; Grisso & Pomiciter, 1977; Grisso et al., 2003; Schmidt, Reppucci, & Woolard, 2003; Viljoen, Klaver, & Roesch, 2005; Woolard, Fried, & Reppucci, 2001). These age-related differences generally hold true across gender, ethnicity, and in or out of juvenile justice custody (Grisso et al., 2003). Deficits in cognitive-based and psychosocial-based reasoning may contribute to these age trends.

Age-based differences in the cognitive process for reaching legal decisions have been identified in a number of studies. For example, younger adolescents are less likely than older adolescents to adequately consider the strength of the evidence against them when deciding to waive legal rights, accept or reject plea agreements, or consult with a lawyer about their charges (Abramovitch et al., 1995; Peterson-Badali & Abramovitch, 1993; Peterson-Badali et al., 1997; Viljoen et al., 2005). Older youth are better able than younger children to explain when and how they have adjusted their decisions based on relevant information (Peterson-Badali & Abramovitch, 1993).

As discussed in Chapter 2, research on decision making among youth has begun to identify ways in which psychosocial developmental factors, including autonomy, perceptions of risk, and time perspective, can influence legal decision making. In addition to being affected by age, many of these threats to sound decisional judgment are also associated with lower intelligence (Grisso et al., 2003; Schmidt et al., 2003; Viljoen et al., 2005).

Autonomy   Some studies have found that younger adolescents are more likely than older adolescents to reach important legal decisions by complying with the requests of authority figures, including their attorneys, parents, and peers (Grisso et al., 2003; Scherer, 1991; Scherer & Reppucci, 1988). One study found no age differences in responses to advice about how to plea, but generally found that the decisions of adolescents at all ages were significantly impacted by the advice of attorneys, parents, and peers (Viljoen et al., 2005).

Perceptions of Risk   Evidence suggests that youth tend to be less able to imagine risky outcomes when making legal decisions (Grisso, 1981; Grisso et al., 2003; Lewis, 1981; Peterson-Badali and Abramovitch, 1993). For example, juveniles 15 and younger were less likely to identify risks than older adolescents and adults when making decisions like entering a plea (Grisso et al., 2003). Also, younger adolescents were more likely than older adolescents and/or adults to assess negative outcomes as unlikely to occur and non-serious if they were to occur (Grisso et al, 2003).

Time Perspective   Adolescents are more likely than adults to iden-tify and overemphasize the short-term consequences, particularly the immediate gains, of their legal decisions, and a more appropri-ate balance with other considerations increases with age (Schmidt et al., 2003; Woolard, 1998). Younger juveniles are also less likely than older youth and adults to identify and consider the long-term outcomes of legal decisions, such as deciding a plea (Grisso et al., 2003; Woolard, 1998).

As has been demonstrated in this section, the influence of age on CST is a robust finding that has held across various research method-ologies and samples. It seems that youth under age 12 are at very high risk of functioning in ways similar to those of IST adults (Otto & Goldstein, 2005). Youth under age 14 or 15 are also at high risk for CST impairments (Grisso, 2000; Grisso et al., 2003), partic-ularly because of idiosyncrasies in developmental trajectories (Grisso, 2000). Juvenile offenders may be at particular risk to demonstrate developmental delays that place them at continued risk for CST vul-nerabilities into this age range. Adolescents older than age 16 are more likely to show abilities similar to those of adults and, when abilities are lacking, it is likely that other factors are involved, such as intellectual functioning, learning and academic functioning, and/or mental illness. The relation between age and CST abilities seems to be due in large part to the immature development of cognitive skills (Viljoen & Roesch, 2005).

Intellectual Functioning

As is true with adults, youth with lower intellectual functioning are more likely to have CST deficits. In most studies (an exception is Burnett, Noblin, & Prosser, 2004), intelligence estimates have been positively correlated and diagnoses of mental retardation have been negatively correlated with the performance of youth on all elements of broad competence assessment tools (Ficke et al., 2006; Grisso et al., 2003; Warren et al., 2003; and verbal abilities, but not some other cognitive skills, by Viljoen & Roesch, 2005). For example, one large-scale study found that 40% of adolescents and young-adult participants with an IQ between 60 and 74 and 25% of participants with an IQ between 75 and 89 showed significant CST impairment (Grisso et al., 2003). Furthermore, youth deemed IST during CST evaluations tend to have lower intellectual functioning than competent youth (Evans, 2003; Kruh et al., 2006), are more likely than competent youth to have diagnoses of borderline intellectual functioning and mental retardation (McKee and Shea, 1999), and are more likely to be diagnosed with mental retardation than a mental illness (Baerger et al., 2003).

UNDERSTANDING AND APPRECIATION

Lower intellectual functioning and diagnoses of mental retardation have been associated with poorer performance on tests of CST Understanding in youth (Burnett et al., 2004; Cooper, 1997; Ficke et al., 2006; Grisso et al., 2003; Pierce & Brodsky, 2002; Savitsky & Karras, 1984; Warren et al., 2003; and verbal abilities, but not some other cognitive skills, by Peterson-Badali and Abramovitch, 1992; Viljoen & Roesch, 2005). IQ has also demonstrated a positive relation with the specific understanding of the role of defense counsel (Pierce &

INFO

Juveniles with lower intellectual functioning are at higher risk for CST deficits.

Brodsky, 2002), understanding of legal rights (Grisso, 1981; Shepard & Zaremba, 1995; Zaremba, 1992), and the ability to develop CST Understanding from brief verbal instruction (Viljoen, Odgers et al., 2007).

Among youth, lower intellectual functioning and diagnoses of mental retardation are also associated with poorer performance on CST Appreciation measures (Ficke et al., 2006; Grisso et al., 2003; Warren et al., 2003; and both verbal and attentional abilities, but not other cognitive abilities, by Viljoen & Roesch, 2005, but not IQ in the context of other variables by Burnett et al., 2004).

ASSISTING AND DECISION MAKING

Lower intelligence scores and diagnoses of mental retardation have been associated with lower scores on measures that assess both Assisting and cognitive Decision Making (Ficke et al., 2006; Grisso et al., 2003; Warren et al., 2003, but not Burnett et al., 2004 in the context of other variables). Examining more specific cognitive abilities, verbal and attentional abilities were significant predictors of scores on one such measure among youth (Viljoen & Roesch, 2005). Similar trends have been found on specific legal decision-making tasks, such as reaching plea agreement decisions (Peterson-Badali & Abramovitch, 1992; Viljoen et al., 2005).

THE AGE–IQ INTERACTION

In addition to empirical evidence that age and intellectual functioning independently predict juvenile CST functioning, the two factors interact such that young age and lower intellectual abilities yield particularly high risk for CST deficits (Ficke et al., 2006; Grisso et al., 2003; Viljoen & Roesch, 2005). In one study, for example, more than one-half of the youth age 13 and younger who also had intellectual functioning below 75 demonstrated levels of CST problems similar to those of IST adults, as was true for more than one-third of the same age group when IQ was between 75 and 89 (Grisso et al., 2003). Among 14- to 15-year-olds in that study, about 40% of those who also had intellectual functioning below 75 and more than 25% of those with an IQ between 75 and 89 demonstrated levels of CST problems similar to those of adults found IST. This age–IQ relationship has also been found specific to Appreciation

INFO

The combined factors of young age and lower intellectual functioning further increase the risk for CST deficits.

abilities (Grisso et al., 2003; Viljoen & Roesch, 2005) and Assisting and Decision-Making abilities (Viljoen & Roesch, 2005). This interaction may occur because legal abilities are less ingrained at a younger age and more vulnerable to the interference of lower intelligence (Viljoen & Roesch, 2005). Also, younger adolescents, who typically have immature cognitive skills, may be doubly handicapped in the cognitive abilities needed for CST functioning when they also have intellectual limitations.

Learning and Academic Functioning

Learning problems also seem to be associated with reduced CST functioning among juveniles, but results have been less consistent than with age and intelligence. Among juveniles referred for CST evaluations, studies have generally found that youth found competent are less likely to have been in special education than incompetent juveniles (Baerger et al., 2003; Cowden & McKee, 1995; Kruh et al., 2006; however, see McKee & Shea, 1999, for a different result), but may be no less likely to be diagnosed with a learning disorder (Kruh et al., 2006). In studies of non-evaluation-referred youth, clear patterns about the relation between learning problems and CST capacities remain unclear. These studies are discussed next.

UNDERSTANDING AND APPRECIATION

Juveniles' specific understanding of rights is related to learning and academic functioning (Lawrence, 1983; Zaremba, 1992). Furthermore, scores on achievement tests have predicted performance on measures of both Understanding and Appreciation (Ficke et al., 2005). Histories of special-education placement or grade retention have predicted Understanding (Cowden & McKee, 1995), but reading level has not (Cooper, 1997).

INFO

Learning problems and CST deficits may be related, though no clear patterns have been identified.

Diagnoses of learning disorders have predicted performance on measures of Understanding but not Appreciation (Warren et al., 2003). Educational level and self-reported grades predicted neither Understanding nor Appreciation (Burnett et al., 2004; Redlich et al., 2003).

ASSISTING AND DECISION MAKING
Performance on CST measures of Assisting and Decision Making have also been related to some measures of learning ability, including diagnoses of learning disorders, education level, and scores on academic achievement tests (Burnett et al., 2004; Ficke et al., 2005; Warren et al., 2003), but not self-reported grades (Redlich et al., 2003).

Mental Illness
Youth referred for CST evaluations are at particularly high risk to have mental illnesses that interfere with CST functioning. As is true with adults, most studies of juvenile CST evaluations have found that youth diagnosed with severe mental illnesses such as psychosis are less likely than other examinees to be found competent (Cowden & McKee, 1995; Kruh et al., 2006; but not McKee & Shea, 1999). As is also true with adults, youth found IST in one sample were more likely than competent youth to have histories of mental health services (Baerger et al., 2003), but no such relationship was found in other samples (Kruh et al., 2006; McKee & Shea, 1999).

One study found that diagnoses of substance abuse among CST examinees were also associated with being found IST, but diagnoses of alcohol abuse and cannabis abuse were not (Baerger et al., 2003). Another study yielded less expected results in that diagnoses of mood disorder, disruptive behavior disorder, and substance abuse were each associated with being found competent, but diagnoses of ADHD, anxiety disorders, adjustment disorders, and personality disorders were unrelated to CST opinions (Kruh et al., 2006).

INFO

Severe mental illness, such as psychosis, is associated with CST deficits in juveniles, but the impact of other diagnoses on CST is less clear.

Most studies examining the relation between CST and mental illness, however, have examined community and/or detained samples of youth who are probably at reduced risk for mental illnesses compared to CST evaluation-referred youth. These studies have not identified clearly discernable patterns. These studies are reviewed next.

UNDERSTANDING AND APPRECIATION

Two studies found few relationships between self-reported acute mental health problems and Understanding or Appreciation among youth (Grisso et al., 2003; Warren et al., 2003). Studies examining clinician-rated acute mental health issues, however, have found that psychotic symptoms and developmental maladjustment are associated with reduced Understanding and Appreciation, withdrawal and hostility with reduced Understanding but not Appreciation, and excitation with reduced Appreciation but not Understanding; internalizing depression and anxiety problems have been found to be unrelated to either (Ficke et al., 2005; Viljoen & Roesch, 2005; Warren et al., 2003). In one study, externalizing behavior problems were associated with lower Understanding and Appreciation (Redlich et al., 2003), but in another study they were not (Ficke et al., 2005). One study found that mental health problems did not predict the likelihood of benefiting from brief verbal Understanding instruction (Viljoen, Odgers, et al., 2007). In another study, diagnoses of mood disorders, behavior disorders, psychotic disorders, and substance abuse disorders did not predict CST Understanding or Appreciation (Warren et al., 2003).

ASSISTING AND DECISION MAKING

Two studies found few relationships between self-reported acute mental health problems and Assisting or Decision-Making abilities among youth (Grisso et al., 2003; Warren et al., 2003). In studies of clinician ratings, hostility, excitation, and developmental maladjustment were associated with reduced abilities, but withdrawal, internalizing emotional problems, and psychotic symptoms were not (Ficke et al., 2006; Viljoen et al., 2005; Viljoen & Roesch, 2005; Warren et al., 2003). Externalizing behavior problems were associated with reduced abilities in one study (Ficke, et al., 2006), but not in another (Viljoen & Roesch, 2005).

When assessing diagnoses in youth, mood disorders, psychotic disorders, and substance abuse disorders did not predict functioning on a test of Assisting and Decision Making, but diagnoses of behavior disorders were associated with reduced abilities (Warren et al., 2003). ADHD symptoms seemed to impact some legal decisions in that they were associated with a greater likelihood of waiving the right to counsel and a lower likelihood of discussing disagreements with counsel (Viljoen et al., 2005).

Multivariate Analyses

Two studies have examined the ability of multiple-variable equations to discriminate youth found CST and IST during clinical evaluations. These studies have reinforced the conclusion that age, intelligence, learning and academic functioning, and mental illness are the most relevant predictors of juvenile CST. Entering data related to these four variables yielded classification accuracy ranging from 74% to 90% (Baerger et al., 2003; Kruh et al., 2006). Several studies have looked at various multivariate models among youth not referred for evaluations that also lend general support to the predictive utility of these four factors (e.g., Warren et al., 2003).

Other Factors and Juvenile CST

EXPERIENCE WITH THE LEGAL SYSTEM

Contrary to conventional wisdom, youth's experience with the legal system—when measured in a variety of ways—is generally not related to CST (Cooper, 1997; Cowden & McKee, 1995; Ficke et al., 2006; Grisso, 1981; Grisso et al., 2003; Redlich et al., 2003; Savitsky and Karras, 1984, but see Burnett et al., 2004; McKee & Shea, 1999; Schmidt et al., 2003; and Viljoen & Roesch, 2005, for some differences). However, Understanding may be better among juveniles who spend more time with their attorney (Viljoen & Roesch, 2005), as well as those who hold greater trust in their attorney (Pierce & Brodsky, 2002).

RACE AND MINORITY STATUS

Most studies have found no relation between race and broad measures of CST, including studies of youth referred for CST evaluations (Cowden & McKee, 1995; Kruh et al., 2006; McKee & Shea,

INFO

No clear relation to juvenile CST has been found for the following factors:

- Experience with the legal system
- Race
- Gender
- Socioeconomic status
- Nature of instant charges
- Court of adjudication (juvenile vs. criminal)

1999; but see Baerger et al., 2003) and non-evaluation-referred youth (Grisso et al., 2003; however, see Burnett et al., 2004, for different findings in a smaller sample). However, minority youth have demonstrated reduced skills compared to those of white youth on their understanding of the role of defense counsel (Pierce & Brodsky, 2002), trust in defense counsel (Pierce & Brodsky, 2002; Schmidt et al., 2003), understanding of legal rights (Lawrence, 1983; Zaremba, 1992), the likelihood of developing Understanding from brief verbal instruction (Viljoen, Odgers et al., 2007), and the willingness to disclose information to defense counsel (Viljoen et al., 2005).

GENDER, SOCIOECONOMIC STATUS, CHARGES, AND COURT

Studies have also failed to find relations between overall CST and gender (Baerger et al., 2003; Burnett et al., 2004; Cowden & McKee, 1995; Ficke et al., 2006; Grisso et al., 2003; Kruh et al., 2006; McKee & Shea, 1999), socioeconomic status (Grisso et al., 2003), the nature of the instant charges (Cowden & McKee, 1995), or the court of adjudication (juvenile vs. criminal; Poythress, Lexcen, Grisso, & Steinberg, 2006). However, Understanding may be less well developed among girls (Viljoen & Roesch, 2005, but not Cooper, 1997) and youth of lower socioeconomic status (Viljoen & Roesch, 2005). Girls may also be more willing than boys to disclose information to counsel (Viljoen et al., 2005).

Juvenile CST Standard

Chapter 2 discussed a number of questions about the appropriate CST standard to be used with juveniles. Researchers have explored some of these issues.

Levels of Capacity

One study provides information about the use of the flexible bar standard discussed in Chapter 2. When presented with hypothetical vignettes in which all other case characteristics were controlled, judges, attorneys, and mental health professionals asked to judge the competence of juveniles more often saw youth facing more serious charges as IST than when the same youth were facing less serious charges (Jones, 2004). The results suggest that participants used a flexible bar approach, apparently raising the bar for CST in cases involving more serious potential sanctions (and potentially more complex trials).

In a study of the potential impact of various juvenile court CST standards, Viljoen, Zapf, and Roesch (2007) examined the rates of youth classified as significantly impaired and at risk to be IST according to the Fitness Interview Test–Revised (FIT-R) when they were compared to available adult norms on the test, to adolescent norms on the test, and to a standard requiring only the most fundamental abilities. The results by age group are provided in Table 3.1. About one-half of the subjects did not show consistent classification across the three standards, and both the adolescent norm standard and the basic understanding and communication

Table 3.1 | Comparing Youth Classified as IST Across Various CST Standards

	11–13 Years (% IST)	14–15 Years (% IST)	16–17 Years (% IST)
Adult norm standard	88%	73%	45%
Adolescent norm standard	20%	6%	2%
Basic understanding and communication standard	80%	59%	33%

Source: Viljoen, Zapf, & Roesch (2007)

standard identified significantly fewer juvenile defendants as impaired relative to the adult norm standard (Viljoen, Zapf, & Roesch, 2007). This study demonstrates that different standards could have very real implications for the outcomes of individual juvenile CST evaluations and for the numbers of youth found IST.

Role of Immaturity

In Chapter 2 it was noted that few jurisdictions have explicitly held that developmental immaturity related to age and/or developmental delays can form a legitimate legal basis for incompetence and there has been no consistent decision on the issue among those jurisdictions that have. Two surveys have provided relevant information on this point. In one study, two-thirds of a national sample of 87 examiners conducting frequent juvenile CST evaluations said that they had recommended juveniles to be found IST on the basis of developmental issues; in fact, one-fifth identified immature development as the most commonly identified basis for their recommendations of incompetence (Grisso & Quinlan, 2005). A survey of 79 juvenile CST examiners revealed that only 22% believed immaturity, in the absence of a mental disorder, is a legitimate basis for an incompetence finding under the laws of their jurisdictions (Ryba et al., 2003a). Most of those surveyed believed there is an age cutoff at which incompetence is more likely, with the modal response being age 12. The contrast in results between the two studies may illustrate confusion about the role of immaturity in juvenile CST among examiners.

Role of Interested Adults

No jurisdictions have explicitly ruled on the role of interested adults in juvenile CST evaluations, but some attorneys have expressed concern that caregivers do not always offer competent assistance to youth. In a study of the competence abilities of child–parent units, 45% of the units showed significant CST impairment in one or both of the members (Woolard, 2006). Further, significant impairments were identified in both members of the unit in 15% of the cases. There were many misconceptions about the role of parents in juvenile adjudications among these units. For example, many youth (35%) and parents (50%) believed that defense attorneys can communicate openly with parents about the youth's case. Over 75% of parents believed that they play the role of final arbiter in their children's cases when they disagree with their child. Younger youth tended to have similar ideas, but older youth increasingly believed that attorneys are supposed to rely on adolescent defendants' preferences.

Forensic Assessment Instruments Developed for Adults

Forensic assessment instruments (FAIs) are structured quantitative interview tools designed for focused assessment of the functional legal abilities of direct relevance to legal questions. Several FAIs have been developed for assessment of CST abilities among adult defendants. Interested readers can access a number of detailed reviews and discussions of these adult CST FAIs (Goldstein, 2002; Grisso, 2003a; Melton et al., 2007; Mumley, Tilbrook & Grisso, 2003; Rogers & Shuman, 2005; Stafford, 2003; Zapf & Viljoen, 2003; and in this series, Zapf & Roesch, 2009). Two of these CST FAIs have been examined in research with juvenile populations, providing the results discussed next. Furthermore, the developers of one (the FIT-R) have increasingly recommended its use with juveniles (Roesch, Zapf, & Eaves, 2006). (Chapter 5 will describe these two instruments in detail.)

MacArthur Competence Assessment Tool–Criminal Adjudication (MacCAT-CA)

RELIABILITY

The MacCAT-CA (Poythress et al., 1999) includes subtests assessing Understanding, Reasoning, and Appreciation, mainly of information related to a hypothetical legal case. The MacCAT-CA administered to youth has produced internal consistency (as measured by alpha) figures ranging from .54 to .92 for Understanding, .37 to .91 for Reasoning, and .33 to .78 for Appreciation (Boyd, 1999; Poythress et al., 2006; Warren et al., 2003). The variability across

INFO

Two forensic assessment instruments—the MacCAT-CA and the FIT-R—have been examined with juveniles in empirical research.

studies may have resulted from sample differences, which ranged from youth being tried in criminal court to psychiatrically hospitalized male adolescents. These results reveal modest to poor internal consistency in some cases, raising some questions about the adequacy of the Reasoning and Appreciation scales when used with juveniles.

With youth, interrater reliability (as measured by intraclass correlation) of the MacCAT-CA has ranged from .63 to .91 for Understanding, .60 to .90 for Reasoning, and .31 to .90 for Appreciation (Boyd, 1999; Burnett et al., 2004; Grisso et al., 2003). Here, too, the discrepant findings between studies might have resulted from the examination of diverse samples. Interrater reliability tended to be stronger for Understanding and Reasoning than for Appreciation.

VALIDITY

The MacCAT-CA has manifested expected relationships with age and intelligence in adolescent samples (Burnett et al., 2004; Ficke et al., 2006; Grisso et al., 2003). As was reviewed earlier in this chapter, studies have also found relations with some measures of learning and academic problems and mental health problems, but not with others.

INTERPRETATION

Detained juveniles performed more poorly on all MacCAT-CA factors than jailed adults in the norming sample (Burnett et al., 2004), a finding highlighting the need for juvenile norms. Although no such norms have been collected, several studies have reported descriptive statistics for juveniles on the MacCAT-CA factors (see Table 3.2).

Fitness Interview Test–Revised (FIT-R)

RELIABILITY

The FIT-R (Roesch, Zapf, Eaves, & Webster, 1998) includes subtests assessing Understanding, Appreciation, and Communication. When used with juveniles, individual items on the FIT-R demonstrated good interrater reliability with intraclass correlations (ICCs) ranging from .60 to .75 (Viljoen, Vincent, & Roesch, 2006). Strong interrater reliability has also been demonstrated when items were summed into FIT-R section and total scores, as follows (as measured by ICC): Understanding = .91; Appreciation = .82; Communication = .83; Total = .91 (Viljoen et al., 2005; Viljoen & Roesch, 2005; Viljoen et al., 2006; Viljoen, Zapf, & Roesch, 2007). When the items were used to yield structured clinical ratings of CST (rather than simply summing the item scores), however, lower but acceptable interrater reliability was obtained (ICCs ranging from .59 to .80).

VALIDITY

An adjusted three-factor model united by a dominant unidimensional factor has been validated with juveniles, indicating that the FIT-R assesses three related but distinct abilities (Viljoen et al., 2006). These factors are Understanding and Reasoning about Legal Proceedings (Items 3, 4, 5, 6, 12, and 13), Appreciation of Case-Specific Information (Items 1, 2, 7, 8, and 9), and Communication with Counsel (Items 10, 11, 14, 15, and 16). These factors have demonstrated adequate internal consistency with alpha values of .85, .78, and .80, respectively (Viljoen et al.,

3
chapter

Table 3.2 Descriptive Statistics for Studies of the MacCAT-CA among Youth by Factor

Study	Sample	Age Category (years)	Understanding X (SD)	Reasoning X (SD)	Appreciation X (SD)
Warren, Aaron, Ryan, Chauhan, & DuVal (2003)	120 male psychiatric inpatients	<14 >13 All	9.70 (1.24) 10.73 (3.33) 10.38 (3.57)	11.48 (3.23) 12.11 (3.14) 11.90 (3.17)	9.80 (2.98) 10.07 (3.14) 10.01 (2.46)
Grisso et al. (2003)	927 youths (offenders & community)	11–13 14–15 16–17	10.45 (3.31) 11.27 (2.97) 12.00 (2.82)	11.30 (2.82) 12.10 (2.55) 12.76 (2.34)	9.68 (2.34) 10.33 (1.79) 10.65 (1.66)
Burnett, Noblin, & Prosser (2004)	110 youths (offenders & community)	10–12 13–14 15–16 17	9.72 (3.25) 9.97 (2.61) 11.04 (2.99) 12.40 (1.67)	10.28 (2.40) 11.00 (2.89) 11.94 (2.88) 13.60 (1.82)	9.67 (0.58) 10.76 (1.37) 11.43 (0.84) 11.44 (1.01)

2006). As was reviewed earlier in this chapter, the FIT-R has also demonstrated expected relationships with age and elements of intelligence, as well as some relationships with various measures of mental health problems when used with juveniles (Viljoen & Roesch, 2005).

INTERPRETATION

There are no published juvenile norms for the FIT-R. It is a structured interview and not a normed test. However, scores obtained by 152 pretrial juvenile defendants have been reported in one study (Viljoen & Roesch, 2005).

Examiner Opinions and Court Determinations

Studies of adults referred for CST evaluations find, on average, that 20%–30% are found IST, but results vary greatly across jurisdictions and time (Melton et al., 2007; Nicholson & Kugler, 1991; Roesch, Zapf, Golding, & Skeem, 1999; Warren, Rosenfeld, Fitch, & Hawk, 1997). Of youth referred for CST evaluations, rates of incompetence between 3% and 41% have been reported (Cowden & McKee, 1995; Evans, 2003; Kruh et al., 2006; Levitt & Trollinger, 2002; McGaha, McClaren, Otto, & Petrila, 2001; McKee, 1998; McKee & Shea, 1999). Given the legal and clinical ambiguities inherent in juvenile CST evaluations, one might also expect that many evaluations yield findings that CST is, for some reason, questionable. In fact, two studies that included a "questionable" category found that 13% to 15% of examinees can be characterized as such (Cowden & McKee, 1995; Kruh et al., 2006).

INFO

Although aggregate rates of IST findings vary across studies, there seems to be a high agreement rate between examiners and the courts on CST opinions.

A study examining agreement between mental health examiner opinions and ultimate judicial decisions found extremely high agreement both when examiners provided clear CST/ IST opinions (kappa = .90) and when cases included "questionable" opinions ($r = .66$; Kruh et al., 2006). Similarly, high examiner–court agreement rates have been found with adults (Cruise & Rogers, 1998; Zapf, Hubbard, Cooper, Wheeles, and Ronan, 2004).

Competence Remediation

Who Is Ordered for CST Remediation?

In a large Florida sample of juvenile court defendants referred for CST remediation, most were male and African American (McGaha et al., 2001). One-half were charged with violent crimes against persons, one-third were charged with property crimes, about one-fifth were charged with criminal mischief, and one-tenth were charged with sex offenses. About one-third of those referred had a diagnosable mental illness alone, about one-third were diagnosed with mental retardation alone, and 40% had both predicates.

Two studies have examined the mental health diagnoses of youth ordered for remediation. In the same Florida sample, 57% of youth with an Axis I disorder were diagnosed with conduct disorder, 37% with ADHD, 35% with mood disorders, 17% with psychotic disorders, and 15% with adjustment disorders (McGaha et al., 2001). In a much smaller Arizona sample of remediation participants, 63% had no diagnosable mental disorder, 25% were diagnosed with ADHD, 8% were diagnosed with a mood disorder, and 4% were diagnosed with a learning disorder (Levitt & Trollinger, 2002). The differences between the samples in these two studies indicate that we do not have a reliable perspective on the disorders of youth sent for remediation and that differences across jurisdictions and settings may be marked.

Where Are Remediation Services Provided?

In the same Florida sample of remediation participants, 83% received at least some of their services on an outpatient basis, 49% received at least some of their remediation services in a secure residential facility, and only 5% received services while being held in juvenile detention (McGaha et al., 2001). Most participants were served on an outpatient basis exclusively.

How Successful Is Remediation?

Nearly 90% of adult defendants referred for CST restoration will be successfully remediated within 280 days (Nicholson, Barnard, Robins, & Hankins, 1994). There has been little research, however, on the efficacy of juvenile CST remediation. Given the role of developmental factors in juvenile CST, it can be expected to be a difficult task (Viljoen & Roesch, 2007). A study of the Florida CST remediation program found that it typically required a 5- to 6-month period of remediation before a final post-remediation CST opinion was offered (McGaha et al., 2001). Although younger defendants required longer remediation periods before clinicians reached a final decision about CST, surprisingly, age did not predict the likelihood of successful remediation. Examining the cases on the basis of the predicate problem causing incompetence, 44% of the juveniles with mental retardation alone, 34% of the juveniles with both mental retardation and mental illness, and 8% of the juveniles with mental illness alone were found to be not remediable. Clearly, the presence of mental retardation was an important impediment to successful remediation.

There has been little effort to identify empirically supported juvenile CST remediation techniques. The Florida study described above examined only judicial decisions and not specific functional deficits and changes, limiting the ability to know which interventions yielded improvement or how they did so (Viljoen & Roesch, 2007).

INFO

There has been little research on juvenile CST remediation interventions and their rate of success.

Studies have found that brief remediation interventions, such as simple verbal instruction or an instructional video, did not adequately improve the functioning of juvenile defendants (Cooper, 1997; Viljoen, Odgers, et al., 2007).

Conclusion

Research on juvenile CST has just begun to appear in the literature, largely because CST has been recognized in juvenile courts only within the past 15 years. During that time, the number of research articles on juvenile CST appearing in professional journals has increased from 2 prior to 1990 to 5 between 1991 and 1995, then 12 more by 2000, and 25 new articles between 2002 and 2005. It is almost certain that research in this area will continue to grow significantly and rapidly. As it does, clinicians evaluating juvenile CST will need to stay abreast of developments.

3
chapter

APPLICATION

Preparation for the Evaluation | 4

Chapters 4, 5, and 6 provide guidelines and recommendations for preparing to conduct a CST evaluation of a juvenile, collecting the data, and interpreting the data. Preparing for the evaluation (this chapter) is among the most important stages of the evaluation, because decisions made early in the process will influence the whole course of the evaluation.

Qualifications for Conducting Juvenile CST Evaluations

As earlier chapters underscored, juvenile CST evaluations pose unique challenges relative to adult CST assessments (Grisso, 2003a; Oberlander, Goldstein, & Ho, 2001). Consequently, juvenile CST examiners must possess a unique blend of expertise, including special training, knowledge, skill, and experience (Grisso, 1998). Juvenile CST examiners must possess expertise in forensic assessment and child development (Borum & Grisso, 2007; Grisso, 2005; Oberlander et al., 2001). Furthermore, they must develop expertise about the functioning of the criminal and/or juvenile justice systems within which they will be serving and about the youth who become involved in them.

Few graduate training programs provide adequate cross-training in the knowledge and skills required for juvenile CST evaluation practice (Borum & Grisso, 2007; Grisso, 1998; Oberlander et al., 2001). Therefore, most juvenile CST examiners will need to develop adequate expertise in other ways. Consistent with this view, some jurisdictions require juvenile CST examiners to obtain specialized training and meet state credentialing requirements. The present volume can only scratch the surface of the information that juvenile CST examiners will need, but the types of knowledge associated with adequate practice can be identified.

Forensic Mental Health Expertise

Forensic mental health evaluations are conducted specifically for use in a legal context or to assist in specific legal decision-making (Grisso, 1998; Melton et al., 2007). Forensic evaluation practice is distinguished from general clinical evaluation practice in critical ways that are thoroughly reviewed in the first volume of this series, *Foundations of Forensic Mental Health Assessment* (Heilbrun, Grisso, & Goldstein, 2009). Forensic mental health examiners must be trained to practice within relevant practice standards, such as those offered by Heilbrun (2001), Grisso (2003a), Rogers and Shuman (2005), and Melton et al. (2007).

Examiners who lack adequate forensic mental health training are at risk of making basic mistakes, such as offering opinions that are inadequately substantiated, inadequately reasoned, and beyond the expertise of the mental health professions, or even failing to recognize the nature of the legal inquiry (Grisso, 2003a). These mistakes can occur from unfamiliarity with relevant laws, specialized ethical standards (Committee on Ethical Guidelines for Forensic Psychologists, 1991; American Academy of Psychiatry and the Law [AAPL], 2005), and/or specialized assessment methods.

Forensic mental health practitioners can avoid such mistakes by adhering to a *legal–empirical–forensic model* in which opinions reflect understanding of the relevant legal standards and the application of empirically grounded methods and procedures to the specific case (Rogers & Shuman, 2005). Of course, this model requires specificity to the type of forensic mental health evaluation, such as juvenile CST. Competence in one area of forensic evaluation practice does not necessarily establish one's expertise in another (Melton et al., 2007).

Child Clinical and Developmental Expertise

Working with children in clinical contexts has long been recognized as a specialty area because of the added complexities and

BEWARE
Lack of adequate training in the application of general forensic evaluation standards to specific types of forensic evaluations can lead to basic mistakes.

need for specialized knowledge. Child clinical evaluations require an understanding of age-specific development; assessment strategies across multiple domains, contexts, and informants; and the diagnostic ambiguity characteristic of developmental psychopathology (Kamphaus & Frick, 2001). For juvenile CST examiners lacking appropriate child clinical and developmental expertise, the risk of making mistakes is so high that such practice is patently incompetent and unethical (Grisso, 2005; Oberlander et al., 2001). For example, Kruh has been involved in juvenile CST cases in which mental health experts, who were trained only with adults, identified a verbally delayed 11-year-old as demonstrating "disorganized psychosis," administered adult assessment measures to children well below the age range on which the test was standardized, and altogether missed important diagnoses, such as Asperger's disorder, because of unfamiliarity with disorders more typically diagnosed in youth. Several types of child clinical and developmental expertise are needed for juvenile forensic assessment.

UNDERSTANDING NORMAL DEVELOPMENT

Developmental psychology involves the scientific study of the common variations of changes in physical, intellectual, emotional, and social development that occur across individuals over the life cycle (Steinberg & Schwartz, 2000). Clinical evaluations of youth must consider that the domains being assessed are always in flux (Lahey et al., 2004). Therefore, juvenile CST examiners should be knowledgeable in the early theories of developmentalists such as Piaget, Erikson, and Kohlberg, as well as in the decades-long research that followed these theories. Study of a commonly used graduate-level developmental psychology text (e.g., Steinberg, 2007) can help in developing this foundation. It can also be fostered through other forms of quality continuing education.

BEST PRACTICE
Acquire child clinical and developmental expertise in the following:

● Normal development

● Developmental psychopathology

● Developmentally appropriate assessment

KNOWLEDGE ABOUT DEVELOPMENTAL PSYCHOPATHOLOGY

Examiners must be familiar with disorders more commonly diagnosed among children (e.g., pervasive developmental disorders, fetal alcohol syndrome) and with the unique childhood presentation and/or diagnostic criteria of other disorders (e.g., the role of irritability in major depressive disorder among youth). They need specialized training in the ambiguities of differential diagnosis among youth because of the true symptom overlap between disorders (e.g., anger and irritability in both behavior and affective disorders; distractibility in both attentional and affective disorders) and the limitations in child mental health diagnostic classification systems that exacerbate diagnostic ambiguity (Grisso, 2005; Mash & Hunsley, 2005; Schwartz & Rosado, 2000). Examiners must also appreciate the high prevalence of comorbid disorders in youth (Jensen, 2003; Youngstrom, Findling, & Calabrese, 2003).

Interactions between mental health symptoms and normal development also make diagnosis of mental illness itself less reliable among juveniles than in adults (Dulit, 1989; Mattanah, Becker, Levy, Edell, & McGlashan, 1995). The appropriate label and conceptualization of a disorder, the characteristics of a disorder, and the impact of a disorder on functioning can vary according to when the disorder emerges during a person's development, but many of the developmental patterns of disorders are not well charted (Grisso, 2005; Kazdin, 2000).

Therefore, examiners should understand childhood disorders from a *developmental psychopathology* perspective. That is, psychopathology is to be understood in relation to normal development and adaptation (Cicchetti, 1990, 1993). Symptoms of pathology result from adaptational compromises or failures in normal development (Cicchetti & Rogosch, 2002). Once they develop, these symptoms continue to interact with patterns of normal development, making the stability and trajectory of identifiable problems difficult to specify (Borum & Grisso, 2007; Grisso, 1998). In short, the lines between normative development and pathology are often unclear.

ABILITY TO PERFORM DEVELOPMENTALLY APPROPRIATE ASSESSMENTS

Juvenile CST examiners must have specialized training in child and adolescent assessment. Interviews must include developmentally appropriate questioning and responses must be placed within an appropriate developmental context (Borum & Grisso, 2007; Mossman et al., 2007). Interviews may need to accommodate information processing, expressive language, and/or attentional weaknesses (Slobogin et al., 1997). Examiners must be skilled at navigating the more complex relational styles demonstrated by youth, such as extreme oppositionality or poorly differentiated attachment. They need to be trained in the selection, administration, and interpretation of tests used in child assessment, including assessment modalities that are uncommon with adults. Examiners must also be skilled at integrating information obtained at different ages, using multiple assessment methods, and data from a variety of informants, as well as addressing functioning in a number of contexts and social systems (Mash & Hunsley, 2005).

4
chapter

Expertise About Justice Systems and Delinquency

To conduct juvenile CST evaluations, examiners need an understanding of the processes and procedures of the justice system(s) within which they work (Grisso, 1998). This includes the history and logic for the existence of criminal and juvenile courts, and knowledge about the general process of cases in each. Additionally, examiners need to know the procedures in the specific courts where they conduct evaluations, including local laws (statutes and case law), local systems of detention, courts, attorneys, and services for adjudicated youth, and contours of the interface between the justice and mental health systems.

Examiners must also have expertise in the patterns of development, psychopathology, and offending that are typical of youth in juvenile justice settings. For example, examiners need to understand the developmental pathways to

BEST PRACTICE
Be familiar with the justice systems in which you are practicing and the typical youth involved with them.

juvenile offending (see, e.g., Loeber, Slot, & Stouthamer-Loeber, 2007), theories about sub-types of children with conduct problems (e.g., McMahon & Frick, 2007), and theories about the psychology of offending (e.g., Andrews & Bonta, 2007). They also require expertise in the relations among offending and disruptive behavior disorders, substance use disorders, affective disorders, posttraumatic stress disorders, developing personality disorders, cognitive disorders, and psychotic disorders.

Examiners need to be knowledgeable in the impact and implications of the life complexities common among youth involved in the justice system, including

- relational and residential disruptions from separation, divorce, incarceration, abandonment, and parental termination;

- variations associated with race, ethnicity, and cultural diversity among delinquent youth;

- varieties of special education classifications, placements, and services; and

- programs within social service, foster care, mental health, chemical dependency, and justice systems.

Ability to Maintain Objectivity

Clinicians who perform forensic evaluations must be able to maintain an objective, dispassionate stance when conducting these evaluations (Greenberg & Shuman, 1997; Melton et al., 2007). Examiners must be particularly sensitive to internal threats to objectivity from beliefs and values. Examiner objectivity can be threatened by a wide range of extreme and inflexible views about child conduct problems (e.g., attachment theories versus behavioral theories), juvenile offenders (e.g., social learning theories versus sociological theories), the juvenile justice system (e.g., "Children with mental health problems don't belong in the juvenile justice system" versus "Juvenile justice is the best way to change troubled kids"), and politics (e.g., "child-saving" child

BEWARE Be sensitive to internal and external threats to objectivity in juvenile CST evaluations.

welfare orientation versus "lock 'em up" punitive orientation) (Kruh, 2006; Schwartz & Rosado, 2000).

Potential threats to objectivity in juvenile CST evaluations can also come from external factors, such as blurred lines between retribution and rehabilitation goals that can make the intent of the juvenile adjudication process unclear. Examiners must be especially sensitive to the potential for the progressive development of biases as a result of establishing closer contact and relationships with either the prosecution or defense communities. For example, examiners may begin to see genuine CST concerns as "an excuse to avoid punishment" or develop an oversensitivity to CST concerns (Grisso, 1998).

4
chapter

Clarifying the Referral

Examiners have an active responsibility to clarify the referral with precision before a CST evaluation begins. Those who fail to do this run a serious risk of straying into unprofessional or even unethical practice. As explained below, discussions with the referral party, the court, and/or other legal entities about a number of issues must be considered. As examiners become more experienced and clearer about the evaluation issues, some of the topics will no longer need to be explicitly discussed. This may especially be true when examiners work in contexts where roles and relationships are well established, clear, and consistent, such as working as a court clinic examiner or as the "go-to" examiner of a given attorney. Examiners in more variable contexts or developing new attorney contacts may need to explore these issues regularly.

Evaluation Authorization

Examiners obtain appropriate authorization for conducting the evaluation before initiating it (Heilbrun, 2001). The authorization

BEST PRACTICE
For CST referrals, be sure to do the following:

● Obtain proper authorization

● Clarify the referral question

● Clarify the clinical concerns

● Clarify any non-CST goals

BEWARE
Whether an
evaluation is
court ordered or conducted
on behalf of an attorney has
implications for how the
evaluation may be carried
out and used.

for a juvenile CST evaluation will usually be a court order or a request from an attorney. The authority for the evaluation must be clear from the outset, as it affects the flow of communication, the limits of confidentiality, the presence of an attorney–client privilege, and the potential uses of the evaluation (Mossman et al., 2007). *Court-appointed evaluations* are "owned by the court," thus authorizing the court to control access to its contents. Either the court will distribute the report to the parties and others as appropriate or relevant statutes may guide the examiner on how to make those distributions. *Ex parte evaluations* (i.e., conducted by a defense-retained or state-retained expert), by contrast, are conducted on behalf of one of the attorneys. In such cases, the evaluation report (sometimes verbal, sometimes written) is shared, not with the court, but with the attorney only. As a privileged work product it can be used at the discretion of the retaining attorney and as specified in law. A retaining party is distinct from the motioning party in a court-appointed evaluation. That is, an attorney raising the concerns that led to the court ordering an evaluation is not the same as an attorney retaining the examiner. Regardless of the motioning party, the court's order is still the authority for conducting a court-appointed evaluation.

Clarifying the Referral Question

Examiners need to be clear about the referral question to determine the appropriate scope of the evaluation, the proper topics to be explored, and ways to provide useful opinions (Melton et al., 2007). First, the examiner should clarify if the referral is for a CST evaluation. Whether written or verbal, the referral may

- include ambiguous legal language (e.g., "competence to know right from wrong"),

- require an opinion on an issue that requires further discussion (e.g., "I want you to tell me if she can understand the plea agreement the state is offering"), or

- be completely unrelated to CST ("I want to know if this youth is mentally ill and needs treatment").

Overlapping legal terminology can add to the confusion, such as use of the term *capacity* in the standard for CST as well as other psycholegal standards. One way to proceed is for the examiner to articulate a basic definition of CST so that the referral source can gauge if that question will address relevant concerns.

Once it is clear that the CST of the juvenile is in question, examiners may need to clarify the relevant legal standard and applicable law for CST as understood by the referral source so that agreement is reached. Clarifying the standard is often a bidirectional discussion and may include instances where the experienced examiner educates the attorney in substantive ways. Examiners who frequently conduct CST evaluations may well be more familiar with the legal concepts and processes than attorneys who encounter these mental health issues in a small proportion of their cases.

The discussion about the referral may also reveal that evaluation opinions, such as risk of violence or rehabilitation planning, may be needed in addition to CST. The mechanism by which the evaluation was ordered may determine the appropriateness of addressing issues above and beyond CST. For example, evaluations that are court appointed pursuant to a specific statute may be legally limited, whereas *ex parte* evaluations may be open to any question that the attorney wishes to raise.

Clarifying the Clinical Issues Raising CST Concerns

The examiner should also clarify the problems demonstrated by the defendant that caused others to question his CST functioning (Melton et al., 2007). Court documents may provide little or no information about the reasons for CST becoming an issue. In some cases, this information can significantly help guide the scope and process of the evaluation. For example, the examiner may determine that the parties have little doubt that the youth understands and appreciates the court process, but have CST concerns regarding communication weaknesses that threaten the defendant's ability to provide information to counsel and to testify. By obtaining these concerns early in the process the examiner can better plan an appropriately targeted evaluation.

Clarifying any Non-CST Goals

It is not uncommon for CST to be questioned for reasons outside valid CST concerns (Bonnie & Grisso, 2000), in part because the threshold for ordering a CST evaluation is low (Melton et al., 2007). Discussions with the referral source may help identify any "hidden agendas." Some of these goals may be specific to the legal case, such as obtaining data for other judicial decisions (such as custody while awaiting trial, suppression of confessions, determinations regarding culpability, or sentencing mitigation) or as a bargaining chip in plea negotiations, to guide defense strategy, or to gain strategic delays in the proceedings (Bonnie & Grisso, 2000; Drizin, 2003; Grisso, 2005; Katner, 2006; Melton, et al., 2007; Mossman et al., 2007; Roesch & Golding, 1980; Tobey, Grisso, & Schwartz, 2000). In other cases, referrals may occur because court personnel want to access mental health information in a way that defense counsel cannot block (Baranoski, 2003; Barnum, 2000; Grisso, 2005). Or the party may want to obtain otherwise inaccessible services outside the justice system (Barnum, 2000; Bonnie & Grisso, 2000; Bonovitz & Bonovitz, 1981; Grisso, 2005; Grisso & Seigel, 1986; Gudeman, 1981; Melton et al., 2007; Mossman et al., 2007; Roesch & Golding, 1980; Warren, Fitch, Dietz, & Rosenfeld, 1991; Zapf & Roesch, 1998). When referrals reflect a misuse of expertise, examiners may consider declining the referral (Mossman et al., 2007).

Ex parte evaluations may provide flexibility so that appropriate goals outside of CST can be made explicit, clarified, and specifically contracted within the scope of the evaluation (Barnum, 2000). In contexts in which such flexibility is not afforded, such as court-appointed evaluations, examiners should refrain from exceeding the appropriate scope of the evaluation but may provide referrals to other appropriate service providers to satisfy other assessment objectives.

Considering Whether to Accept the Referral

As the information discussed above is obtained, examiners become better able to consider the appropriateness of accepting the referral. Examiners will need to determine if they have the appropriate expertise required for the specific case (Grisso, 1998; Melton et al.,

BEST PRACTICE
Accept referrals only for which you have the relevant experience or can call on others with the required expertise.

2007). For example, referrals involving complex psychopharmacological issues may be beyond the expertise of many psychologists and cases involving complex psychological testing issues may be beyond the expertise of many psychiatrists. Examiners should hold themselves to a higher standard than would courts when determining if they have adequate expertise (Grisso, 1998). In many cases, expertise gaps can be appropriately navigated through consultation, subcontracting with another provider, or recommending that the referring attorney add another examiner to address circumscribed issues. In other cases, however, the examiner may need or prefer to decline the referral and refer the attorney to a provider with appropriate expertise.

In discussions with the referral source examiners should also seek to determine if there are case-specific threats to objectivity, such as dual-role concerns. For example, conducting a juvenile CST evaluation of a youth with whom one has had a previous therapeutic alliance can severely threaten the objectivity needed for the evaluation (Grisso, 1998; Melton et al., 2007) and/or raise ethical concerns about accessing and disclosing information (Mossman et al., 2007). Dual-role concerns are also raised when clinicians accept referrals for CST evaluations knowing that they may be the provider of later treatment services for the same youth, as the examiner may benefit from certain evaluation opinions (Melton et al., 2007).

Clarifying Relevant Procedures, Methods, and Products

Once the examiner and the referring party have agreed on the appropriateness of proceeding with the evaluation, they will need to address the procedures, methods, and rigor intended for the evaluation (Grisso, 1998; Melton et al., 2007). Some of this discussion will be guided by applicable statute and case law, but some cases may require further discussion with the referring party. For

BEWARE
Playing dual roles (examiner and therapist) can raise concerns about objectivity and/or other ethical problems.

4
chapter

example, timelines for completing CST evaluations are often specified by statute. However, these statutes may be intended for criminal court and application to juvenile court cases may be uncertain. When timelines are not clearly set by law, they will need to be negotiated with the referral source, keeping in mind that time demands must not be so short that they prevent examiners from conducting an evaluation that meets practice standards.

The examiner and referring party may need to address other issues as well, such as the location of and best ways to make contact with the youth, possible locations for conducting the interview of the youth and caregivers, expectations about the number of sessions that will be needed, and the nature of any tests that will be used. They should also identify the possible collateral informants to be contacted and the third-party records that will be needed. The referring party may be able to help identify and obtain needed records, as well as schedule interviews or alert possible interviewees about the legal context of the examiner's contact. The referral source may offer suggestions, request limitations, or even insist on or object to elements of the plan, which the examiner can ultimately accept or reject.

INFO

Clarification with the referral party may address the following:

- Timeline for completing the evaluation
- Locations for interviews
- Number of sessions with youth
- Nature of tests to be used
- Collateral informants
- Third-party records
- Need for a written report
- Need for court testimony

If the evaluation parameters are not specified by statute, the referral discussion will also need to address the need for a written report and/or court testimony. Particularly in *ex parte* evaluations, the attorney may not want to invest in the writing of a report until she is certain it will support her client's position or otherwise be of use. Although accurate prediction is difficult, the referring party may also have some early sense of the likelihood that court testimony will be needed and when the hearing may occur.

BEST PRACTICE
Document the evaluation parameters as agreed to by the referral source.

Discussion of the report and testimony also provides an opportunity for the examiner to be certain that the referring attorney understands his role as an objective examiner who may reach opinions that do not support the position of the referral source (Grisso, 1998).

When these evaluation parameters have been negotiated, examiners should consider memorializing the agreement and having it signed by the referral source (Heilbrun, 2001). At the very least, the agreed-to parameters should be documented in the examiner's notes. Record forms for documenting this process in juvenile CST evaluations have been offered by Grisso (2005).

Contacting Defense Counsel

Regardelss of whether defense counsel is the referral source, she should be contacted prior to any evaluation contact with the defendant (Grisso, 1998). In fact, this step is legally required in some jurisdictions. When defense counsel is contacted, several issues should be discussed.

Notify and Confirm Legal Representation

It is unethical to initiate an evaluation with a defendant who is not legally represented (AAPL, 2005; Committee on Ethical Guidelines for Forensic Psychologists, 1991). Contacting defense counsel is important, therefore, to confirm representation. Even when representation seems apparent, such as when a defense attorney's signature appears on the court order for the evaluation, counsel might not have been assigned (e.g., a temporary attorney may have been assigned to represent the youth at a specific hearing). The examiner should always confirm that defense counsel is aware that a CST evaluation has been ordered. If the evaluation is court appointed or state retained, the defense attorney may not have been alerted and the examiner's contact may be her only mechanism for finding out about the referral (Grisso, 1998).

BEST PRACTICE
Once legal representation has been confirmed, notify defense counsel of the evaluation.

The notification allows the defense attorney to discuss the issue with her client, support him, and prepare him for the evaluation.

Assess Expectations About Attorney's Involvement

Defense attorneys should also be asked if they plan to be present at the interview with the youth (Grisso, 1998, 2005). Some jurisdictions, based on the right to assistance of counsel at critical pretrial stages, mandate the right for defense counsel to be present during the interview (Melton et al., 2007). Some of these jurisdictions also limit the level of involvement of the defense attorney (e.g., observation only). Other jurisdictions have explicitly held that the defendant does not have the right to have counsel present at the interview. That position may be based on cases (e.g., *Estelle v. Smith*, 1981), in which courts have expressed concerns that an attorney's presence could disrupt the evaluation (Melton et al., 2007).

In other jurisdictions, however, the law is silent on attorney presence at the evaluation or the examiner is expressly permitted to decide if defense counsel will be invited. Defense attorneys vary in their preferences about being present (Grisso, 2005). Some attorneys prefer to directly observe and document the interview (Frost & Volenik, 2004; Grisso, 1998). This may be for strategic reasons, such as allowing them to better assess and possibly challenge the examiner in later proceedings, or to learn more about their clients or the evaluation process. When these are the goals, alternatives include videotaping the evaluation or sending a designee to observe the interview.

On the other hand, attorneys may want to be present to protect their client's rights, such as avoiding self-incriminating statements, especially since developmentally limited or verbally impulsive youth may not heed examiner instructions to refrain from such statements. Any objections by defense counsel to questioning about the alleged offense should generally be honored by the examiner (Grisso, 2005). When other objections by defense counsel jeopardize the quality of the evaluation, they may need to be discussed directly with the attorney, preferably outside the presence of the youth.

There is no consensus among examiners on defense attorney presence during juvenile CST evaluations; some refuse, some accept, others encourage, and still others insist on the presence of defense counsel whenever possible (Grisso, 1998, 2005). There are a number of advantages and disadvantages to either option (see Table 4.1). Examiners must make decisions on the issue, based in part on local law and in part on the likely impact in light of the specific youth's characteristics.

When a defense attorney is present, examiners may wish to discuss "ground rules" with the youth and attorney prior to the interview (Grisso, 2005). For example, examiners may reach agreement with attorneys about certain limitations to their presence, such as having the attorney seated behind and out of eyesight of the juvenile or restricting interruptions to efforts to protect the youth from incriminating statements. Examiners may also request that attorneys not be present for the administration of any psychological testing so as to avoid violating standardized administration.

4
chapter

Obtain Attorney's Perceptions of Child's Problems, Case, and CST Concerns

Collecting evaluation data from the defense attorney is an important component of CST evaluations with juveniles (Frost & Volenik, 2004; Grisso, 1998; Slobogin et al., 1997; Viljoen & Roesch, 2007). Defense attorneys may be able to provide critical information about

- CST concerns they have directly observed during previous meetings and in the courtroom, including communication problems, unusual thinking or behavior, or unmanageable or inappropriate behavior;
- the charges and likely penalties;
- the length, substance, and nature of previous attorney–client meetings;
- the likely demands of the specific adjudication the youth will face;

Table 4.1 | Advantages and Disadvantages of Defense Attorney Presence During Juvenile CST Evaluations

---

DISADVANTAGES

- Juvenile may be made uncomfortable with presence of multiple adults, particularly silent observers

- Juvenile may be overly dependent on helpful adults and not demonstrate true functional abilities

- Juvenile may be easily distracted by the attorney's interruptions

- Juvenile's presentation may be distorted by the presence of someone about whom the youth has strong positive or negative feelings

---

ADVANTAGES

- Juvenile may be more comfortable with attorney's presence, which can facilitate examiner rapport

- Juvenile may be more cooperative with the presence of someone known from court

- Attorney may offer suggestions for the best ways to question the defendant

- Examiner can observe attorney–client interactions for additional evaluation data

- Attorney may help compare the juvenile's interview presentation with typical presentation

- Attorney-guided questioning may help address certain issues

- Enhanced protection of juvenile's rights

- Attorney may better understand areas in which juvenile needs additional support or remediation

---

Source: Grisso (1998, 2005); Mossman et al. (2007).

- qualities of the attorney–client relationship; and
- their skill in working with the kinds of youth who are at risk to be IST.

Whenever possible, communicating with defense counsel to collect this information should occur at the outset of the evaluation to inform the meeting with the defendant. Having the defense attorney put his thoughts in writing can help him conceptualize his concerns and provide focused, digestible information to the examiner. Further, a written document reduces the likelihood that the attorney will change his representation at a later point in the process, such as during a contested CST hearing. Kruh, Sullivan, and Dunham (2001; as provided and discussed in Grisso, 2005) have developed a checklist form, specifically for juvenile CST evaluations, that allows for easy written communication of these issues, either by having attorneys complete the form or using it to guide a telephone interview. However, defense attorneys may resist providing information seen as privileged when the evaluation is not defense retained, such as plans for defense strategy or observations made during consultation meetings, and examiners should respect this.

Contacting Caregivers

Juveniles almost always have caregivers involved in their lives, including parents, stepparents, relatives, foster parents, case workers, and/or group-home social workers. Caregivers should also be contacted early in the evaluation process to notify them that their child is being evaluated for CST. Most caregivers would want to be provided this notification, it may be ethically required and, in some jurisdictions, is legally required (Grisso, 2005). It may be best for the initial notification to come from one of the legal parties to the case, such as the defense attorney or probation officer, to reduce confusion about the role of the examiner. Alternatively, examiners may need to contact the caregivers directly. Once contact is made, examiners should explore the evaluation expectations of the caregiver early in the contact and be prepared to explain their role.

BEST PRACTICE

Collect information, possibly in a written document, from the defense attorney before interviewing the defendant.

BEST PRACTICE
Notify caregivers of the evaluation, clarify their expectations, and discuss the evaluation process.

If the youth is residing with the caregiver, the evaluation interview of the youth can be scheduled during this contact. Some families of youth involved in the justice system have limited resources and chaotic lives, issues that may be beyond the direct control of the youth. Therefore, examiners may consider offering greater scheduling flexibility than might be offered in other contexts. These same factors may cause appointment no-show rates to be high (Levitt & Trollinger, 2002). When no-shows occur, especially repeatedly, some courts may order the youth into custody to assure her availability to the examiner.

Caregivers can also be helpful in identifying and accessing records. They can authorize the release of records to the examiner or provide copies they have maintained. They may be able to provide these records prior to the interview or bring them with them when the youth is being interviewed. Caregivers should be informed of the limits of confidentiality and the intended uses of the information obtained from these records (Grisso, 2005).

Planning the Evaluation

Having established the evaluation goals and made contact with the relevant parties, examiners can begin to make choices about approach and method. Choices must be guided by general practice standards for forensic evaluations that are discussed in detail in the first volume of this series (Heilbrun et al., 2009). Those guidelines will not be repeated here, but a few points that pertain specifically to juvenile CST evaluations are worthy of mention.

BEST PRACTICE
Approach the evaluation process by proceeding from a conceptual model that guides the data gathering, data interpretation, and communication processes in a manner consistent with scientific, empirical, and ethical standards.

Use the Guidance of an Evaluation Model

Building on the forensic concepts discussed in Chapter 2, forensic examiners must translate the basic question, "Does this juvenile defendant possess CST?" into an evaluation framework that will facilitate a focused, clear, organized, and relevant evaluation.

The most widely accepted model for conducting CST evaluations was developed by Grisso (1986, 2003a), and a modified version was tailored specifically to juvenile CST evaluations (Grisso, 2005). The model includes five questions, as follows:

1. *Functional question:* Does the defendant demonstrate deficits in CST functioning?

2. *Causal question:* What are the clinical and/or developmental causes of any deficits?

3. *Contextual question:* How will the deficits impact the defendant in her adjudication?

4. *Conclusory question:* Does the impairment rise to a level rendering the defendant IST?

5. *Remediation question:* If the defendant is IST, can the deficits be remedied? If so, how?

4
chapter

Another CST evaluation model was proposed by Morse (1978). However, that model focuses exclusively on mental disorders as a source of CST deficits and does not consider CST remediation, so it is less well-suited to the juvenile CST context than Grisso's model. Morse's model also omits any contextual question. The contextual question is somewhat controversial. Some have suggested that recent court cases, like *Godinez v. Moran* (1993), define CST in general terms applicable across diverse cases (Heilbrun, 2001; Perlin, 1996; Zapf & Roesch, 2008; Zapf, Viljoen, Whittemore, Poythress, & Roesch, 2002). However, the *Dusky* standard is typically seen as case specific (Rogers & Shuman, 2005), and subsequent cases have reinforced this impression. In *Wilson v. United States* (1968), for example, the court held that case-specific issues, such as the availability of sources of information about the alleged incident, must be considered

CASE LAW
Wilson v. United States (1968)

● Delineated six factors that need to be considered for evaluating competence when a defendant claims amnesia (e.g., the extent to which the evidence could be reconstructed in view of the defendant's amnesia)

● Generally related the specific deficits of the defendant to the particular legal context when deciding CST when they are relevant to determining CST. Most scholars, in fact, highlight the importance of the contextual issue in CST determinations (Barnum, 2000; Dawson & Kraus, 2005; Golding & Roesch, 1988; Otto & Goldstein, 2005; Poythress, Bonnie, Monahan, Otto, & Hoge, 2002; Redding & Frost, 2001; Roesch, Zapf, Golding, & Skeem, 1999; Zapf & Roesch, 2008; Zapf & Viljoen, 2003).

Obtain Relevant and Reliable Information

Examiners should seek to help courts obtain the appropriately relevant and reliable data with which to reach CST decisions. Relevance requires that there is a logical and/or empirically demonstrated connection between the data and the issue of juvenile CST (Heilbrun, 2001). If there is not, then the data need not be obtained, even if it might seem clinically interesting. For example, one might learn that a youth may have enuresis (i.e., bedwetting). In a juvenile CST evaluation, data about this typically would not be pursued because it has no logical connection to an opinion about juvenile CST. Pursuing irrelevant data can cause distraction for the examiner and even invade the privacy of the examinee.

Planning should also focus on obtaining data in ways that enhance reliability (i.e., dependability and credibility). A critical way to enhance data reliability is the use of multiple data sources to corroborate hypotheses and conclusions. The potential for error is greatest when a conclusion is based on one fact obtained from one source. Potential error is greatly reduced when conclusions are based on multiple facts obtained from multiple sources.

Another important method for focusing the evaluation on relevant and reliable data is the use of standardized and objective data collection methods whenever possible, such as manualized interview schedules, observational checklists, and sound psychological testing instruments (Grisso, 2005; Rogers & Shuman, 2005). Where applicable, various standardized assessment methods for juvenile CST evaluations will be discussed in the following chapter.

In particular, developmentally appropriate assessment methods enhance relevance and

BEST PRACTICE

Collect only data relevant to CST, corroborate data through multiple sources, and use standardized and developmentally appropriate assessment approaches.

reliability and should be considered a practice standard in the context of juvenile CST evaluations (Grisso, 2005; Oberlander et al., 2001). The overall strategy for data collection should be developmentally sensitive, such as pursuing information about school functioning or other domains less commonly pursued in adult CST evaluations. Focused data-gathering strategies must also be developmentally appropriate, such as interviewing the defendant using questions that are responsive to developmental level (Grisso, 2005).

Target Relevant Domains

To conduct the CST evaluation, examiners need to consider three fundamental data domains: historical information, current developmental and clinical status, and current CST functioning.

HISTORICAL INFORMATION

Collecting historical information is critical in conducting juvenile CST evaluations. Life experiences can have great impact on the behavioral, emotional, cognitive, and social functioning of youth.

A historical context is critical to generating and testing valid hypotheses about current functioning, current developmental status, and psychopathology. Take, for instance, a youth with profound social withdrawal. Knowing if the youth always rejected socialization or was socially engaged until he witnessed his best friend's murder will yield different understandings. The former may represent a severe delay in social development such as that associated with a pervasive developmental disorder, whereas the latter may represent a setback in normal social development due to posttraumatic stress.

Juvenile CST examiners should consider historical information and the impact of that history on the child's development in

BEST PRACTICE

Consider all of the following historical information:

- Significant features of the youth's cognitive, social, emotional, and behavioral development across stages and within different social contexts, such as school and peer groups

- The implications of any major life experiences

- Any medical, mental health, or other conditions

- The family context within which all of this development occurred

BEST PRACTICE
Assess current functioning through the following:

● Direct observations

● Mental-status questioning

● Symptom interviewing and/or psychological testing

● Collecting information form caregivers and third-party sources (through interviewing, records, and/or testing)

every evaluation (Grisso, 2005). This is accomplished through interviewing the youth and caregivers, reviewing third-party information, and, as needed, taking into account the results of relevant retrospective psychological testing.

CURRENT DEVELOPMENTAL AND CLINICAL STATUS

Whereas the youth's history provides critical contextual insights, CST is a current mental-state question and requires focused assessment of current functioning (Grisso, 2005). Examiners must consider the youth's current cognitive, emotional, motivational, and perceptual status.

Examiners should assess symptoms of mental, emotional, or cognitive disorders, and whether or not they cluster together in a manner consistent with specific diagnoses. For example, in an evaluation of a youth recently placed into foster care, an examiner may need to consider an array of factors such as immature coping skills to deal with the situational distress, depressive symptoms that limit motivation and attention, and immature abstraction skills relative to adults that limit the conceptualization of the legal process. Identifying current levels of functioning and how they relate to developmental status and/or psychopathology is critical to identifying the causes of any deficits in current CST functioning.

CURRENT CST FUNCTIONING

Of course, at its core, CST evaluations must include the direct assessment of legally relevant CST functional abilities (Grisso, 2005; Heilbrun, 2001). Statements about current developmental status or psychopathology are necessary but inadequate in and of themselves to answer the question of CST. Regardless of the specific CST model chosen to guide the evaluation, the youth's abilities within each of the four capacities—Understanding, Appreciation, Assisting, and

BEST PRACTICE
Consider the youth's abilities in relation to the legally relevant capacities: Understanding, Appreciation, Assisting, and Decision Making.

Decision Making—must be considered. The most typical assessment procedures include functional CST observations and interviewing of the youth, and functional CST reports of lawyers, caregivers, and other informants.

Use a "Flexible Battery" Approach

The underlying model guiding the evaluation and the basic methods used to obtain data may be very similar across cases, but examiners should avoid using an overly rigid approach to selecting specific methods for the evaluations (Grisso, 2005). Borrowing terminology from the field of neuropsychology, juvenile CST examiners should use a *flexible assessment battery*. That is, they should select specific tests and tools for a purpose relevant to the unique aspects of the examinee and the presenting concerns. Such an approach is in contrast to a standardized protocol that comprehensively samples all aspects of the examinee's functioning, regardless of the unique issues that precipitated the evaluation.

Like flexible neuropsychological evaluations, juvenile CST evaluations must target the unique questions of each case for clinical, consumer, and practical reasons (Grisso, 2005). Clinically, assessments must accommodate different ages, genders, cultural backgrounds, clinical presentations, and CST deficits. These factors can affect the number, duration, and contents of interview sessions, the degree of reliance on third-party information sources, and the selection of psychological tests. The evaluation design should also consider the needs of the consumer, where the complexity of the evaluation may need to match the complexity of the court considerations and concerns. The pragmatics of individual evaluations, such as the time frame for the evaluation and the ability to access recent mental health records or recent psychological testing, will also require flexible structuring and allocation of resources.

Approach Data Collection as an Ongoing Process

Even when the goals and plans for data collection are well constructed, examiners must respond to the demands of a case as it

BEST PRACTICE

Be flexible in designing the evaluation to suit the needs of the specific case.

BEWARE
There is no single data collection sequence that will apply in every case.

unfolds and make necessary adjustments to data collection (Grisso, 2005; Melton et al., 2007). Hypotheses should be generated and evaluated as the evaluation progresses through an analysis of the consistency of the findings (Heilbrun, 2001). Adequately corroborated data can decisively rule out an early hypothesis and eliminate the need for more data, or a new data point can generate unanticipated hypotheses that require the pursuit of data not previously considered.

The process of data collection will also be impacted by data availability. Sometimes third-party records, for example, will be provided to the examiner at the outset of the evaluation. In other cases the examiner will not identify relevant third-party sources until later in the evaluation after interviewing the caregivers. Similarly, clinical factors, pragmatic reasons, or other issues may determine that caregivers be interviewed prior to the youth in some cases, at the same time as the youth in other cases, and after the youth in still others. Inevitably, some cases will require that the same data collection method be used more than once because new information has come to light. For example, a caregiver may neglect to discuss a problem that becomes evident when interviewing the youth, so the caregiver will need to be contacted again to clarify what was observed.

The evolving process of data collection and differences in data availability require flexible data collection. Each of the major sources of data, including third-party sources, caregivers, the youth, and psychological testing, are discussed in the next chapter. Whereas the order in which they are discussed may be an ideal evaluation sequence in some cases, it will not be ideal or appropriate in all cases.

Keep Careful Records

To meet ethical requirements, detailed, organized, and accurate evaluation records must be maintained. Examiners must be able to

BEST PRACTICE
Keep careful records of the evaluation process.

provide the information that evaluation consumers need, so that they, in turn, are able to consider the specific facts that served to form the evaluation opinions. Grisso (2005) has provided a number of forms to facilitate the record-keeping process in juvenile CST cases.

Conclusion

This chapter has highlighted the need for juvenile CST examiners to conduct evaluations from an adequately developed knowledge base about forensic, child clinical and developmental, and juvenile justice–related mental health issues and with an ability to maintain objectivity throughout the evaluation. To prepare for the evaluation, examiners must clarify the referral with the referring party(ies) and discuss the referral with defense counsel. The evaluation is best approached using a carefully considered evaluation model with a plan to gather relevant and reliable data from relevant domains. Examiners should maintain flexibility when planning and while they are conducting the evaluation to meet the unique demands of the instant case. Careful records of the data collection process should be maintained.

Data Collection | 5

Data collection involves gathering information and administering relevant procedures so that the evaluation is built around valid facts (Heilbrun, 2001). An appropriate approach to data collection is critical for forming valid and useful opinions. General considerations for the data collection process were discussed in Chapter 4. In Chapter 5, the fundamental methods of data collection will be detailed, including the collection of third-party information, interviewing caregivers, interviewing and observing the youth, and administering psychological testing.

Third-Party Resources: Reviewing Records and Interviewing Collaterals

Juvenile CST examiners must skeptically appreciate the potential for distortions in the information obtained from youth and/or caregivers, as a result of genuine difficulties providing accurate information and/or purposeful manipulations. Third-party data, including written records and interviews with collateral informants, allow critical comparisons that enhance data accuracy (Heilbrun, 2001; Heilbrun, Warren, & Picarello, 2003; Mossman et al., 2007; Otto, Slobogin, & Greenberg, 2007). Care must be taken to pursue third-party information in ways that meet legal and ethical requirements (see Otto et al., 2007, for a thorough discussion). As the evaluation progresses, examiners should carefully track the third-party information that has been sought and obtained. Grisso (2005) has provided forms to facilitate that process.

The Value of Third-Party Information

Obtaining third-party information is particularly important in the context of juvenile CST evaluations. Youth may be less able than adults to provide adequately detailed and accurate information (Grisso, 2005). Further, youth function differently in different settings, requiring information from multiple contexts for an accurate assessment (Kamphaus & Frick, 2001). For example, caregivers and teachers may have discrepant perspectives on a child's functioning.

Examiners must likewise be sensitive to threats to the veracity of the third-party information itself, including (Heilbrun et al., 2003)

- distorting biases (e.g., defense counsel stressing competence weaknesses over abilities),

- poor insight (e.g., counselor providing an odd conceptualization),

- suggestibility (e.g., teacher pressured by school administrators),

- and/or memory limitations.

Suggestions for managing these threats have been offered (American Prosecutors Research Institute [APRI], 2006; Austin, 2002; Heilbrun, 2001; Heilbrun et al., 2003), such as using structured interview tools, asking about easily observed behavior, and considering how the third-party source is related to the youth or is otherwise invested in the case.

Analysis of third-party information should also consider data "shelf life." The functional abilities of the youth may be developing rapidly and influenced by life events such that older information may not reflect current abilities (Grisso, 2005). Yet when considered chronologically, even much older information can help examiners gain insights into developmental trajectories of youth's functioning. For example, testing conducted when a 17-year-old youth was 8 may seem minimally relevant—until the data are also compared to testing conducted at 11 and 15 and reveal deteriorating functioning as school attendance

BEWARE Though invaluable to the evaluation process, information from third parties can be difficult to obtain and verify.

dropped and substance abuse increased. Older data can also provide a longitudinal view of current mental health symptoms that can help clarify diagnoses (Mossman et al., 2007).

Despite the importance of third-party information, juvenile CST examiners often do not seem to consider it (Otto, Borum, & Epstein, 2006). One reason may be that accessing records is often very challenging. Release of records may be protected by various laws, regulations, and ethical guidelines (Grisso, 2005). Caregivers, attorneys, probation officers, or the court may assist in accessing records (Grisso, 1998, 2005; Melton et al., 2007; Viljoen & Roesch, 2007). Examiners must sometimes (or even frequently) obtain records directly using signed Releases of Information or statutory authority, but some caution it should be a last resort (Melton et al., 2007).

Collecting interview data may also be challenging. Incorrect telephone numbers, telephones that are disconnected or lack messaging capabilities, and unreturned phone calls occur frequently. Unique challenges also arise, such as contacting school officials during summer months. Once contact is made, face-to-face interviews may be difficult to coordinate, but telephone interviews yield comparable information (e.g., Rohde, Lewinson, & Seeley, 1997).

Given the limited time frame for juvenile CST evaluations in many settings, even minor obstacles to accessing third-party data can stymie an evaluation. Therefore, many examiners begin pursuing records and interviews early in the evaluation process (Grisso, 2005; Viljoen & Roesch, 2007). Examiners should try to obtain at least basic clinical data before interviewing the youth, but they must often conduct that interview without most third-party information (Grisso, 2005).

Sources of Third-Party Information

A standard list of specific types of third-party data that must always be reviewed is not possible, as availability and relevance will vary between cases. However, within their analysis, examiners might consider obtaining information from four primary third-party sources: mental health and medical providers, teachers and school officials, social service representatives, and probation officers (Grisso, 2005; Heilbrun, Goldstein, & Redding, 2005; Otto & Goldstein, 2005).

MENTAL HEALTH AND MEDICAL PROVIDERS

Mental health providers may be able to provide important information relevant to past or present mental health conditions of the youth, past psychological testing and past and current interventions, such as medication regimens or psychiatric hospitalizations, and youth's responses to them (Grisso, 2005). Medical professionals may provide information about illnesses and/or injuries that could have direct or indirect relevance for CST. For example, brain tumors, fetal alcohol syndrome, or traumatic brain injuries may help explain observed cognitive deficits. Medical information may also indicate delays or abnormalities in the course of physical development.

Information from any past CST examiners referencing earlier charges or from experts involved in the current case can provide helpful information specific to CST functioning. Results from past evaluations can place the current observations in a better context. Disagreements with an examiner on the current case can help examiners generate and analyze alternative hypotheses.

TEACHERS AND SCHOOL OFFICIALS

Teachers and school officials can provide information about the youth's history of academic functioning. Teacher interviews, report card grades, results on statewide tests, and results on psychoeducational tests can offer insights into past and current CST-relevant functional abilities. Information can be obtained about in-class functioning, such as attention problems, motivation to learn, cooperation with adults, and response to intellectual frustrations. Individualized Education Plans (IEPs) can be especially helpful for assessing the age-appropriateness of academic goals. Attendance information can also shed light on the youth's academic motivation and/or the family context. Teachers and school officials can sometimes provide insight into the developmental trajectory of the youth's functional problems. For example, a youth may have been a very good student until a specific period when he began to exhibit withdrawal, make odd statements, and, eventually, have prodromal psychotic symptoms. Another youth, by contrast, may have demonstrated poor grades during a chaotic early upbringing that stabilized as she matured.

SOCIAL SERVICE REPRESENTATIVES

Social service representatives can describe the history of the youth's relationships with family members and other important people as well as document residential and placement changes that can impact social functioning. Responses to past services might be available when social service agencies have put services in place for the family and/or the youth.

BEST PRACTICE

As relevant, collect third-party information from the following:

- Mental health providers and medical professionals
- Teachers and school officials
- Social service representatives
- Probation officers
- Family members
- Other caregivers (e.g., foster parents, case managers)

PROBATION OFFICERS

Probation officers may provide information about the youth's development, especially behavioral (e.g., offense history) and social (e.g., peer relationships) aspects, and his response to past court-mandated services. "P.O.s" often accompany juvenile court defendants to hearings and may be another source of interview information about the youth's courtroom functioning. If the youth is being held in custody, probation officials (or detention staff) can describe how the youth is managing the stress of detention and describe other aspects of recent functioning (Slobogin et al., 1997).

Interviewing Caregivers

Although the defendant's family members are typically considered a third-party data source in adult CST evaluations (Mossman et al., 2007), information from juvenile defendants' caregivers warrants special attention. The setting for youth's caregivers can range from intact families, to families with multiple divorces and remarriages, to broad caretaking systems (e.g., foster care, case managers, etc.). Caregiver input is probably needed in most juvenile CST evaluations (Grisso, 2005; Viljoen & Roesch, 2007). Such input is a cornerstone of child mental

BEST PRACTICE

Obtain information about three primary domains from caregivers:

● Historical information about the youth

● Relevant observations of the youth

● Caregiver influence on the youth's CST-related functioning

health evaluations because it often augments other available information in important ways (Kamphaus & Frick, 2001). Youth are inherently more dependent upon adults for their financial, social, and psychological needs and thus should be understood within the context of the adults in their lives and the care these adults provide (Grisso, 2005; Kamphaus & Frick, 2001). Furthermore, caregivers sometimes provide more reliable information than the youth, such as observations of the youth's behavioral functioning (Barnum, 2000; Kamphaus & Frick, 2001).

Examiners may consider interviewing caregivers and the youth together when they are available at the same time. Because many of the interview questions that will be asked of the caregivers will also be asked of the youth, this strategy is certainly a feasible one, as well as efficient. The presence of caregivers may also enhance comfort in some youth (Barnum, 2000). However, there are also limitations to interviewing caregivers with youth, as discussed later in this chapter.

Historical Information

Caregivers are often uniquely able to provide certain historical information (e.g., early developmental history) or direct the examiner to others who can. Caregiver reports also provide an important contrast with youth reports. Consistency in information suggests that the youth and caregivers are able and forthcoming historians. Discrepancies, however, may suggest that the youth is a poor historian, sees her life in different terms than do the caregivers, or is purposefully providing misinformation. Alternatively, discrepancies may point to caregivers with weaknesses in ability and/or motivations to distort the information.

Standardized tools for collecting historical information from caregivers have not been reported by juvenile CST examiners in studies of their practices. Some

BEST PRACTICE

Note any discrepancies between youth and caregiver reports and possible reasons for the inconsistencies.

semistructured interviews are commercially available for general
clinical use (e.g., Structured Developmental History [SDH] of the
Behavior Assessment System for Children – Second Edition
[BASC-2]; Reynolds & Kamphaus, 2004). However, these guides
may be broader than is necessary for a CST evaluation. Grisso
(2005) provided a semistructured interview guide specifically
designed to target historical information relevant to CST.

Observations of the Youth's Current Functioning

The interview of caregivers can yield useful information about a
youth's typical functional abilities in domains relevant to CST, such as
learning ability, decisional style, and attentional capacity (Grisso,
2005). For example, caregivers can be asked about how often the
youth requires reminders to pay attention and how the youth copes
with boredom (Oberlander, Goldstein, & Ho, 2001). Information
about the youth's everyday decision-making approaches can also be
obtained, and Grisso (2005) has provided suggested questions for
doing this. The caregiver interview can also target symptoms relevant
to diagnosing psychopathology. Structured interviews are available for
this purpose (e.g., the Diagnostic Interview Schedule for Children,
Version IV–Parent [DISC-IV-P]; Shaffer, Fisher, Lucas, Dulcan, &
Schwab-Stone, 2000), although time constraints may require more
efficient methods. Caregivers may also be able to describe observations
of the youth during attorney meetings or court hearings, compare
what was observed to typical daily functioning, and describe how accurately meetings and hearings are reflected in the youth's daily discussions (Institute of Law, Psychiatry, and Public Policy [ILPPP], 1998).

Caregivers' Influence on CST Functioning of Youth

Caregivers need not be assessed for their potential as proxy decision
makers because CST requires autonomous functioning by youth.
However, caregivers may participate in meetings with counsel, educate the youth, clarify legal concepts and issues for the youth, or
directly advise the youth about important legal decisions. More
subtly, caregivers sometimes may make off-handed comments or
create a certain emotional environment surrounding the case.
Through such processes, caregivers may impact the youth in good

BEWARE In some cases, caregiver involvement can threaten independent decision making by the youth.

(supportive, helpful, and facilitative), bad (intrusive, hostile, or sabotaging), or a mix of ways (Barnum, 2000; Grisso, 1998, 2005; Slobogin et al., 1997; Tobey, Grisso, & Schwartz, 2000; Viljoen & Grisso, 2007; Viljoen & Roesch, 2007). Other youth will have little support from adults for a variety of reasons, such as an adult's substance abuse, mental illness, or lack of facility with the English language (Tobey et al., 2000).

The court is likely to be particularly interested in situations in which caregivers, through direct or indirect means, threaten the autonomy of the youth's legal decisions (Grisso, 2005; Grisso & Ring, 1979; Viljoen, Klaver, & Roesch, 2005; Woolard, 2005). This can occur when parents themselves have limitations in their legal abilities (Grisso & Pomiceter, 1977; Tobey et al., 2000; Woolard, 2005) or when parents have conflicts of interest with the youth (Frost & Volenik, 2004; Tobey et al., 2000). Grisso (2005) has provided a guide for interviewing caregivers about their attitudes toward the case that may influence the youth.

Some elements of caregiver influence may be determined by the general relationships between the youth and caregivers. For example, overly controlling parents can be expected to take an overcontrolling stance in relation to the case. Therefore, questioning the caregivers about those relationships can be important. The examiner can also observe youth–caregiver interactions to assess factors such as the caregiver's ability to understand the youth's needs and the effectiveness of communications and advice from the caregiver (Grisso, 2005). Caregivers may also influence the youth through the ways they relate to the youth's legal predicament. Their stances may include empathic support, defensiveness and denial, distant disinterest, anger at the youth or justice system, or distress (Grisso, 2005).

Preparation for Interviewing the Youth

A core component of every CST evaluation will be time spent interviewing and directly assessing the youth. Of course, there may be rare reasons that an interview cannot take place (e.g., the youth is too limited or too impaired to participate) or does not take place (e.g., the youth refuses to participate). If an interview is expected, examiners should consider several preliminary matters.

The main goals in interviewing youth are obtaining and integrating their social history, obtaining lifelong diagnostic information, assessing their current developmental and clinical status, and assessing their current CST abilities (Grisso, 1998, 2005). Most youth interviews can be completed in one session lasting about 45 to 90 minutes, but longer interviews and/or multiple interviews are sometimes necessary. Multiple interviews can be uniquely advantageous in juvenile CST contexts because (a) they allow for direct assessment of the youth's retention of legal information over extended periods, and (b) they protect against a single contact being an outlier compared to typical functioning (Grisso, 2005). When a single interview is conducted, observations should be compared to third-party information about typical functioning to enhance reliability.

Interview Conditions

Interviews with and testing of the youth must be conducted in physical conditions that minimize threats to the validity of the findings (Grisso, 1998; Heilbrun, 2001). Settings like detention facilities and hospitals may require examiners to balance competing privacy and security needs. For example, a glassed interview space can protect the youth's verbal communications while allowing security staff to monitor his behavior.

Oberlander, Goldstein, and Ho (2001) have suggested that, when possible, efforts be made to create age-appropriate interview space to enhance the comfort and interest of the examinee. As with any rapport-development strategy, balance must be maintained so that youth do not misinterpret the purpose or the seriousness of the evaluation. Having toys available is often encouraged in other kinds of clinical interview situations with preadolescent youth. But in this forensic context it can inappropriately lead youth

BEST PRACTICE

Consider the following factors for interview conditions:

- Environmental factors, such as privacy, noise level, room temperature, and adequacy of space

- Physical factors, such as restraint of the youth

- Psychological factors, such as medication levels or acute stressors to believe that the purpose of the interview is to have fun and may provide potential distraction. Overall, the best interview conditions are comfortable, but simple.

Caregiver Participation

As discussed earlier in this chapter, when caregivers are present for the youth interview, examiners may want to consider interviewing the youth and caregiver together. However, because the assessment of CST is focused primarily on the youth's own abilities, the examiner may want to observe these abilities in the youth alone, to better match the demands the youth will face in her adjudication. For this reason, some examiners opt to exclude caregivers from the youth interview. Case-specific factors may also need to be considered, such as excluding a clearly intrusive caregiver from the interview but inviting the presence of a supportive caregiver with an extraordinarily anxious youth. Examiners may also want to invite caregivers to be present or participate at specific stages of the youth interview. Advantages and disadvantages of caregiver presence will be examined in the discussions of each relevant stage.

Developmentally Appropriate Interviewing

All phases of the youth's interview should be developmentally appropriate, using language suited for the youth's age and verbal development (Barnum, 2000; Slobogin et al., 1997). With younger and/or developmentally delayed youth, for example, the examiner might need to avoid using overly abstract concepts, complex and compound questions, complex verb structures, too many pronouns, and complex or multiple negatives (Oberlander et al., 2001). Examiners may find it particularly challenging to discuss legal terms and procedures in age-appropriate ways. Walker (1994) has written an excellent text guiding developmentally appropriate interviewing in legal contexts that is recommended reading for juvenile CST examiners (see Appendix B). To enhance developmental appropriateness, interviews may sometimes include drawings, diagrams, or

BEST PRACTICE

Tailor the interview to the youth's developmental age and functioning.

other props that help younger or more limited youth better express themselves (Barnum, 2000).

Developing Rapport

Juvenile defendants may present with a broad array of interpersonal stances that can challenge the examiner's ability to develop an appropriate evaluation relationship. Such stances may include complete disengagement, overt hostility, acquiescence, or passivity (Melton et al., 2007; Slobogin et al., 1997). When examiners introduce themselves in a friendly manner and explain the most basic parameters of the interview, some of these presentations may begin to soften. These introductions should be sensitive to the fears or concerns that may arise in the youth from the specific demand characteristics of the interview. For example, when an interview is being conducted in a medical setting, it may be relevant to explain that the evaluation will simply involve talking and activities, and no uncomfortable medical procedures.

In some cases, initial efforts to develop rapport will fail and an overly oppositional stance will persist. Examiners will need to have strong child-behavior management skills to establish acceptable limits (Grisso, 2005). They also may need to use other strategies for cultivating rapport, such as using a low-key, conversational tone, extended "warming up" to begin and "patching up" to end the interview, the presence of caregivers for part or all of the interview, and clarifying explanations about the evaluation process (Grisso, 2005; Melton et al., 2007; Oberlander et al., 2001).

Rapport, however, can be overdone in the context of juvenile CST evaluations. Rapport-building efforts might actually increase the risk of a youth's misunderstanding of the purpose of the evaluation. It is important, therefore, to avoid offering youth the impression that a clinician–client relationship exists between the examiner and the youth. Use of a *notification of rights* can help to avoid that potential misunderstanding.

Notification of Rights

A notification to the youth (and caregivers) about the conditions and limits of

BEWARE While developing rapport may be necessary to facilitate the evaluation interview, be sure that the youth understands you are not there in a therapeutic role.

BEST PRACTICE
Warn youth about the possible uses of self-incriminating information obtained through the evaluation.

confidentiality for the CST evaluation is an ethical requirement, and in many jurisdictions it is a legal requirement. CST evaluations conducted under court order and/or statutory mandate do not require the youth's or caregiver's *informed consent* (i.e., a waiver of one's right to privacy). No CST evaluations require waiver of confidentiality. In defense-retained *ex parte* evaluations, confidentiality is protected through attorney–client privilege and should not be waived. Court-appointed evaluations inherently provide no confidentiality so there is nothing to be waived. However, examiners should provide appropriate notification about the evaluation at the beginning of each interview contact with the juvenile. Some examiners also have the examinee sign a form to memorialize the process (Slobogin et al., 1997); this is not a "consent form," but simply affirms that the examinee has been provided an explanation of the purpose of the evaluation and limits of confidentiality.

SELF-INCRIMINATING STATEMENTS

One issue that should be considered during the notification is the use of self-incriminating statements. If examiners obtain incriminating statements that are unavailable from other sources, they could inadvertently assist the state's investigation of the case or, even worse, be called as a fact witness at trial (Melton et al., 2007). Incriminating statements made during a compelled CST evaluation cannot be used at trial (*Estelle v. Smith,* 1981), but when the defense joins the motion for the evaluation, as is typical, they forfeit that protection (*Buchanan v. Kentucky,* 1987). There may be local protections against the use of incriminating statements at trial, or language establishing such protections can be inserted into the court order for the evaluation. Examinees should be made aware of the potential consequences of self-incriminating statements at the outset of the interview and, perhaps again, when questions about the court case are commenced.

RECOMMENDATIONS FOR NOTIFICATION

General descriptions of appropriate notifications for adults are common in the literature (Barnum, Silverberg, & Nied, 1987;

Dawson & Kraus, 2005; Gagliardi & Miller, 2007; Grisso, 1998, 2005; Heilbrun, 2001; ILPPP, 1998; Melton et al., 2007; Mossman et al., 2007; Slobogin et al., 1997). Typical recommendations are provided in Table 5.1. As is evident from this list, a comprehensive notification would be long, complex, and confusing to many youth.

Several strategies should be considered to enhance comprehension of the notification by youth. In some cases, it may be best to simply focus on the essential points to the exclusion of others, especially when a defense attorney is present to protect the youth's interests. In other cases, a more comprehensive notification can be given, with significantly greater emphasis placed on these essential points to increase the likelihood that they are grasped. Creating an outline or rough script for the notification can help the examiner explain the issues in a clear and developmentally appropriate manner. A sample notification script is provided in Appendix A (also see Grisso, 2005, for a sample notification outline). Still, the notification should be explained in a natural style (Heilbrun, 2001).

BEST PRACTICE

In providing notification, emphasize the most essential points that must be understood by the youth:

● The evaluation is focused on both general functioning and court-related abilities.

● The information will be shared with specific people.

● The information will be used in court to help the judge make important decisions about the case.

5
chapter

COMPREHENSION

After the notification is provided, the youth's comprehension should be assessed (Barnum et al., 1987; Grisso, 1998, 2005; Heilbrun, 2001). In fact, one of the best ways to help youth sift through a complex notification and focus on grasping the essential points is to assess their comprehension of the most critical issues. Their limits of understanding can be tested using open-ended requests to paraphrase, as well as more focused questions (Grisso, 2005). Of course, any comprehension difficulties also provide data for the examiner addressing the CST question itself.

Table 5.1 | Information Typically Provided to Youth Prior to Interview

- Who the examiner is and what the purposes and goals of the evaluation are

- Who has requested the evaluation

- The atypical role of the forensic examiner and a clear statement that the evaluation is not being conducted within a treatment relationship

- The types of information that will be sought and the procedures that will be used to conduct the evaluation

- The limits of confidentiality

- Legally allowable ways the evaluation data may be used or accessed, including self-incriminating statements

- Whether the youth and her attorney will be allowed to determine any use of the information in legal proceedings or if the information will be shared directly with the court

- The possibility of testimony at court hearings

- The youth's rights during the evaluation, such as the right to decline to answer questions where that is applicable

- Any situations in which the law requires that other parties would need to be notified (e.g., disclosures about child abuse)

- Explanations of any known potential for dual-role relationships

- Any consequences of declining to participate

If comprehension of the notification is poor, examiners can re-explain the information in various ways, obtain advice from others about how to best explain such issues to the youth, or even have those other individuals provide the explanation (Grisso, 2005). For this reason, regardless of whether caregivers are invited to remain present for the entirety of the youth's interview, it may be advisable to invite them to participate in the notification process whenever possible.

PARTICIPATION

Even with such efforts to enhance comprehension, some examinees will remain confused by the notification, which can cause concern or ambivalence about participating, or even full noncompliance with the evaluation. Examiners must avoid any coercive tactics to improve participation (Melton et al., 2007). Even subtle gestures, such as an expression of frustration, can become coercive with a confused or anxious juvenile. Examiners will also need to be sensitive to potentially coercive actions by caregivers or other interested adults. For example, an adult may tell the youth that the evaluation is intended to help him and encourage him to participate. Examiners should correct any misinformation immediately, such as explaining or reiterating that the evaluation is intended to assist the court and not necessarily the youth.

The best approach to managing such concerns is for examiners to seek to educate the youth. The examiner can discuss the youth's concerns, inform him of available legal protections, and/or assist him in discussing his concerns with his attorney or other interested adults. The examiner may need to inform the youth that the evaluation will still need to be conducted, but opinions will be based on more limited information without the youth's participation (Grisso, 1998, 2005; Heilbrun, 2001; Melton et al., 2007; Slobogin et al., 1997). If refusal to participate persists, it should be honored and defense counsel should be made aware of the youth's decision.

In some cases, it will be evident that the youth did not adequately comprehend the notification but may elect to participate nonetheless. In most jurisdictions, one may proceed to the interview despite the youth's poor comprehension of the notification, but

BEWARE
Avoid coercing the youth into participating in the interview and address any attempts by other adults to do so.

certain protective steps may be appropriate. For example, if a youth does not seem to understand the right to decline to answer questions, one can remind the youth of that right periodically during the interview or at moments when the youth demonstrates evidence of ambivalence about answering.

Clinical and Developmental Interview of the Youth

Once notification has been provided, the CST interview can begin. Questions typically focus on obtaining two types of data. This section addresses the first broad interview stage pursuing clinical and developmental information. Later, the collection of information about abilities specifically relevant to CST will be explained.

Historical Information

Examiners often begin the youth interview with a historical inquiry. This helps to develop rapport because it involves less threatening information that is relatively easy for many youth to provide. Historical information may be available from sources other than the youth, but examiners are encouraged to interview the youth directly when possible. The youth may provide

- information that others cannot (e.g., substance use history),
- more reliable information than that provided by others due to personal knowledge (e.g., sexual abuse) or lack of bias (e.g., relative to frustrated caregivers), or
- corrections to information obtained elsewhere.

Sometimes the youth will be the only available source of information, such as when third-party information cannot be accessed. In addition, conducting the social history interview of the youth provides a context for observing the youth's current mental status and their communication skills. Nonetheless, examiners may abbreviate or forego the history interview of the youth if it is clear that the youth is a poor historian, that other reliable data sources are available, or when the examiner has placed a premium on interview brevity

because of pragmatic evaluation limitations or other factors.

As discussed earlier, some examiners collect historical information from the youth and the caregiver(s) simultaneously (Grisso, 2005). Doing so allows the informants to fill in one another's information gaps or highlight differences of opinion. It also provides an ecologically realistic view of family dynamics and the youth's level of autonomy. However, conducting the interview together creates the possibility that one or both parties will be reluctant to discuss certain sensitive issues (e.g., adoption history). The interpersonal dynamics may also be disruptive to gathering accurate information, such as when an overbearing parent refuses to allow the youth to speak up about issues. Alternatively, the youth can be questioned alone and information obtained from the caregiver separately.

Standardized tools for conducting historical interviews of youth have not been reported by juvenile CST examiners in studies of their practices. Commercially available interview guides developed for general clinical use may be too broad for CST evaluations. Grisso (2005) has provided a semistructured interview guide designed for targeting CST-relevant history with youth.

Symptom History and Diagnostic Information

The interview of the youth will also include collection of past and present mental health symptoms to facilitate diagnostic decision making. Available evidence suggests that juvenile CST examiners are likely to use unstructured approaches when asking about clinical symptoms. However, such approaches have been shown to be idiosyncratic and unreliable in other contexts (Garb, 1989; Murphy & Davidshofer, 1988; Siassi, 1984), too often yielding diagnoses that are not genuinely present and missing relevant

5
chapter

BEST PRACTICE
Consider using standardized and empirically supported diagnostic interviews when asking about clinical symptoms.

diagnoses that are present (Rogers, 2003; Rogers & Shuman, 2005). Although time intensive, examiners may consider using standardized and empirically supported diagnostic interviews, such as the Diagnostic Interview Schedule for Children, Version IV–Youth (DISC-IV-Y; Shaffer et al., 2000). The Achenbach System of Empirically Based Assessment (ASEBA) offers a briefer (60- to 90-minute) Semistructured Clinical Interview for Children and Adolescents (SCICA; McConaughy & Achenbach, 2001) that examiners may also want to consider.

Youth's Current Mental Status

Because CST is a current mental-state question, the youth interview should include an assessment of the youth's current mental status and functioning (Grisso, 1998, 2005; Otto & Goldstein, 2005). This assessment does not merely duplicate similar observations of the youth in records, because historical records may not adequately describe the youth's current mental state. First of all, observations made across the entirety of the interview with the youth provide relevant information, such as appearance, attitude, behavior and activity level, and communication skills. Sattler (2001b) has provided an observation-based behavior and attitude checklist that is a good model for documenting this process.

Most examiners also include a period of focused mental-status questioning to increase the likelihood that an adequate range of data is collected regarding the following (Grisso, 2005):

- motivation,
- emotions (such as mood, range and appropriateness of affect, energy level, and suicidal or violent thoughts or feelings),
- thought processes (such as unusual perceptions, intrusive thoughts, thought organization, and problem-solving process), and

- mental capacities (such as memory, attention and concentration, abstraction abilities, spoken vocabulary, and general fund of information).

The field of child clinical assessment has provided little by way of standardized and commercially available mental status exams designed specifically for youth. The Kaufman Short Neuropsychological Assessment Procedure (K-SNAP; Kaufman & Kaufman, 1994) includes a very brief version. Grisso (2005) has offered a broader basic child mental-status exam guide appropriate for juvenile CST evaluations.

Presented next are clinical recommendations for mental status questioning within juvenile CST evaluations provided by several writers (Evans, 2003; ILPPP, 1998; Levitt & Trollinger, 2002). Notably, many suggestions are based on items from verbal subtests of the Wechsler intelligence tests. This has two implications. First, examiners should not use actual items from the current versions of these tests or they risk having their examination impacted by practice effects from recent test administrations or causing practice effects on future test administrations. Second, if the Verbal Scale of a Wechsler or other intelligence test is administered during the CST evaluation, some of the domains below will be assessed there and need not be asked during a focused mental-status exam.

MOOD

To assess mood, current depressive symptoms should be screened with an appreciation that some depression may be expected given the examinee's legal situation. Youth are commonly asked to rate their mood on a scale from 1 (very depressed) to 10 (very happy) and to explain their rating. Questioning about mood might sometimes reveal risks of harm to self or others. Occasionally the results might require that the examiner

BEST PRACTICE

Assess the youth's current mental status through observations across the interview and through focused questioning in the following domains:

- Mood
- Orientation
- Fund of information
- Memory abilities
- Abstraction skills
- Social and practical judgment
- Psychotic symptoms

BEWARE
Don't neglect to meet local requirements for acting on risk of imminent harm to the youth or others.

consider notifying others regarding the risk of imminent harm to the youth or others.

ORIENTATION

In assessing orientation, youth should be able to state who they are, where they are, what the date is, and, broadly, what the purpose of the contact is (e.g., "An evaluation" or "To get to know me"). Some youth may have minor difficulties with such questioning, such as trouble providing the exact date—especially when they are being held in custody. Only extreme inability to answer these questions or frankly erroneous responses that are not otherwise explainable should be considered evidence of disorientation. Disorientation suggests a major compromise to current mental status.

FUND OF INFORMATION

To assess examinees' fund of information, they can be asked to name common objects, define words in age-appropriate ways, identify famous people (e.g., the current president), or discuss current events. This information helps the examiner estimate their understanding of and involvement in the world.

MEMORY ABILLITIES

Mental status questioning should address memory abilities, including immediate memory and concentration, recent memory functioning, and remote memory. Assessment of immediate memory and concentration may include asking examinees to repeat the names of common objects listed by the examiner or to repeat digit strings forward and backward, as on the Digit Span subtest of the Wechsler tests. Recent memory can be assessed by testing the youth's memory for information presented some time earlier (e.g., the objects used to assess immediate memory) and/or by asking about recent information that can be corroborated later (e.g., the contents of recent meals). Remote-memory abilities will likely need to be assessed by corroborating remote information provided by the youth (e.g., what happened during a major medical incident).

ABSTRACTION SKILLS

Abstraction skills can be a critical component of adequate CST functioning and are commonly assessed by asking examinees to compare similar items, such as on the Wechsler Similarities subtests, or by asking them to interpret proverbs. Abstraction skills can also be assessed through classic Piagetan tasks, such as the Water Conservation Test, in which water is poured from a broad beaker to a thin beaker and the youth is asked which container held more water.

SOCIAL AND PRACTICAL JUDGMENT

Some sense of youth's social and practical judgment is also helpful. Questions about how they would respond to certain circumstances, such as those posed in items on the Wechsler Comprehension subtests, may help gauge youth's ability to interpret basic social situations.

PSYCHOTIC SYMPTOMS

Although psychotic symptoms are a less common concern among juvenile CST examinees than adult CST examinees, they can and do arise. Youth should be asked whether they have recently experienced delusions or hallucinations (worded in a way they can understand).

Direct Observation of CST Functioning

At the heart of a CST evaluation is an inquiry regarding things that the youth "knows, understands, believes, or can do" in reference to his court case (Grisso, 1986, 2003a). Whereas relevant functional descriptions may be obtained from other data sources, direct evidence of youth's CST functioning is also essential.

Observing Throughout the Evaluation Process

Although direct questioning about CST abilities is necessary (and subsequently discussed), clinicians should be making observations throughout the evaluation process that offer information about CST abilities. For example, mental status observations, such as communication abilities, attentional skills, and behavioral controls, may be directly relevant to the functional CST assessment (Barnum, 2000; Grisso, 2005). With careful consideration of generalizability issues, such observations can yield insights into how the youth will manage attorney consultations and court hearings.

Observing Attorney–Client Interactions

Direct observations of attorney–client interactions can provide ecologically valid functional observations. The examiner may observe the youth's abilities to attend to discussions, assert uncertainty about confusing issues, adequately respond to attorney questions, ask independent questions, discuss difficult topics, and balance compliance and autonomy in relating to the attorney (Barnum, 2000). Transcripts or recordings of recent hearings can also provide some of this information (Mossman et al., 2007). The attorney's ability to support the youth, encourage openness, and engage in developmentally appropriate communications will also help assess the adequacy of the attorney–client match. There are no standardized assessment schemes to guide the observations. Also, examiners must consider the impact of the observation process itself (i.e., Hawthorne effect).

Observing Court Hearings

Occasionally examiners might have an opportunity to directly observe the juvenile's functioning during "status hearings" that update the court. Such observation can help the examiner assess the youth's understanding and appreciation of factual elements of the hearing, as well as her overall ability to track and make sense of what happened. When such data are critical in a case and observing a hearing is not possible, examiners may consider creative observational approaches that approximate courtroom situations.

BEST PRACTICE

If possible, directly observe the youth's interaction with the attorney and during court hearings.

Discussions can be play-acted in an actual courtroom. Alternatively, youth can be shown courtroom scenes from movies (e.g., *My Cousin Vinny; Liar, Liar*), television programs (e.g., *Judging Amy*), or, ideally, films of actual or reenacted local proceedings, and asked to discuss what they observe. However, such steps are rarely a necessity. Furthermore, no standardized methods of observational assessment have been developed.

Functional CST Interview With the Youth

Certainly the most common method for collecting functional data regarding CST capacities is with questioning, sometimes called a *functional CST interview*. In only the most extreme cases, such as with a nonverbal or psychotic youth, will this interview be purposefully omitted from the evaluation process. This interview poses questions directly to the youth to explore abilities relevant to CST.

Functional CST interviewing with juveniles should be developmentally sensitive. CST interview questions are typically posed quite directly (Grisso, 1998; e.g., "What is the job of your defense attorney?"). But verbal language problems, discomfort, or shyness may signal the need for alternative interview approaches (Oberlander et al., 2001). Sometimes an underlying understanding can be revealed through less formal questioning based on actual events (Melton et al., 2007; e.g., "What was the defense attorney doing the last time you were in court?") or concrete examples (Grisso, 1998; e.g., "Let's say that there's a kid who is accused of a crime and tells the judge, 'I plead guilty.' What would that mean?"). Examples of how CST-related questioning might be adjusted for younger and older adolescents are a key component of the Juvenile Competency Assessment Procedure (Otto, 1996).

Developmentally sensitive interviewing may also require specialized strategies, such as using agreed-upon terms that are easier for children (e.g., "your lawyer" for defense attorney or "punishment" for disposition), discussing multiple data points (e.g., multiple charges) one at a time, and avoiding "Why" questions that may be perceived as confrontational by less sophisticated youth (Oberlander et al., 2001). Multimodal interviewing, such as asking questions while referencing relevant pictures, diagrams, or dolls representing courtroom personnel, may also facilitate effective

responses, especially in younger or verbally impaired defendants (Grisso, 1998; Mossman et al., 2007; Ryan & Murrie, 2005). No standardized interview aids for juvenile CST evaluations have been developed (Oberlander et al., 2001), although some tools have been developed by clinicians in Virginia (see Ryan & Murrie, 2005, for a description).

Various questioning methods may also improve developmentally sensitive interviewing. For example, recognition formats, such as multiple-choice questions, can help differentiate lack of knowledge from difficulty verbally demonstrating knowledge. An ideal questioning format for juvenile CST interviewing is to begin questions at a level that requires youth to express what they know with minimal cues, often called "open-ended questioning." If knowledge deficits seem apparent at this level, one can move to easier formats—for example, simplifying the wording of one's questions and then, if necessary, using multiple-choice questioning, to find the level at which the youth is capable of expressing what he knows (Kruh & Lexcen, 2007).

The primary goal of the functional CST interview is the systematic evaluation of the youth's abilities within each of the *Dusky* prongs. Interviews should be guided by one of the CST models, such as the discrete abilities model (Grisso, 2005; Rogers & Shuman, 2005). Continuing with the approach recommended in this volume, questions should address the four capacities discussed in Chapter 2. The Juvenile Adjudicative Competence Interview (JACI: Grisso, 2005) includes developmentally sensitive questioning of each of the four capacities. Examples are provided in the following sections, which review various points of focus in the functional CST interview.

Preliminary Questioning

Preliminary questioning in the functional CST interview may address the youth's past experience with court adjudications. Youth may obtain information about court from their own previous cases, cases of friends or family members, or television programming. Asking about those sources can help focus youth on experiences from which to draw their responses to subsequent interview

questions. It can also help examiners place youth's responses in context. For example, the JACI asks examiners interviewing first-time defendants to "Explore whether the youth has been in other people's court hearings or seen courts on television." Examiners may need to be particularly sensitive to the context of any direct experiences the youth has had with the legal system (Grisso, 1998, 2005). For example, a youth who was convinced by counsel to take a past case to trial and lost may reasonably be more likely to decline to take the current case to trial. The JACI instructs examiners interviewing youth with past court experience to "Determine whether the youth remembers having a lawyer and, if so, youth's recollections and perceptions of the lawyer."

5
chapter

Assessing Understanding

Questioning should assess whether the youth can provide reasonably accurate definitions of relevant legal terms and concepts. There has been general consensus about the issues that youth should be asked about to assess their Understanding, discussed in Chapter 2. As an example, to assess understanding of the role of defense counsel, the JACI asks youth what a defense lawyer is, what a defense lawyer does, and/or what a defense lawyer's job is.

What a youth specifically needs to understand about court may vary depending on the case. For example, if defense counsel has made clear that the youth will or will not testify at a trial, the examiner may emphasize or limit questioning about the process of testifying. The venue of juvenile court can also affect the content of questioning. That is, questioning will typically need to accommodate the absence of a jury, the expanded role of the judge as trier of fact and of law, and the expanded role of probation officers.

Questions about possible consequences may need to emphasize treatment services in addition to aversive sanctions (Barnum, 2000). Also, juvenile court defendants will usually not need to understand mental state defenses, because they are rarely raised in juvenile court.

On the other hand, if the youth is being evaluated for competence to participate in a hearing about transfer to criminal court, local standards might require that the youth understand all aspects of criminal trials as well. For example, if a juvenile is offered a plea agreement to plead guilty in juvenile court to avoid transfer, the youth's agreement has not been made competently if the youth does not understand the legal circumstances she would face if she did not accept the plea agreement and was transferred.

Assessing Appreciation

Appreciation pertains to the youth's ability to consider his own legal predicament. Beyond a surface, concrete understanding of legal matters, competent youth must also be able to use information so that they can appropriately apply it to actual circumstances that arise as they progress in their case (Grisso, 2005). Appreciation questioning should require the youth to use the facts and definitions assessed with Understanding questioning to determine if he can grasp the implications of the fact (Grisso, 2005; Otto & Goldstein, 2005). Further, questioning should require the youth to explain the reasons for holding particular beliefs so that the examiner can assess the extent to which they are a consequence of mental illness, cognitive delays, or immaturity.

As discussed in Chapter 2, delusional beliefs and other psychotic symptoms pose the greatest threat to adequate Appreciation in traditional conceptualizations of CST. Juveniles may also experience Appreciation problems caused by concrete thinking and other weaknesses related to cognitive delays and/or immaturity that can impair the ability to appropriately consider and apply information, increasing the risk of overgeneralizations, undergeneralizations, confusion, immature presumptions, and, frankly erroneous beliefs (Grisso, 2005).

Because youth are susceptible to traditional Appreciation threats (e.g., youth who are older or abusing certain drugs) and development-based Appreciation threats, questions should be posed that are sensitive to both. For example, in

assessing youth's appreciation of the role of defense counsel, the JACI includes the questions, "What are some ways a juvenile defense lawyer might help a youth?" and "Imagine that your defense lawyer said to you, 'I want you to tell me what happened the night you were arrested.' Why would the lawyer want to know that?"

Assessing Decision-Making Ability

Competent youth will be expected to make decisions regarding important court issues, such as entering a plea, deciding to testify, or waiving rights, as well as more subtle decisions, such as how much information to communicate to counsel, whether to testify against others in the pursuit of leniency, and how much effort to put into psychological evaluations that may be conducted for the case (Barnum, 2000). Therefore, examiners should question about decision-making abilities. Questioning should be sensitive to both cognitive and psychosocial threats, including weaknesses in abstraction skills, perceived autonomy, perceptions of risk, and time perspective (Grisso, 1998; 2005; Oberlander et al., 2001; Viljoen & Roesch, 2007).

Examiners should directly assess decision-making style through hypothetical decision-making tasks, such as asking for plea decisions in situations that vary the available evidence against a hypothetical youth (Grisso, 1998, 2005; Levitt & Trollinger, 2002). Juveniles should also be asked about actual case-based decisions to examine their decision-making process for weaknesses, such as poor awareness of one's choices, poor awareness of reasons for making various choices, or extreme overreaction to certain factors, like adult

recommendations (Barnum, 2000; Rogers & Shuman, 2005). For example, asking a youth how he will decide whether or not to testify in his case could reveal that he insists on waiving his right to testify because of profound embarrassment about facial acne.

As an example of decision-making questioning, youth being interviewed with the JACI are asked, "Let's imagine that you actually did what the police said you did. The juvenile court judge asks you whether you want to plead guilty or not guilty. What do you think you might decide to do . . . plead guilty or not guilty? What would be the main reason you would do that?"

Assessing Ability to Assist Counsel

Recalling the discussion of CST models in Chapter 2, Decision-Making abilities are sometimes conceptualized as falling within the Assisting capacity. Here, we have separated out decisional abilities from Assisting. Examiners must still consider the youth's ability to accurately and coherently communicate details of the alleged incident to counsel during consultations and on the witness stand (Otto & Goldstein, 2005).

ASKING ABOUT THE ALLEGED INCIDENT

Because communication concerns are most significantly in reference to the facts of the case, the most straightforward method for assessment is to ask the youth to provide a basic narrative of the incident and to assess its qualities (Barnum, 2000; Grisso, 1998; Slobogin et al., 1997). If asked, questions about the alleged incident should generally be open-ended and phrased in a manner that does not presume guilt (Melton et al., 2007). For example, the JACI includes an optional question that can be posed: "Describe to me what happened that got you arrested by the police." Given the additional stress of cross-examination, examiners may also engage in some confrontational questioning to assess the youth's ability to cope.

BEST PRACTICE
Carefully consider local laws in weighing the risk of youth self-incrimination against the risk of losing potentially important evaluation data.

As discussed earlier in this chapter, however, asking about the alleged incident can yield incriminating statements that are not protected in some jurisdictions. In such situations, the examiner can ask about and document the statements in her notes but protect that information in the evaluation report (which will be discussed in Chapter 7; Grisso, 1998, 2005; Oberlander et al., 2001; Viljoen & Roesch, 2007). However, interview notes are easily accessed by the parties in many jurisdictions. Therefore, some examiners choose not to ask the youth for a narrative of the offense, but instead gather data about his ability to provide such an account, based on his ability to provide a detailed narrative of another incident and/or his overall verbal communication skills throughout the interview. Examiners may also ask defendants, in general, how well they recall and think they can speak of the incident (Mossman et al., 2007).

ATTORNEY–CLIENT RELATIONSHIP

Another important element of assisting counsel is the attorney–client relationship itself. The youth should have reasonable expectations and beliefs about the relationship that are not compromised by factors such as delusional beliefs or development-based misunderstandings. For example, a threat to CST might be a youth's belief that her attorney is "mean" and will provide the judge negative information about the youth if she resists the attorney's suggestions. Examiners should determine if the youth can identify his attorney. They should ask about the quantity and quality of previous contacts with counsel, perceptions of his relationship with the attorney, and expectations of how well he will be served by counsel (Barnum, 2000; Melton et al., 2007; Rogers & Shuman, 2005). For example, the JACI asks examiners to discuss "Whether the youth has a lawyer now and, if so, youth's impressions of the lawyer."

Teaching

Another type of questioning that should be used by examiners could be called Teaching. Chapter 1 noted that the *Dusky* standard requires an assessment of the youth's *capacity* to know, appreciate, and do, rather than

BEST PRACTICE

Factor in the attorney–client relationship when assessing the youth's ability to assist counsel.

BEWARE
Lack of knowledge is not, in and of itself, grounds for incompetence. For IST consideration, the youth must also be unable to readily learn or adequately retain the information.

actual knowledge, appreciation, or behavior, at the outset of the interview. Ignorance from lack of familiarity with court and/or the instant case is not, in and of itself, a legitimate basis for incompetence. Juvenile defendants are more likely than adults to have distorted, incomplete, or even no awareness of the legal system (Grisso, 2005; Levitt & Trollinger, 2002), so their ability to learn is critical to assess. In such cases, examiners must explain the information to the youth and then assess the youth's ability to learn, apply, and retain this information (Barnum, 2000; Grisso, 1998, 2005; Slobogin et al., 1997; Viljoen & Roesch, 2007). If the youth can adequately do so, it would typically not be considered a significant CST concern.

As discussed in Chapter 6, the duration of learned information retention for competent functioning is not clear. At the very least, immediate retention should be assessed just after new information is taught. Ideally, delayed retention should be assessed about 10 or 15 minutes later after further questioning has been conducted (Grisso, 2005). In some cases, it may also be warranted to assess longer-term retention, such as asking about the taught information in a subsequent interview several days later.

Case-Specific Interviewing and Standardized Interviewing

Many examiners believe that it is best to integrate two methods within the functional CST interview (Grisso, 1998; Rogers & Shuman, 2005; Zapf & Roesch, 2008; Zapf & Viljoen, 2003). One is a flexible style of case-specific questioning, guided by the recommendations just discussed, targeting issues that are of greatest concern in the youth's own case. The other method is use of a predetermined set of questions commonly considered relevant to CST. The use of both methods should always be considered because each approach has certain weaknesses that the alternative approach can help resolve.

Case-specific questioning is important during the CST interview because it can better assure that a youth can appropriately apply information to his own situation than can standardized questioning.

Case-specific questioning can also better assess the varied and complex contextual considerations common in juvenile cases. For example, initial evidence that family issues are significant may require targeted questioning to adequately determine if caregivers are likely to detract from the juvenile's functioning. Case-specific questioning can also help examiners address the spectrum of complexity of juvenile cases themselves. For instance, detailed questioning about understanding complex evidence, responding to various types of witnesses, and understanding various mental-state defenses may be necessary in a complex rape trial, but may be overkill in a simple assault case.

A flexible approach to CST interviewing is also needed to consider various definitions and standards across jurisdictions (Grisso, 1996, 2003a). As discussed in Chapter 1, both of these issues arise in challenging ways in the juvenile CST context. For example, some juvenile courts may use a threshold consistent with that in adult court, whereas others may reduce that threshold in one of a variety of ways. Some jurisdictions may expand definitions of juvenile CST to include immaturity-based CST deficits, whereas others may not. Interviewing may need to be adjusted to match the standard. For example, in a jurisdiction where juvenile CST standards are set at a low threshold (e.g., basic understanding and communication standard) and immaturity has been excluded as a basis for incompetence, only very basic questioning may be necessary. Examiners are advised to limit questioning to match any established standards to best inform the court. However, when standards remain unresolved, as is common, questioning should err toward being overinclusive so that courts may have information available to set the standards as seen fit.

Adequate interview flexibility is also needed to accommodate the variability in youth who present for juvenile CST evaluations. For example, youth who present with severe attentional impairment may require more extensive questioning to assess their ability to attend across different situations, whereas youth who present with pervasive developmental disabilities may need more extensive questioning to

BEST PRACTICE

Combine a flexible, case-specific approach with standardized CST interviewing to gain the benefits of each.

5
chapter

assess how interpersonal relatedness may impact CST. Younger juveniles may need simplified questioning or use of props that might be demeaning to an older juvenile.

On the other hand, the exclusive use of idiosyncratic, case-specific questioning leaves the examiner vulnerable to missing important deficits because they are not asked about. When structured around an explicit operational definition of CST, standardized CST interviews reduce error and bias by reducing the variability in what is asked about (information variance) and what is recorded during the interview (criterion variance; Grisso, 2003a). In doing so, such interviews likely reduce inter-examiner disagreements in CST opinions (Rogers & Shuman, 2005; Rogers, Ulstad, Sewell, & Reinhardt, 1996; Zapf & Viljoen, 2003). They also help examiners communicate their findings to the court. Therefore, examiners must know how to effectively select standardized interview tools as well. The next section identifies one's options.

CST Assessment Tools for Use With Juveniles

A number of standardized CST assessment tools are available for possible use in juvenile CST evaluations. These tools are not interchangeable, as they vary in their structure, administration rigor, detail and objectivity of scoring criteria, breadth of CST domain coverage, empirical support, conceptual quality, and generalizability (Grisso, 2005; Melton et al., 2007; Rogers & Shuman, 2005). Despite broad similarities between instruments, different tools acquire somewhat different types of data. Moreover, as with any tool, CST assessment tools can be misused and misinterpreted, such as interpreting the results as determinative of CST itself. This can lead to unethical misrepresentations in court and miscarriages of justice in individual cases, as well as erosion of confidence in mental health experts and their techniques across cases (Grisso, 2003a). Therefore, examiners must be knowledgeable about available CST assessment tools and make careful choices.

BEWARE
Assessment tools are not interchangeable and can be misused and misinterpreted.

Examiners have two broad options for tools that standardize CST interviewing, each with unique limits. One option is the use of a semistructured interview recently developed for specific use with juveniles (the Juvenile Adjudicative Competence Interview [JACI]; Grisso, 2005). The JACI provides a developmentally sensitive interview strategy, but no mechanism for standardized scoring or evidence of its ability to improve clinicians' judgments about youth's competence abilities.

Another option is to employ standardized, quantitative CST assessment tools (called forensic assessment instruments, or FAIs; Grisso, 2003a). CST FAIs provide mechanisms for rating interview responses and generating composite scores, and, ideally, allow for norm-based interpretation. These features reduce subjectivity and examiner disagreement, yielding more reliable CST opinions than unstructured judgments (Golding, Roesch, & Schreiber, 1984; Grisso, 2003a; Nicholson & Kugler, 1991; Rogers & Shuman, 2005; Skeem & Golding, 1998; Viljoen, Vincent, & Roesch, 2006).

However, all available CST FAIs were initially designed for use with adults. They may miss important content areas unique to juvenile CST (Barnum, 2000; Cauffman & Woolard, 2005; Otto & Goldstein, 2005; Otto et al., 2006). They may lack developmentally appropriate wording and questioning techniques (Oberlander et al., 2001). They may emphasize psychosis-based threats to CST and not adequately assess youth with other clinical presentations. Furthermore, no juvenile norms have yet been published for any CST FAIs, and the use of adult norms for gauging the functioning of youth is not appropriate, eliminating one of the main benefits of FAIs when they are used with juveniles. Consequently, all available CST assessment tools that can be used with juveniles are really structured interviews that allow for clinical interpretation, but are not "tests" that provide norm-based interpretation.

Selecting Assessment Tools

As this discussion suggests, examiners should consider several issues when selecting CST assessment tools. First, the best tools

5
chapter

BEWARE Currently available CST FAIs were designed for use with adults, and no juvenile norms have yet been collected for these tools. Therefore, they are not true FAIs when used with juveniles.

are structured around a definition that adequately focuses the inquiry on the functional abilities required by the *Dusky* standard (Cruise & Rogers, 1998; Grisso, 2003a; Heilbrun, Rogers, & Otto, 2002; Rogers, Grandjean, Tillbrook, Vitacco, & Sewell, 2001). Tools should demonstrate strong coverage of the four capacities required to address the Functional question—Understanding, Appreciation, Decision Making, and Assisting.

Well-structured CST assessment tools will reduce error variance that could impair the quality of examiner opinions. Tools should offer standardized scoring criteria and evidence of psychometric rigor with the target population (Cruise & Rogers, 1998; Grisso, 2003a; Heilbrun et al., 2002; Rogers et al., 2001). The greater the structure, however, generally the greater the need for additional case-specific questioning to address the diversity of developmental, clinical, and legal issues presented by juvenile CST examinees. Because of these concerns, examiners might wish in some cases to use standardized tools in nonstandardized ways, varying the questioning so that it is more case specific. This practice is generally not problematic, since there are no normative comparisons that require standardized administration. Still, such adjustments must be thoughtful and clearly communicated to the court.

Ideally, CST tools used with juveniles will also target the particular developmental and clinical concerns associated with CST in youth. Tools should include developmentally appropriate questioning, mechanisms for assessing unique development-based threats to CST (e.g., psychosocial reasoning), and developmentally sensitive interpretation of the results of the interview. Similarly, tools used with youth demonstrating particular clinical symptoms and disorders should be sensitive to the CST threats that these problems can raise. For example, the use of a tool with strong sensitivity to psychosis-based threats to CST but lacking in developmental sensitivity may yield responses that are difficult to interpret when used with a cognitively immature defendant. More extensive case-specific interviewing will be needed than with a tool that has more appropriate sensitivity. Tools that are not developmentally sensitive may be best suited for use with older adolescents who, in studies, have tended to demonstrate adult-like functional abilities.

In the following sections, available CST assessment tools sometimes used in juvenile CST evaluations are described and reviewed on the basis of the criteria mentioned earlier (see Table 5.2 for a summary).

Specific Assessment Tools

JUVENILE ADJUDICATIVE COMPETENCE INTERVIEW (JACI)

General Description   As the item examples presented earlier in this chapter illustrate, the JACI (Grisso, 2005) is a semistructured interview designed to guide the collection of developmentally sensitive juvenile CST data. The interview opens with questions about the youth's past experience with legal proceedings and continues with questioning addressing "Juvenile Court Trial and its Consequences" and "Roles of the Participants," covering topics such as the purpose of a trial and the role of the judge. Within each topic, both Understanding and Appreciation are assessed through discrete questions. Teaching items are built into the interview through several "Capacity Checks" that guide inquiries regarding information that the examinee was taught during the interview, allowing for the assessment of both immediate and longer-term retention. A third section of questioning, "Assisting Counsel and Decision Making," assesses Understanding and Appreciation items of relevant concepts (e.g., plea agreements), as well as posing hypothetical decisional scenarios that allow the examiner to observe whether cognitive or psychosocial immaturity might be influencing youth's decision making. A final section, "Participating at the Juvenile Court Hearing," helps examiners structure their functional observations of the youth during the evaluation interview on relevant capacities such as attentional abilities, self-control, and capacity to testify.

Content   Items on the JACI were developed and refined through considerable consultation with clinical and legal experts. The result

Table 5.2 | Comparison of CST Assessment Tools Used With Juveniles

	JACI	MacCAT-CA	FIT-R	CAST*MR	ECST-R
Content	Strong	Strong	Good	Fair	Strong
Structure	Semi	High	Semi	High	Semi
Scoring	None	Explicit	Basic guidance	Explicit	Detailed guidance
Psychometrics	None	Mixed	Good	None	None
Developmental	Strong	Limited	Good	Good	Limited
Clinical	Strong (not psychosis)	Psychosis	Good	MR	Psychosis

JACI, Juvenile Adjudicative Competence Interview; MacCAT-CA, MacArthur Competence Assessment Tool–Criminal Adjudication; FIT-R, Fitness Interview Test–Revised; CAST*MR, Competence Assessment Screening Test for Persons with Mental Retardation; ECST-R, Evaluation of Competence to Stand Trial–Revised; MR, mental retardation.

includes items designed to assess Understanding, Appreciation, and Decision Making. Observational guidance for assessing Assisting is also provided, but there are no interview items for direct assessment of the youth's Understanding or Appreciation of testifying, tracking the proceedings, and maintaining appropriate behavior. This consensus development did not include any empirical approaches to content selection.

Structure   The JACI is a semistructured interview guide that balances structure and flexibility. It is adequately structured to help examiners focus their questioning on the most relevant information needed to make juvenile CST judgments. However, it also allows flexibility to accommodate differences across evaluations in clinical presentations, court systems (juvenile vs. criminal), and jurisdictional definitions. For example, examiners may omit more complex items or sections when youth cannot adequately respond to more straightforward content. Examiners are also invited to simplify the wording if they maintain the intent of the item, and add their own questions, including the use of alternative questioning strategies.

Scoring   The JACI provides no item scoring system and no rating guidance beyond brief descriptions of what each item is targeting (e.g., "Understands advocacy nature of counsel"). Consequently, there is also no quantitative system provided for measuring or summarizing functioning within each of the four capacities or overall CST. Examiners must rely on qualitative analysis using clinical judgment.

Psychometrics   The tool has strong conceptual basis and face validity. Other measures of reliability and validity are not available. The JACI is merely an interview schedule. It offers no specific "measures" of the abilities that it assists the examiner to identify.

Developmental Appropriateness   The JACI's greatest strength is its developmental appropriateness, the result of extensive piloting with youth. Item wording was designed to be developmentally appropriate. When items are still too complex for younger or more limited youth, further simplification is invited. Examinees are asked about past legal experience, which helps younger and more limited youth frame their reference. The JACI also helps examiners target the questioning to issues of legal relevance in juvenile court, such as asking juvenile court defendants about the expanded role of the probation officer.

The JACI offers opportunities to identify CST problems caused by developmental immaturity. Decision-Making items help assess developmentally based psychosocial threats to decisional abilities. Appreciation items provide excellent focus on development-based misconceptions and confusion (Grisso, 2005;

Viljoen & Roesch, 2007). Teaching items assess both short-term retention of information after brief instruction and longer-term retention, which can be more of an issue for younger youth. Detailed guidance for interpretive sensitivity to developmental weaknesses in youth responses is provided. However, there is no specific empirical basis to guide these interpretations.

Clinical Appropriateness   In targeting developmental issues, the JACI is also well suited for youth with developmental delays and/or developmental disabilities. The manual, in fact, provides specific guidance on how mental retardation may affect interview responses. The JACI manual also gives guidance on how other common childhood disorders, such as attention-deficit/hyperactivity disorder (ADHD), mood disorders, and anxiety disorders, may impact JACI responses. Here, too, there is no empirical guidance for these interpretations. The JACI was not specifically designed to be sensitive to psychosis-based CST weaknesses. For example, it includes no Appreciation items designed to assess traditional threats caused by disordered thinking. Examiners using the JACI when psychosis is suspected may need to ask case-specific questions to assess this.

MACARTHUR COMPETENCE ASSESSMENT TOOL–CRIMINAL ADJUDICATION (MACCAT-CA)

General Description   The MacCAT-CA (Poythress et al., 1999) is a structured and highly standardized 22-item interview that consists of three sections assessing different domains, with each employing a different type of questioning. The Understanding Scale includes eight items assessing basic understanding of legal concepts in reference to a fictional case about two individuals involved in a bar fight (a "vignette methodology"). Six of the eight items require the teaching of examinees unable to answer adequately and an assessment of their ability to comprehend that teaching. The Reasoning Scale includes eight items that also reference the fictional vignette, including five Assisting items in which the examinee must identify which of two facts from the fictional case would be more relevant to share with counsel and why, as well as three Decision-Making items that assess cognitive decision-making about a hypothetical plea agreement. The Appreciation Scale includes six items assessing expectations about how the court processes will occur in one's own case that are designed to elicit implausible beliefs relevant to CST.

Content   The MacCAT-CA is based on a combination of Bonnie's and the discrete abilities models. It includes items assessing Understanding, Appreciation, Decision Making, and Assisting. However, the latter two concepts are covered on a single scale (Reasoning) and some elements of Assisting (e.g., ability to provide relevant facts about the instant case) are not well covered. The MacCAT-CA allows for the assessment of "capacity" by including Teaching items.

Structure   The vignette methodology has been criticized because it offers little opportunity to assess Understanding and Appreciation in the context of the defendant's own case (Rogers, 2001; Rogers & Shuman, 2005; Zapf & Viljoen, 2003). Consequently, it is important for examiners using the MacCAT-CA to conduct case-specific questioning as well (Poythress et al., 1999; Grisso, 2003a).

The vignette methodology nonetheless offers distinct strengths in allowing for a highly standardized interview, which can help remove youth from the emotionality of their own case to assess their underlying abilities. The result is a highly standardized and structured tool. For example, items are to be read verbatim and in a specified order. Standardized administration, therefore, requires that questions be asked that may not be applicable in most juvenile court CST cases, such as questioning about the role of the jury. The verbatim questioning may not be well suited for immature youth. The standardized administration encourages the use of certain follow-up probes to more fully assess the examinee's abilities, but these do not include simplified versions of the items that might yield better responses by youth.

Scoring   Another advantage of the vignette methodology of the MacCAT-CA is that it offers explicit scoring criteria to help examiners differentiate the quality of responses, producing ratings of

2 (adequate), 1 (questionable), or 0 (inadequate). However, these criteria were developed on the basis of studies with adults. Additionally, norm-based interpretations described in the manual were based on studies with adults and cannot be generalized to juveniles at this time.

Psychometrics   The test manual specifies that the MacCAT-CA was not validated with juveniles in its development. However, the tool has been extensively studied in juvenile populations, including in one study in which it was administered to more than 900 juveniles (Grisso et al., 2003), providing some support for its use with juveniles. Many of these studies found adequate to strong psychometric results (see Chapter 3). For example, validation studies have demonstrated expected relations with variables such as age and intelligence. However, some psychometric weaknesses were also revealed. Internal consistency has not been consistently adequate (Boyd, 1998; Poythress, Lexcen, Grisso, & Steinberg, 2006). Also, the Appreciation scale has demonstrated weak interrater reliability with youth (Burnett, Noblin, & Prosser, 2004; Grisso et al., 2003; Poythress et al., 2006), which may call into question the appropriateness of its use with juveniles.

Developmental Appropriateness   The MacCAT-CA was not designed to be developmentally appropriate. Items were not structured or worded with the goal of comprehension by youth. It does not assess issues such as the unique decision-making approaches of juveniles or developmentally based problems with Appreciation (Grisso, 2005; Woolard & Harvell, 2005). Given these limitations, in juvenile CST evaluations the MacCAT-CA must be used with caution (Grisso, 2005; Heilbrun et al., 2002; Woolard & Harvell, 2005). It is probably best suited for older adolescents presenting with issues other than significant cognitive limitations.

The Appreciation scale raises particular concerns for use with youth. In addition to focusing on psychosis-based Appreciation weaknesses, the scoring criteria do not distinguish between distorted beliefs and the "I don't know" responses that may be common among youth faced with the grammatically complex questions on the scale (Ficke, Hart, & Deardorff, 2006; Grisso et al., 2003). Given these concerns, examiners will need to conduct qualitative analysis of the responses to assess the cause of any low scores or consider omitting the Appreciation scale when assessing youth with development-based threats to CST (Burnett et al., 2004; Grisso, 2005; Warren, Aaron, Ryan, Chauhan, & DuVal, 2003; Woolard & Harvell, 2005).

Clinical Appropriateness   Given the concerns about use of the MacCAT-CA with younger youth, its use with developmentally delayed or disabled youth is also not well supported. The measure has not been validated with mentally retarded adults (Poythress et al., 1999), let alone intellectually limited youth. Moreover, the rigidly standardized wording of items is not well suited for cognitively limited youth. The strength of the MacCAT-CA is in its assessment of traditional clinical threats to CST, such as delusional beliefs and other psychotic symptoms (Grisso, 2005), which may generalize to youth with psychosis. The MacCAT-CA manual provides no specific guidance on its use with other clinical populations, adult or juvenile. Studies, though, have shown that the tool is sensitive to problems associated with learning disorders in youth (Ficke et al., 2005; Warren et al., 2003).

FITNESS INTERVIEW TEST–REVISED (FIT-R)

General Description   The FIT-R (Roesch, Zapf, Eaves, & Webster, 1998) is a semistructured clinical interview developed for the assessment of CST with adult defendants in Canada by means of four "background questions" and 16 items. Questions are asked in a standardized sequence, with discretionary probing. Items are grouped into three sections that have been assigned various titles, including (1) Understanding, (2) Appreciation, and (3) Communication.

Content   The items on the FIT-R were rationally selected by the authors to match the Canadian CST definition. Some commentators have questioned use of the measure in the United States, since the Canadian standard does not precisely follow the *Dusky* standard (Rogers et al., 2001). However, the three sections of the measure parallel the discrete abilities model of CST (Viljoen et al., 2006). The FIT-R provides good coverage of the *Dusky* abilities. The Communication scale covers both Assisting and Decision

Making abilities, but does not include decisional vignettes, as many have recommended for assessing Decision Making. Examiners may want to supplement the tool with such vignettes.

Structure   The FIT-R is a semistructured interview that provides strong structure for the functional CST interview (Grisso, 1998). However, the FIT-R does not restrict examiners to specific wording of items, and probing for better understanding of examinees' responses is encouraged. Although this approach may sacrifice reliability, its strength is in its enhanced sensitivity to more individualized threats to CST (Grisso, 2003a), which may enhance its utility with juveniles.

Scoring   Examinee's responses to items are rated on a 3-point scale. Descriptions of the meaning of each item are provided, but examples or scoring criteria are not provided. Items are scored using a structured clinical judgment based on all of the relevant information available and the examiner's sense of the defendant's abilities, rather than strict analysis of the words used to respond. Item scores are totaled within each section to yield scores on each of the three sections. The three sections are then also rated on a 0–2 scale using a structured clinical judgment, which feed into overall judgments of "Fit; Questionable; or Unfit." Formulas are not provided for synthesizing this information into these ratings, in part because the ratings must include case-specific considerations.

Psychometrics   Studies with youth have revealed good interrater reliability on items, strong interrater reliability on scale and total scores, and weaker, yet acceptable, interrater reliability on clinical ratings (see Chapter 3). In addition to expected relationships with age and intelligence, validation of the measure with youth revealed a three-factor model (Viljoen et al., 2006). Thus, significant steps have been taken toward validating the FIT-R for use with youth (Viljoen & Roesch, 2007).

Developmental Appropriateness   The FIT-R was not specifically developed for use with adolescents. However, its authors have supported its use with juveniles (Roesch, Zapf, & Eaves, 2006). The simple wording of items lends the FIT-R to use with younger and more limited populations. Furthermore, the minimal standardization of items enables examiners to pose questions in developmentally appropriate ways. The tool is not explicit about assessing development-based threats to CST (Viljoen & Roesch, 2007), such as immaturity-based Appreciation problems. Psychosocial developmental threats to decision making are also not explicitly covered because of the lack of clarity about their applicability to juvenile CST (Roesch, Zapf, & Eaves, 2006). Consequently, when such issues are of concern, examiners will need to include questioning about such issues in their case-specific questioning.

Clinical Appropriateness   The FIT-R manual provides general guidance for considering the impact of disorders most likely to threaten CST among adults: mental retardation and formal thought disorder. The manual also offers some guidance on considering issues such as concentration deficits, rapid thinking, and memory deficits, which may generalize to certain childhood disorders (e.g., ADHD, learning disorders). In addition, studies have demonstrated that the measure is sensitive to problems associated with ADHD in youth (Viljoen & Roesch, 2005).

COMPETENCY ASSESSMENT FOR STANDING TRIAL–MENTAL RETARDATION (CAST*MR)

General Description   The CAST*MR (Everington & Luckasson, 1992) is a structured interview developed specifically for assessing CST with adult defendants who have mental retardation. The measure includes 50 items organized into three sections: (a) Basic Legal Skills, (b) Skills to Assist Defense, and (c) Understanding Case Events. The first two sections have 40 multiple-choice items (with three possible choices) that assess defendants' knowledge of the criminal justice process (25 items) and the defendants' understanding of the client–attorney relationship (15 items). The third section includes 10 open-ended items assessing defendants' abilities to discuss the facts of their case with coherence and an understanding of how the facts of the case relate to the arrest and charges. The items read at a second- to sixth-grade reading level (Grisso, 2003a).

Content   The CAST*MR was rationally developed by the authors and rated by experts in criminal disability law for appropriateness. The content focuses on matters of Understanding, Appreciation, and Assisting. The Appreciation items emphasize applying knowledge to hypothetical courtroom situations. The tool has been criticized for the informality of item selection (Rogers & Shuman, 2005), its narrow coverage of relevant CST capacities, and its particularly poor coverage of Decision Making (Melton et al., 2007).

Structure   The CAST*MR is a highly structured interview. Examinees are given a subject form to read the questions as the examiner reads them. There are rules about how many times each item can be repeated and possible prompts that can be used to obtain more information. Two of the three scales contain multiple-choice items that must all be administered. Multiple-choice items were used to compensate for the greater difficulty persons with mental retardation may have expressing what they know in the context of open-ended questioning yet be able to do when they need only identify correct and incorrect information. However, multiple-choice questioning is a step removed from the actual abilities required by *Dusky,* risking overestimates of functioning compared to the deeper comprehension and adequate verbal skills needed in actual court proceedings (Grisso, 2003a, 2005; Melton et al., 2007; Viljoen & Roesch, 2007).

A third subtest includes open-ended questions asked verbatim with allowable repeating, prompting, and/or rephrasing, which can enhance developmentally appropriate questioning. Examiners are instructed to ask all questions regardless of the quality of responses to earlier items. This standardized administration requires questioning about issues that may not be applicable to all juvenile CST cases, such as asking juvenile court defendants about the role of the jury.

Scoring   The CAST*MR provides highly detailed scoring criteria. The correct answers to multiple-choice items are provided. Detailed scoring criteria are provided for the open-ended questions so that they can be scored 0, 1/2, or 1.

Psychometrics   There have been no studies of the CAST*MR with juvenile samples, so its psychometric properties in this population are unknown.

Developmental Appropriateness   Although the CAST*MR was not developed with developmental sensitivity in mind, it was developed for use with cognitively limited defendants, thus it may have some generalizability to youth. This design has led some to recommend its use in juvenile CST evaluations (Barnum, 2000; Schwartz & Rosado, 2000). For example, youth are likely to be comfortable with the first two sections' multiple-choice format from other contexts, such as school exams. This format may limit acquiescent response styles common in youth and may help them demonstrate knowledge without reliance on verbal skills (Evans, 2003; Grisso, 1998; 2005). However, the multiple-choice items may require other unique skills, such as reception and retention, as well as review and comparison of various options (Grisso, 2003a). The open-ended section of questions has been criticized for using unnecessarily complex wording (Rogers & Shuman, 2005).

The CAST*MR does not include items assessing development-based threats to CST, such as immature Appreciation, thus requiring supplemental questioning when that is at issue.

Clinical Appropriateness   The CAST*MR was designed specifically for defendants with mental retardation. The test developers report that the measure can be used with defendants with IQs as low as 35, but the instrument was only studied with individuals in the range of mild mental retardation, casting doubt upon those claims (Rogers & Shuman, 2005). The tool was not designed to be sensitive to psychosis-based threats to CST and is a less appropriate choice when psychosis is a significant concern. Its appropriateness for use with youth experiencing other childhood mental disorders is untested and no guidance for its use with other disorders is provided.

EVALUATION OF COMPETENCE TO STAND TRIAL–REVISED (ECST-R)

General Description   The ECST-R (Rogers, Tillbrokk, & Sewell, 2004) is a structured CST interview composed of a small set of background questions and four main sections. The Consult with Counsel Scale evaluates the attorney–client relationship, the Understanding Scale addresses the role of key figures in courtroom proceedings, the Rational Understanding Scale addresses the capacity to make unimpaired decisions and logical judgments, and the Atypical Presentation Scale evaluates possible feigning.

Content   Preliminary items were selected on the basis of high prototypicality ratings for each of the *Dusky* prongs—an important empirical approach to FAI development that other CST FAIs have not used (Rogers & Shuman, 2005). Therefore, it corresponds well to the *Dusky* standard and includes coverage of all four capacities, at least as they are typically applied with adults in criminal court. The Consult with Counsel Scale evaluates Assisting, the Understanding Scale addresses Understanding, and the Rational Understanding Scale evaluates Appreciation and Decision Making. However, the research guiding item selection was conducted on traditional conceptualizations of CST, and its generalizability to the juvenile CST context is unknown.

Structure   Some sections of the ECST-R use a semistructured interview approach designed to allow for individualized inquiry. The examiner is encouraged to "evaluate each defendant's capacities as extensively as he or she feels is required in order to provide sufficient relevant data for the court's determination of competency to proceed" (Rogers et al., 2004, p. 16). A gradual testing of limits is encouraged by asking examinees standard questions, followed by optional probes as needed, which are then followed by unstructured queries when necessary. This balance of structure and flexibility might assist juvenile CST examiners in obtaining responses in developmentally appropriate ways.

Scoring   The manual provides detailed discussion of each item and guides clinical ratings with explanations of scoring procedures, which vary from scale to scale. While this approach risks interrater disagreements, the tool's flexibility may be a strength for use with juveniles. Item scores are used to calculate scale scores, but no score estimating overall CST is recommended.

Psychometrics   There have been no studies of the ECST-R with youth, so its psychometric properties with youth are unknown.

Developmental Appropriateness   Although the ECST-R was not designed to be developmentally sensitive, items are worded simply to manage receptive and expressive language deficits (Rogers et al., 2004). Therefore, the item wording may be appropriate for use with juveniles. The item selection did not contemplate development-based threats to CST. The ECST-R manual specifies that it was not validated with juveniles and discourages careless application to juvenile court cases.

The inclusion of methods for screening feigned incompetence is a strength of the measure when used with adults, but the content of those scales focuses on malingering strategies common among adults and may not be as sensitive to feigning among youth. It is probably necessary to omit the feigning screening scales in clinical use until research with juveniles is conducted.

Clinical Appropriateness   The ECST-R is clearly designed to focus on impairments related to psychotic illnesses and its clinical use is most appropriate when such concerns arise. The manual specifies that the measure should not be used with adults with tested IQs below 60. Although the manual provides significant guidance for case-specific interpretation of responses, these are not explained in terms of specific mental health problems or disorders. Beyond psychosis and intellectual functioning, the tool has been studied with adults in reference to depressive

INFO

As these reviews suggest, available CST tools have strengths and weaknesses when used with juveniles. The JACI is probably a better choice for younger or more immature youth, whereas the MacCAT-CA or the ECST-R may be better choices with some older adolescents. More flexible tools, like the JACI, FIT-R, or ECST-R, may be more appropriate when efficiency is stressed, and the MacCAT-CA is a more reasonable choice in some cases when there is adequate time for more extensive case-specific questioning. Examiners might also consider augmenting one tool with another to expand the breadth of coverage and capitalize on the strengths of each tool. For example, if examiners want to use alternatives to the open-ended questioning on the JACI, they may consider supplementing it with the multiple-choice subtests of the CAST*MR.

symptoms. It has not been studied in reference to any childhood disorders. Therefore, use of the tool with child clinical populations requires significant interpretive caution.

Psychological Testing

Psychological testing may be useful in juvenile CST evaluations when examiners need to reduce examiner-based errors in identifying youth's cognitive capacities, psychological traits, and clinical conditions. The use of testing can help meet the heightened demand for documentation, reliability, and verification in forensic evaluations. However, examiners must consider the delays that may be caused by preparation for the testing, the possible need for multiple interview sessions, the additional report-writing time, the heightened demands placed on the youth, and any increased monetary costs that will arise from the use of testing.

Therefore, psychological testing is not required in every juvenile CST evaluation. The use of psychological testing in juvenile CST evaluations should be considered an optional practice to be determined using case-by-case considerations that seek to balance comprehensiveness and efficiency (Grisso, 2005). Some experts claim that testing is rarely cost-effective in adult CST evaluations

(Rogers & Shuman, 2005), but it seems to be more common in CST evaluations with juveniles than with adults (Grisso, 1997, 1998), perhaps because of the increased importance of cognitive and developmental characteristics in understanding a youth's CST deficits.

When deciding whether to administer psychological tests, an important consideration is whether testing will provide additive information relative to other available data. It is less likely to be additive when examiners can access recent testing of the youth that was conducted in other contexts (e.g., special education assessments; psychotherapy). Using testing conducted elsewhere has obvious time–cost benefits and reduced potential for the influence of court-specific motivations. Relying on the testing of others, however, may limit the examiner's ability to assure that the tests were administered and interpreted in a valid manner and eliminate direct observation of the examinee's behaviors during testing. When relying on testing from other sources, it is best to obtain as much detail as possible. That is, actual scores provide more detail than narrative descriptions of the results, and actual test protocols provide more detail than scores.

All psychological tests administered during a CST evaluation should target constructs that are relevant for explaining deficits in CST abilities, especially domains of developmental maturity, general and specific cognitive abilities, learning and academic functioning, and symptoms of mental illness. Tests should not be administered during juvenile CST evaluations without a clear rationale for doing so. For example, intelligence testing is not recommended unless intellectual deficits are, in fact, a suspected cause of the youth's CST limitations (Slobogin et al., 1997). As discussed in Chapter 4, rigid test batteries are inappropriate.

BEST PRACTICE

Any psychological tests used for juvenile CST evaluation should

- Be relevant to identifying CST deficits or the causes of deficits

- Be standardized and empirically supported

- Comply with professional and ethical standards

- Be appropriate for the youth's age, ethnicity, and clinical problems

5
chapter

Tests should be commercially available and provide a manual describing development, psychometric properties, and standardized administration procedure. They should have demonstrated reliability, validity (including face validity and ecological validity), and potential for normative comparison, and have passed peer review (Slobogin et al., 1997; Heilbrun, 1992; Heilbrun et al., 2002; Marlowe, 1995; Melton et al., 2007; Otto & Heilbrun, 2002). The use of tests must also comply with relevant professional and ethical standards. Additional factors that must guide test selection are the youth's age, ethnicity, and clinical problems.

The following list of domains and tests is offered to help examiners begin their considerations. The discussion begins with the domains identified in Chapter 3 as areas most commonly associated with juvenile CST (intellectual functioning, learning ability, maturity, and mental illness) followed by other more specific domains.

Intellectual Functioning

Intellectual functioning may be the most important of domains to consider assessing in juvenile CST evaluations. Empirical links to juvenile CST have been demonstrated in many studies. Wechsler tests, such as the Wechsler Intelligence Scale for Children, 4th edition (WISC-IV; Wechsler, 2003), are commonly used by juvenile CST examiners (Ryba, Cooper, & Zapf, 2003b). Tests like the Woodcock-Johnson Tests of Cognitive Abilities, III (WJ-III COG; Woodcock, McGrew, & Mather, 2001) might also be considered (see Sattler, 2001a, for guidance on selecting intelligence tests). It can be particularly useful to score IQ tests to compare youth to mature cognitive development, as well as use the more typical approach of comparing to age-peers. For example, the "W score" on the WJ-III or mental-age estimates on other tests can estimate absolute cognitive abilities (Sattler, 2001a).

When time constraints are a concern and only a broad estimate or a recheck of intellectual ability is needed, the use of a reliable and valid intelligence screening test may be warranted (Grisso, 2005). For example, the Wechsler Abbreviated Scale of Intelligence (WASI; Psychological Corporation, 1999), which has been empirically linked to juvenile CST (Grisso et al., 2003), may be useful. When a language-free test is needed, the Universal Nonverbal Intelligence Test (UNIT; Bracken & McCallum, 1998) is recommended for use in "high-stakes assessments" (DeThorne & Schaefer, 2004) like CST evaluations. Examiners may also administer individual subtests of broader intelligence tests to assess domains of greatest relevance and concern.

Learning Ability

Learning ability can be assessed with academic achievement tests that measure educational progress. In particular, the Wide Range Achievement Test (now WRAT-4; Wilkinson and Robertson, 2006) has been specifically used in research to assess juvenile CST deficits (Ficke et al., 2006) and was the most commonly cited achievement test used by juvenile CST examiners (Ryba, Cooper, & Zapf, 2003b). Focused tests of memory and learning, such as the Wide Range Assessment of Memory and Learning, Second Edition (WRAML-2; Sheslow & Adams, 2003), may provide a direct assessment of relevant learning abilities.

Developmental Maturity

Developmental maturity offers a unique measurement challenge, because there is no clear consensus among clinicians about how to best measure maturity for juvenile CST evaluations (Ryba, Cooper, & Zapf, 2003a; Slobogin et al., 1997). As discussed in Chapter 2, examiners should think about specific domains of maturity (e.g., cognitive maturity, emotional maturity, etc.) and not a global construct. For example, intelligence tests provide data about cognitive maturity.

In Chapter 3, research was discussed that suggested that abstraction abilities and domains of psychosocial maturity, such as perceived autonomy, risk perceptions, and time perspective, may be particularly relevant to CST (Grisso, 2005). Subtests of intelligence tests (e.g., Similarities on the Wechsler tests) may provide reliable and valid measures of abstraction abilities. The measurement of features of psychosocial maturity is less clear. One might consider the "Sophistication-Maturity" section of the Risk-Sophistication-Treatment Inventory (RSTI; Salekin, 2004), which has items that help examiners focus on autonomy, time perspective, self-concept, ability to anticipate consequences, self-reflection, and other maturity factors that could impact CST.

Measures of adaptive behavior, such as the Vineland Adaptive Behavior Scales, Second Edition (Vineland II; Sparrow, Cicchetti, & Balla, 2005), provide information about maturity of skills that may be relevant to CST, such as socialization and communication. Also, some omnibus rating scales, such as the Behavior Assessment System for Children, Second Edition (BASC-2; Reynolds & Kamphaus, 2004), include adaptive behavior scales together with other relevant measures, including behavioral measures that can help assess social–emotional maturity.

Mental Disorders

Mental disorders can be assessed with a wide range of instruments. These include multi-informant measures of social–emotional functioning (e.g., the Achenbach System's Child Behavior Checklist/ Teacher Report Form/Youth Self-Report; Achenbach & Rescorla, 2001; BASC-2; Reynolds & Kamphaus, 2004) and examiner ratings of mental health symptoms (e.g., Brief Psychiatric Rating Scale for Children [BPRS-C]; Hughes, Rintelmann, Emslie, Lopez, & MacCabe, 2001). Some rare cases may warrant the use of comprehensive psychopathology and personality measures (e.g., Minnesota Multiphasic Personality Inventory–Adolescent [MMPI-A]; Butcher et al., 1992; Millon Adolescent Clinical Inventory [MACI]; Millon, 1993).

In some cases, symptoms of a particular disorder will be critical to conceptualizing the case and focused measures of psychopathology will be useful. Examples may include the assessment of anxiety (e.g., Revised Childhood Manifest Anxiety Scale [RCMAS]; Reynolds & Richmond, 1985), depression (e.g., Children's Depression Inventory [CDI]; Kovacs, 1992), posttraumatic stress (e.g., Trauma Symptom Checklist for Children [TSCC]; Briere, 1996), or communication disorders (e.g., Oral and Written Language Scales [OWLS]: Listening Comprehension and Oral Expression Scales; Carrow-Woolfolk, 1995). A number of excellent texts are available to guide test selection in such cases (e.g., Kamphaus & Frick, 2001; Mash & Barkley, 2007; Sattler, 2006).

Neuropsychological Testing

Neuropsychological testing may sometimes be relevant. Examiners may target specific domains, such as executive functioning (e.g., Behavior Rating Inventory of Executive Functioning [BRIEF]; Gioia, Isquith, Guy, & Kenworthy, 2000) or attentional capacity (e.g., Continuous Performance Test [CPT]; Riccio, Reynolds, & Lowe, 2001). Other times, broad screening measures may be most helpful (e.g., the Kaufman Short Neuropsychological Assessment Procedure [K-SNAP]; Kaufman and Kaufman, 1994).

Response Style Testing

Every forensic mental health evaluation should include consideration of the impact of both subtle and overt *response styles* that might invalidate the meaning of test scores (Heilbrun, 2001). The use of testing to assess such response sets is strongly recommended whenever feasible in forensic contexts (see Rogers & Shuman, 2005, for a discussion and helpful guide to assessment methods). However, there are few standardized tests with adequately documented reliability and validity to assist with this assessment for adults, and even fewer for use with juveniles (McCann, 1998).

Preliminary research on two focused measures of cognitive effort is promising. The Test of Memory Malingering (TOMM; Tombaugh, 1996) is designed for use with individuals as young as 16, and there is evidence that it is similarly useful with children (Constantinou & McCaffrey, 2003; Donders, 2005; Palav, 2004). Several studies have also demonstrated that the Word Memory Test (WMT; Green, Allen, & Astner, 1996; Green & Astner, 1995) is useful with children older than 10 (Courtney, Dinkins, Allen, & Kuroski, 2003; Green & Flaro, 2003; Palav, 2004). In addition, the Structured Interview of Reported Symptoms (SIRS; Rogers, Bagby, & Dickens, 1992) is a test of feigned psychosis and has demonstrated initial utility with adolescents (Rogers, Hinds, & Sewell, 1996). However, excluding 16- and 17-year-olds with the TOMM, none of these tests have been adequately validated or normed on youth. Therefore, any use in juvenile CST evaluations should be interpreted cautiously, and the limitations of their use should be clearly communicated to the court.

5
chapter

Broad-based personality measures, such as the MMPI-A or the MACI, may also have utility in the assessment of response style (Grisso, 2005; McCann & Dyer, 1996; Rogers, Hinds, & Sewell, 1996). Other self-report tests, such as the BASC-2, include scales targeting response styles that are of unexamined utility in juvenile CST evaluations.

Conclusion

This chapter provided detailed guidance on methods for collecting data needed to form CST opinions, including use of third-party information, interviewing caregivers, interviewing and observing the youth, and the use of psychological testing. Once the data are collected, examiners must sift through the information and organize it in ways that allow adequately supported opinions to be reached. This process of data interpretation will be discussed in the next chapter.

Interpretation

6

Once examiners have collected all of the data relevant to the evaluation, that data must be interpreted in order to offer useful opinions to the courts. Irrelevant data should be excluded and the remaining data must be "sorted, considered, compared, and configured to arrive at conclusions that are logically consistent with the pattern of case facts that the evaluation has uncovered" (Grisso, 2005, p. 87). The complexity of the interpretation process varies from case to case, so examiners must use an interpretive model that is structured enough to provide guidance, but flexible enough to accommodate a variety of possible scenarios.

The process of synthesizing the data must be informed by scientific reasoning (Heilbrun, 2001). At the core of this process is the generation of hypotheses that might be consistent with the data, combined with consideration of alternative hypotheses, in a search of the "best hypothesis"—the one that is most consistent with the full array of data. For example, if a youth with CST deficits has a history of learning problems, the examiner may well hypothesize that the two are related. But the test of this hypothesis is whether the types of CST deficits the youth manifests are theoretically consistent with the known learning problems, and whether there are any other hypotheses that would better explain the youth's CST deficits. This process requires that examiners be open to the possibility that they will be unable to form a reasonably certain

BEST PRACTICE

Generate alternative hypotheses and pursue the "best hypothesis" to help form opinions. Recognize that in some cases there may be no "best hypothesis."

opinion because, for example, competing hypotheses are similarly supported by the data or because no hypothesis is adequately supported (Heilbrun, 2001).

At the heart of the interpretive process in juvenile CST cases is the need to answer five types of guiding questions, as offered by Grisso's (2003a) model for evaluating legal competencies. That model is used to guide the following discussion of data interpretation.

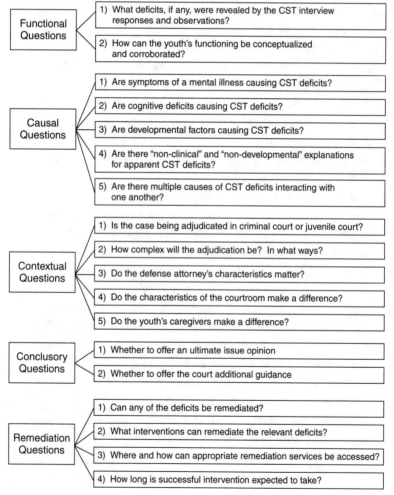

Functional Questions

1) What deficits, if any, were revealed by the CST interview responses and observations?

2) How can the youth's functioning be conceptualized and corroborated?

Causal Questions

1) Are symptoms of a mental illness causing CST deficits?

2) Are cognitive deficits causing CST deficits?

3) Are developmental factors causing CST deficits?

4) Are there "non-clinical" and "non-developmental" explanations for apparent CST deficits?

5) Are there multiple causes of CST deficits interacting with one another?

Contextual Questions

1) Is the case being adjudicated in criminal court or juvenile court?

2) How complex will the adjudication be? In what ways?

3) Do the defense attorney's characteristics matter?

4) Do the characteristics of the courtroom make a difference?

5) Do the youth's caregivers make a difference?

Conclusory Questions

1) Whether to offer an ultimate issue opinion

2) Whether to offer the court additional guidance

Remediation Questions

1) Can any of the deficits be remediated?

2) What interventions can remediate the relevant deficits?

3) Where and how can appropriate remediation services be accessed?

4) How long is successful intervention expected to take?

Figure 6.1 Interpretive Model

Functional Questions

The main functional question asks what the youth is capable of knowing, understanding, believing, doing, and deciding within the role of being a defendant at the current time and as the adjudication proceeds (Grisso, 1998, 2003a, 2005; Otto, Borum, & Epstein, 2006). The analysis should consider the defendant's functional strengths and weaknesses in Understanding, Appreciating, Assisting, and Decision Making, without reference (yet) to the likely causes of any functional impairments (Barnum, 2000; Grisso, 1998, 2005). To allow for appropriate analysis by the court, examiners should clearly identify the severity of both major and minor functional deficits (Slobogin et al., 1997). They should also consider functional strengths that may compensate for any deficits.

The two questions discussed next will help examiners respond to the main functional question. The data sources most likely to assist examiners answering these questions include functional CST observations, the functional CST interview, and reports from third-party information (Barnum, 2000). Third-party sources may be specific to the case, such as observations by defense counsel, caregivers, or probation officers (Grisso, 2005). Or they may relate to general functioning, such as information from school officials or mental health providers.

What Deficits, if any, Were Revealed by the CST Interview Responses and Observations?

Prior to evaluation, examiners will have identified the specific functional abilities that are relevant for CST in their own jurisdiction. As interpretation begins, examiners should focus on the defendant's discussion and demonstration of each ability during the functional CST interview and observation periods. Several aspects of this process deserve special mention.

BEST PRACTICE

When interpreting functional abilities, make sure to

- Be developmentally sensitive

- Distinguish between Understanding and Appreciation

- Assess the underlying rationale for Decision Making

- Consider the extent of benefit from teaching

DEVELOPMENTAL SENSITIVITY

Interpretations must be developmentally sensitive. Focusing only on the issues of typical concern in adult CST evaluations is inadequate. For example, the assessment of Assisting with adults is more typically focused on the interference of psychotic thinking that can yield nonsensical explanations of the facts of the alleged incident or delusional mistrust of counsel. Even if the juvenile is psychotic, the assessment of Assisting in youth must include attention to possible concerns rooted in developmental immaturity or delays. For instance, such concerns may involve explanations of the offense that omit critical information or inject irrelevant or even fantastical information (Oberlander, Goldstein, & Ho, 2001; Ryan and Murrie, 2005). They may also include limits in interpersonal relatedness and social skills.

DISTINCTION BETWEEN UNDERSTANDING AND APPRECIATION

During the interpretation phase, examiners must take care to distinguish between Understanding questions and Appreciation questions. Again, *Understanding* refers to knowledge of or an ability to readily learn basic facts about the legal process. *Appreciation* refers to an ability to apply that information to one's case in a rational manner. For example, a juvenile has demonstrated Understanding if he knows that pleading not guilty means one is not admitting to the offense. But he shows poor Appreciation if he believes that he himself would have to plead guilty if he actually committed the offense, because to plead not guilty would be lying and thus wrong.

RATIONALE FOR DECISIONS

Examiners who have assessed decisional abilities using hypothetical decision-making tasks should focus on the underlying rationale for the decisions rather than simply what the youth chooses. No choice itself is right or wrong, or mature or immature. Those characteristics only pertain to *reasons* for one's choices and *processes* for arriving at them. How the decision was made—not the choice to which it led—is the main issue. Did the youth appear to understand that she had options? Did she seem to recognize advantages

...
...

and disadvantages of each option? Did she have a distortion-free understanding of how each option would impact the case? Did she appear to reach a nonimpulsive choice?

BENEFIT FROM TEACHING

When the interview includes teaching information to the youth, examiners should not merely conclude that the youth did or did not benefit from teaching. Rather, they should note how well and how quickly the youth responded. Did the youth respond positively to straightforward explanations of the type an attorney can provide? Or did the youth respond positively only after more extensive explanations and training (suggesting inadequate but potentially remediable abilities)? Or did the youth respond poorly to even extensive explanations and training?

How Can the Youth's Functioning Be Conceptualized and Corroborated?

After individual responses have been analyzed, patterns of functioning across the CST interview should be considered (Grisso, 2005). A disorganized laundry list of highly specific difficulties (e.g., "She said that a probation officer is always on her side"), alone, is of minimal use to the court. To the extent possible, examiners should organize the findings in a more useful conceptualization. For example, the examiner may indicate that the analysis revealed that the youth demonstrated adequate Understanding of most issues, but demonstrated less well-developed Appreciation, Assisting, and Decision Making.

The functional analysis also should be expanded beyond the functional CST interview and observations to include other relevant data from third-party sources. These data may or may not corroborate the functional conceptualization. For example, when the defendant demonstrated poor ability to assist counsel during the interview, and the defense attorney also reported difficulty understanding and communicating with her client at their last meeting, the conclusion that there are

BEST PRACTICE

Organize the findings on the youth's CST abilities, corrobating the conceptualization with collateral information.

Assisting deficits is reinforced. On the other hand, when a youth demonstrates poor memory of the charges immediately after they are explained, yet was recently praised by educators for learning complex lines in a school play, the examiner must begin to question the validity of the interview results.

Causal Questions

The main causal question asks the examiner to opine about the sources of any deficits that were identified when answering the functional question and the manner in which a given source and deficits are related (Grisso, 2003a). The answer to the causal question helps the court limit findings of incompetence to the most relevant cases, such as when a predicate requirement such as "mental disease or defect" has been met (Viljoen & Roesch, 2007). The answer to the causal question will also help the examiner to later assess the likelihood of successful CST remediation (Goldstein, Thomson, Osman, & Oberlander, 2002; Grisso, 1998, 2003a; Schwartz & Rosado, 2000; Viljoen & Roesch, 2007).

Once any problems have been identified, the examiner should assess whether one or more of the problems, either in isolation or in combination with other problems, best account for the weaknesses identified in the functional analysis. The identified problems are only relevant when there is a plausible causal connection with (in contrast to mere coexistence with) the CST deficits (Barnum, 2000; Grisso, 2003a; Schwartz & Rosado, 2000; Slobogin et al., 1997). For example, the fact that a young juvenile is demonstrating CST deficits does not necessarily mean that the development-based cognitive immaturity associated with her age is causing the deficits. It may be, for example, that the deficits are best accounted for by the combination of a severe attentional disorder and significant depression.

An important step toward assessing the plausibility of the causal connection is to consider it in specific and not just vague terms. Examiners should think in terms of the specific impacts of a given problem, such as symptoms (e.g., distorted social perceptions), deficits (e.g., memory), or developmental lags (e.g., social abilities), to see if they plausibly explain the CST limits. So, identifying that a young juvenile has deficits in both general abstraction abilities and Appreciation capacities helps establish a logically sound and clear connection between the cause and the deficits.

Answering the main causal question requires consideration of each of the five questions discussed next (Barnum, 2000; Grisso, 1998, 2005; Viljoen & Roesch, 2007). Usually hypotheses are generated from the interview of the defendant (both historical and current mental status), interview of caregivers, third-party data, and psychological testing (Grisso, 2005).

Are Symptoms of a Mental Illness Causing CST Deficits?

Some examiners do not offer specific diagnoses to courts and simply identify impairment (e.g., concrete thinking). However, it is generally accepted that a diagnosis should be offered whenever relevant; doing so helps the court to determine if a predicate requirement has been met, helps the court to appreciate when the defendant's weaknesses are an element of a well-established syndrome, and provides a firmer foundation for making estimates of remediation success (Mossman et al., 2007). Juvenile offenders show high rates of mental illness, so the potential threats to CST from mental illnesses are significant.

6
chapter

DIAGNOSING MENTAL ILLNESS IN JUVENILES

As explained in Chapter 4, diagnosing mental illnesses with youth is challenging for many reasons, including high rates of comorbidity that can cloud symptom patterns and reduce diagnostic reliability, and interactions between symptoms of pathology and normal development. Further complicating the issue is that mental health symptoms that do not rise to the level of meeting criteria for a full disorder ("subthreshold diagnoses") may still impair functioning (Kazdin, 2000). For example, children with depressive symptoms that do not meet criteria for a depressive disorder still tend to show deficits in psychosocial functioning compared to that of other youth (Gotlib, Lewinsohn, & Seeley, 1995). So, the relation between mental

BEST PRACTICE
Offer diagnoses when feasible, but focus on specific symptoms and how they affect the youth's functioning.

BEWARE
Do not
simply rely
on diagnoses offered by
others; consider the specific
symptoms to form your own
diagnostic conclusions.

illness and CST is often more complex than in adult CST cases, where concerns are often relatively overt psychotic symptoms.

For all of these reasons, the causal analysis involving childhood mental illnesses may be most useful when examiners offer the best diagnostic picture possible, but then move beyond the disorders themselves to discuss problems at the level of symptoms and functional impacts. This creates a reduced need for complete diagnostic specificity in juvenile CST evaluations (Grisso, 2005). For example, clearly determining if a defendant's weaknesses in attention are associated with attention-deficit/hyperactivity disorder (ADHD) or dysthymic disorder may be less critical in some cases than identifying that attention deficits are present. The closer the examiner can get to precise diagnoses, the easier for the court to reach sound decisions, such as determining when deficits are more likely due to a mental disorder or developmental immaturity. However, some differential diagnoses will be complex and beyond the scope of the CST evaluation. Uncertain and "not otherwise specified" diagnoses are not uncommon in juvenile CST evaluations. In reaching any diagnostic conclusions, examiners should never merely accept the diagnoses offered by other professionals without appropriate consideration of the specific symptoms that led to the professional's diagnosis (Rogers & Shuman, 2005).

COMMON CST-RELATED SYMPTOMS AMONG JUVENILES

There has been little research regarding the impact of various symptoms on CST functioning among juveniles. Although a comprehensive discussion is beyond the scope of this book, certain common childhood symptoms may have clear relevance to CST (Kazdin, 2000). For example, *impulsivity,* which may be associated with disorders such as ADHD, bipolar disorder, posttraumatic stress disorder (PTSD), and behavior disorders, can yield poorly reasoned and short-sighted decision making and inaccurate responses to questioning (Grisso, 1998, 2005; Kazdin, 2000). *Inattention* and *distractibility* that can be associated with disorders like ADHD, mood disorders, and anxiety disorders may increase the risk of difficulties with remaining on task, appropriately responding to questioning, and experiencing interference with the reception and integration of new information, as is required when assisting counsel or in decision making (Barnum, 2000; Grisso, 1998, 2005; Kazdin, 2000; Viljoen & Roesch, 2005). Depressive, anxiety, behaviorial, and psychotic disorders can all yield *poor interpersonal relations* (Barnum, 2000; Grisso, 2005; Kazdin, 2000; Viljoen & Grisso, 2007). *Cognitive slowing* associated with depression can yield apathy and poor motivation during attorney consultations and in court (Grisso, 1998, 2005; Kazdin, 2000).

Some disorders may yield irrational conceptualizations of one's legal situation and can contribute to irrational legal decisions. Depressed and anxious youth may be influenced by pessimism, hopelessness, detachment, negative self-attributions, and external locus of control that can limit the options seen as viable (Barnum, 2000; Fletcher, 1996; Grisso, 2005; Kazdin, 2000). They may experience ruminative thoughts and concerns that yield idiosyncratic perceptions of case-related situations (Barnum, 2000). Acute delusions, as well, can distort perceptions of the adjudication process in odd, illogical, or even bizarre ways (Barnum, 2000).

Are Cognitive Deficits Causing CST Deficits?

The broad and extreme deficits in cognitive functioning associated with disorders like mental retardation are often associated with incompetence in adults. This is also true with juveniles. However, youth's functioning can also be impaired by more focused cognitive limitations, such as memory impairment, executive dysfunction, or learning difficulties, as well as less severe weaknesses, such as developmental delays or borderline intellectual functioning (Grisso, 2005; Kazdin, 2000). For example, weaknesses in executive functioning can impair abstract reasoning, goal setting, anticipating and planning, self-monitoring and self-awareness, inhibiting of impulsive behavior, and interrupting of ongoing behaviors to initiate more adaptive behaviors (Barkley, 1996; Kazdin, 2000; Moffitt, 1993). Cognitive weaknesses can impair the

BEST PRACTICE

In addition to severe intellectual deficits, be sensitive to cognitive limitations less commonly associated with adult IST.

understanding of and ability to learn even fundamental aspects of court functions such as the purposes, procedures, and participants in trials (Grisso, 1998, 2005). Cognitive impairments can also reduce abstraction abilities necessary for adequate Appreciation, impair cognitive decision-making skills, and/or impair the language skills needed for Assisting (Grisso, 1998, 2005).

Are Developmental Factors Causing CST Deficits?

Some youth may evidence functional CST deficits due to immature development. Most preadolescent youth will be less cognitively mature than adults, so they are at greater risk of relatively poorer ability to think about abstract concepts (e.g., guilt as a legal concept). As discussed in earlier chapters, immature psychosocial functioning can yield poor coping skills and immature decisions, such as when young defendants are in denial about their charges and overly passive with their attorneys. The social roles of childhood can also limit the functioning of younger defendants in the legal context. For example, some youth may have difficulty conceptualizing their attorneys' advocacy role because they have rarely experienced adults who take their side against other adults. As discussed in chapter 2, examiners are most helpful to courts when they analyze maturity in terms of specific domains, contrast incomplete development and delayed development, and explain psychosocial factors such as perceived autonomy, time perspective, perceptions of risk, and abstraction abilities (Barnum, 2000; Grisso, 2005).

Examiners may feel uncertain about whether to include considerations of developmental immaturity in jurisdictions that have not yet determined its relevance as a predicate cause of incompetence. When in doubt, we recommend "casting a wide net that is clearly marked." That is, err on the side of overinclusion, but make sure that the inclusion of matters about which there may be controversy are clearly identified and obvious. It is better to be able to explain to the court the role of developmental immaturity in a defendant's relevant functioning and have that information viewed as less compelling by the court than to be unprepared to address the issue in a court that does see development-based capacities as relevant.

BEST PRACTICE

Include considerations of developmental immaturity in your evaluation, clearly identifying them if the court may find them controversial.

Are There "Nonclinical" and "Nondevelopmental" Explanations for Apparent CST Deficits?

OTHER FEATURES OF THE DEFENDANT

Sometimes functional impairments are due to static and dynamic features of the defendant that are not typically associated with incompetence. For example, sensory deficits such as poor vision or hearing can impair the ability of the defendant to perceive information, and recent sleep deprivation or poor nutrition can reduce attentional capacity and cognitive efficiency. Many of these causes can be readily reme-

died, such as providing a sign language interpreter in a case involving a deaf youth. However, there have been criminal court cases in which extreme sensory impairment has yielded a finding of incompetence based on *Dusky* (e.g., *State v. Burnett,* 2005).

Membership in non-majority cultures can also impact court functioning in unique ways (Mossman et al., 2007; Tobey, Grisso, & Schwartz, 2000; Viljoen & Roesch, 2007). Intractable cultural expectations about court corruption, for example, are common in some U.S. and immigrant populations. Languge barriers that are difficult to remedy can also occur, such as when defendants speak unusual foreign dialects. Cultural issues are not typically considered grounds for a finding of incompetence, but some of these extreme cases may be difficult or even impossible for courts to resolve (see Associated Press, 2007).

RESPONSE SETS AND UNWILLINGNESS TO COOPERATE

Examiners must also consider response sets in the causal analysis. Juvenile defendants are at considerable risk to disengage the CST evaluation by presenting as bored, passive, defensive, hostile, oppositional, or tough, and by challenging the examiner, "shutting down," or habitually using responses of "I don't know" (Melton et al., 2007; Slobogin et al., 1997). Such presentations often appear to reflect poor motivation, although assessment of this is difficult. There are no reliable means to assess "optimal effort" (Rogers & Shuman, 2005). When juveniles are capable of adequate CST functioning but purposefully put forth little effort to do so for reasons not related to identifiable impairments, they are not typically found IST (Otto & Goldstein, 2005). As discussed earlier in this section, however, what appears as poor motivation may also be due to mental health problems, such as anxiety, paranoia, or depression, or to other factors, such as sleep deprivation (Barnum, 2000; Rogers & Shuman, 2005).

The distinction between inability and unwillingness to cooperate can be difficult to discern (Otto et al., 2006). In practice, lines between "mental disorder," "developmental limitations," and "choosing not to cooperate" are often unclear. Especially difficult to decipher are impairing patterns of negativity, hostility, and noncompliance, such as those associated with oppositional defiant disorder (ODD). In some cases, severe oppositionality is clearly rooted in another disorder (such as pervasive developmental disorder; see Ryan & Murrie, 2005) and should probably be considered related to a mental illness for purposes of assessing CST. In other cases, however, the oppositionality is a discrete, yet ingrained, pattern of interacting that has resulted from a combination of temperamental factors and environmental circumstances (Patterson & Forgatch, 1987). It is legally unresolved whether such cases of ODD should be seen as "intentional" and not a basis for incompetence (as is typically true with antisocial personality disorder in adult CST considerations; Mossman et al., 2007) or seen at least in part as related to the limited judgment and insight that is characteristic of developmental immaturity and distinct from noncompliant adults.

MALINGERING

Although they are by most reports rare among youth, some evaluations will reveal evidence of exaggerated or feigned incapacities, such as memory deficits, in an effort to illegitimately be found IST

(Grisso, 2005). Examiners are vulnerable to missing such attempts by youth (Faust, Hart, Guilmette, & Arkes, 1989). There has been little research on youth's malingering or feigning of disabilities, and none focused specifically on feigning in CST evaluations (Grisso, 2005; Viljoen & Roesch, 2007). In general, however, signs of possible malingering may include

BEWARE
When a conclusion of malingering is reached, elements of the defendant's report may need to be weighed less heavily or even disregarded. A conclusion of malingering, though, does not mean the youth is necessarily competent— there may still be legitimate CST threats, and other sources of information will need to be considered.

a. an overplayed and dramatic presentation;

b. deliberateness and carefulness;

c. inconsistency of symptom history, onset, or nature relative to typical clinical and developmental presentations;

d. inconsistency in self-report when symptoms are questioned in detail at different points in the interview;

e. the endorsement of symptoms rarely seen together;

f. discrepancies in abilities at various points during the evaluation interview; and

g. endorsement of obvious symptoms and problems (Heilbrun, 2001; Rogers, 1997; McCann, 1998).

6
chapter

Are There Multiple Causes of CST Deficits Interacting With One Another?

Adding to the complexity of the causal analysis are the potential interactions among symptoms of mental illnesses, cognitive deficits, developmental immaturity, and/or nonclinical causes. When multiple problems co-occur, such as a youth who is both 11 years old and suffers from PTSD, distinguishing between the relative contributions of the two factors is often complex and sometimes impossible (Ambrosini, 2000; Rudolph, Hammen, & Burge, 1994; Schachar & Logan, 1991). Examiners should always limit their conclusions to what can be said of the data. It is also important for examiners to remember the importance of specifying all of the interacting factors. For example, if an examiner believes an 11-year-old is IST due to both

immaturity and PTSD but focuses exclusively on the former, the defendant may be found competent on purely legal grounds in a jurisdiction that does not recognize immaturity as a basis for being found IST (Oberlander et al., 2001).

Contextual Questions

The contextual questions address the significance of a youth's deficits in light of the specific circumstances (i.e., the *context*) of her adjudication. Incompetence depends in part on comparing the degree of the defendant's CST deficits to the actual demands of the case-specific circumstances. Therefore, juvenile CST examiners should consider the fit between the types and degrees of the youth's deficits and the demands that the particular court situation will place on her (Grisso, 1998; Roesch & Golding, 1980; Schwartz & Rosado, 2000; Viljoen & Roesch, 2007).

As a question of defendant–case fit, the contextual analysis can begin with the case or the defendant. Examiners might identify case factors that can impact the importance of deficits in the instant case (e.g., the need for testimony from the defendant), then determine if the defendant's abilities are likely to meet the demands. Alternatively, the examiner can consider the defendant's CST deficits (e.g., poor communication skills), then consider the likelihood that the function in question will be needed in the particular case (Grisso, 2003a). Either way, the question is of fit, but there is no ready formula with which to compare the trial demands and the defendant's ability (Grisso, 1998).

As discussed in Chapter 4, there is controversy over whether it is necessary for examiners to address contextual questions in CST analyses. We again suggest that examiners cast a wide net that is well marked, offering the information and allowing the court to determine whether it is relevant from a legal perspective. To forego this step could deprive the court of relevant information (Christy, Douglas, Otto, & Petrila, 2004; Grisso, 2005). The five broad considerations in the contextual question are typically addressed using data obtained from the defense attorney, the defendant, the caregivers, the probation officer, and/or police reports (Grisso, 2005).

Is the Case Being Adjudicated in Criminal Court or Juvenile Court?

An important contextual consideration in juvenile CST evaluations is the venue in which the case will be heard (Schwartz & Rosado, 2000). It has been argued that juveniles require a higher level of CST functioning when they are being adjudicated in criminal court rather than in juvenile court (Bonnie & Grisso, 2000; Grisso, 1997). Juveniles tried in criminal court will face the same fully adversarial system and court procedures and need to be versed in the same legal concepts as all criminal defendants. In some jurisdictions, by contrast, courts are clear that juveniles tried in juvenile court are held to a reduced adolescent norm standard (see Chapter 2).

However, it is not necessarily true that juveniles tried in juvenile court are facing an "easier" process. Juveniles tried in juvenile court may face hearings of ambiguous demands in which the level of formality and adversarial qualities may vary from jurisdiction to jurisdiction, courtroom to courtroom, and sometimes case to case (Barnum, 2000; Grisso, 1997; Heilbrun, Hawk, & Tate, 1996). In fact, some investigators have argued that juvenile proceedings are often *more* complex than criminal proceedings, because of greater complexity and a wider variety of offense types, dispositions, and hearings (Viljoen & Roesch, 2007; Wynkoop, 2003). Lawyers and judges may be less likely to slow the proceedings and use layman's terms when there is no jury (Buss, 2000). Furthermore, many juvenile proceedings lack the procedural trappings that can help the defendant cognitively structure and track what is happening (Buss, 2000).

6
chapter

How Complex Will the Adjudication Be? In What Ways?

Another important contextual issue is the expected complexity of the youth's case, which may have an influence on the demand placed on the youth as a defendant (Grisso,

BEWARE
The mere fact that a juvenile's case is being heard in juvenile or criminal court does not automatically translate into greater or lesser demands on the youth.

1998, 2003a, 2005; Heilbrun et al., 1996; Schwartz & Rosado, 2000; Skeem & Golding, 1998; Slobogin et al., 1997). Simply knowing the charges can help determine if the number and complexity of the charges and types of possible penalties (e.g., sex offender registration) may increase the likelihood of confusion. Further, more serious charges tend to yield more complex issues, decisions, and proceedings (e.g., transfer hearings). Examiners should also consider the availability of reliable evidence about the facts of the case, such as may be available from objective witnesses, since this information places less demand on the defendant to provide facts of the case to counsel.

The nature of the plea that will be selected can also be important for assessing complexity. A guilty plea requires adequate plea agreement decision-making skills and a not-guilty plea adds the need for adequate trial skills. If the case is going to trial, other considerations may include the likelihood that trial will be lengthy, taxing, and/or emotionally arousing, involve many witnesses, require a complex legal defense, and/or require the presentation of complex evidence. Examiners should also consider the likelihood that the defendant's testimony will be needed, as certain skills, such as verbal communication, may be less relevant if testimony is unlikely for other reasons.

There currently are no focused techniques for systematic assessment or descriptions of future trial demands or for assessing the match between defendants and their cases. Examiners are left to conduct this analysis on logical and speculative bases (Grisso, 2003a).

Do the Defense Attorney's Characteristics Matter?

The *Dusky* standard requirement that defendants be able to assist counsel makes clear that CST is interactive and should consider the relationship between defendant and attorney (Grisso, 2003a; Dawson & Kraus, 2005; Melton et al., 2007). The mere fact that a particular attorney may be difficult for a defendant to work with is never a reason to declare incompetence. But attorneys are active participants in the relationship, and some may have the ability to improve defendant functioning (Redding & Frost, 2001; Slobogin et al., 1997; Tobey et al., 2000). Some attorneys, for instance, skillfully provide careful and simplified explanations, augment explanations in developmentally appropriate ways, and adjust courtroom situations, such as requesting frequent breaks, to assist their clients (Bonnie & Grisso, 2000; Buss, 2000; Tobey et al., 2000). Some attorneys are also able to enhance the active engagement of their clients by getting advice from others who relate well to the youth, spending more time together, demonstrating loyalty, and forming strong collaborative relationships (Buss, 2000; Melton et al., 2007; Viljoen & Roesch, 2005).

BEST PRACTICE
Consider the defense attorney's ability to improve the defendant's functioning as part of the contextual analysis.

Other attorneys will be untrained, unmotivated, or otherwise unable to offer extraordinary assistance and cannot be expected to enhance the functioning of their clients (Grisso, 2003a). In fact, despite many calls for juvenile defense attorneys to gain such skills (American Bar Association Center on Children and the Law, 2006; Buss, 2000; Grisso & Schwartz, 2000; Katner, 2006; Margulies, 1996; Sentencing Project, 2000; Tobey et al., 2000; Ventrell, 1995), few attorneys have done so (American Bar Association Center on Children and the Law, 2006; American Bar Association Juvenile Justice Center, 1995b; Federle, 1988). The reality is that even fundamental assistance is often limited by factors such as large caseloads (Katner, 2006).

To the extent that the examiner can determine where the defense attorney representing the defendant falls on some of these dimensions, she may be able to estimate the likelihood that the attorney can enhance the defendant's functioning. Data sources for this analysis might include observations of and information about attorney–defendant interactions, as well as information about defense counsel's past behavior and relations to clients in general (Grisso, 2003a).

Do The Characteristics of the Courtroom Make a Difference?

Judges and the courtrooms they run may vary in how well they accommodate the needs of juvenile defendants (Heilbrun, Hawk, & Tate, 1996). Too often, sophisticated language is used, and time

6
chapter

demands create a harried, rushed, and stressful environment that can detract from adequate functioning of youthful defendants (Tobey et al., 2000; Viljoen & Grisso, 2007). Courtroom procedures can be modified, though, to enhance the functioning of juveniles (Tobey et al., 2000). In a case in which Kruh was involved, for example, the court commissioner spent time at the outset of the hearing reminding the juvenile defendant of accommodations that could be offered, such as taking a break if she felt herself becoming frustrated, and instructed the attorneys that they would not be permitted to question the juvenile in an aggressive or purposefully confusing manner if she chose to testify.

Do the Youth's Caregivers Make a Difference?

As discussed in Chapter 2, caregivers may influence defendants in obvious and/or subtle ways that support functioning, detract from functioning, or include a mix of influences. Nonetheless, the appropriate ways to consider this influence in the CST evaluation are not fully clear. Attorneys and judges may tend to place less emphasis on the supportive role of caregivers because CST requires independent functioning by the defendant; that is, there is no accepted role for "surrogate" case assistance. In fact, including caregivers in communications about the case may be seen as an infringement of attorney–client confidentiality (Grisso, 2005; Tobey et al., 2000). Whereas the role of caregivers should rarely be weighed by the examiner in arriving at their CST opinions, it may be important for examiners to alert the court when adults seem particularly likely to detract from the defendant's functioning. Kruh recalls, for example, a case in which a parent caused severe confusion in a young, cognitively limited defendant by insisting that he lie.

BEST PRACTICE

Inform the court of interference by caregivers that could significantly limit a youth's functioning.

General Thoughts About the Contextual Question

Examiners are likely to find the contextual analysis particularly challenging. Even knowledgeable examiners cannot fully anticipate the demands, supports, and obstacles that will arise as the adjudication unfolds. At the time of evaluation, it is often too early in the case for many plans to have been made. Defense attorneys may consider case-specific information privileged and be reluctant to share it. Finally, the case context is a "moving target," in that attorneys, judges,

BEST PRACTICE
Use conditional statements to explain the different ways in which the case may unfold and the possible demands on the defendant in various scenarios.

and/or interested adults may or may not respond to the needs of a particular youth (Barnum, 2000).

Given the difficulties inherent in this process, the contextual analysis should be conducted cautiously and with a focus on more extreme concerns (Grisso, 1998, 2005). Furthermore, examiners should consider the many possible ways the case may unfold and form their contextual concerns using "if-then" statements (Barnum, 2000; Grisso, 2005). For example, the examiner may note, "If testimony is required in this case, then the court may consider that the defendant becomes very anxious and verbally inept when authority figures seem angered, as could occur during cross-examination"; or "If the court can slow the proceedings and the attorney can attentively check the defendant's understanding, the defendant's functioning will be enhanced." Analyses like these provide the relevant information to the court and allow those directly involved to consider the likelihood that the contextual concern will arise and that the deficit can or will be accommodated, as well as the appropriate weight to assign to the concern in the overall CST analysis.

6
chapter

Conclusory Question

The conclusory, or ultimate, question refers to the last step in the process of deciding about the youth's CST. It involves a synthesis of all of the preceding questions. Specifically, are the defendant's functional deficits caused by legally relevant factors and are they so limited that the defendant should be considered incompetent to proceed to adjudication in her case? Addressing this conclusory question requires awareness of a controversy often called the "ultimate issue." The *ultimate issue* refers to the final, most central point that the trier of fact is seeking to decide, which is competence vs. incompetence. The ultimate issue is the controversy over whether examiners should offer an opinion specific to that ultimate issue (e.g., "It is my opinion that he is competent to stand trial").

Debate Over Offering Ultimate Issue Opinions

The ultimate issue has been widely debated (see, for example, Fulero & Finkel, 1991, and Melton et al., 2007, for differing opinions). Surveying board-certified forensic mental health examiners, Borum and Grisso (2003) found them to be split three ways: one-third believed that such opinions should always be offered, one-third believed that they should never be offered, and one-third believed that such opinions are acceptable but not mandatory. Otto (2006) concluded that the controversy will never be resolved.

Those who suggest that examiners can provide ultimate issue opinions argue that laws usually allow examiners to speak to an opinion on the ultimate legal question, and that judges and attorneys expect it, recognizing that the court will ultimately reach the legal determination (Heilbrun, 2001; Redding, Floyd, & Hawk, 2001). They argue that there is no evidence that offering such opinions usurps the factfinder's legitimate role, as some critics have suggested, and that advances in forensic practice allow examiners to reach sound ultimate issue opinions (Rogers & Shuman, 2005). In fact, examiners in some jurisdictions are directed to provide ultimate issue opinions regarding CST (e.g., Texas: Tex. Crim. Proc. 46B.025), and they are encouraged or allowed to provide such opinions in many others (Rogers & Shuman, 2005).

Those who recommend against examiners offering ultimate issue opinions point out that doing so requires the examiner to engage in a legal analysis for which there is no clinical answer: specifically, whether the youth's deficits in abilities are of sufficient magnitude to conclude that putting the youth on trial would violate fundamental fairness (Grisso, 2005). In other words, this is a legal, social, and moral fairness question that reaches beyond the bounds of mental health expertise (Barnum, 2000; Grisso, 1998, 2003a, 2005; Melton et al., 2007; Tillbrook, Mumley, & Grisso, 2003).

Based on this reasoning, some jurisdictions prohibit examiners from offering ultimate issue opinions (e.g., Virginia: *Llamera v. Commonwealth*, 243 Va. 262, 264, 414 S.E. 2d 597, 598 [1992]).

Ultimate Issue in the Context of Juvenile CST

Special consideration of the ultimate issue is warranted within the context of juvenile CST evaluations. First, the assertion that forensic practices have advanced adequately to warrant ultimate issue opinions seems inapplicable to the juvenile CST context. Currently, no true juvenile CST FAIs are available, there are no psychometrically sound tests to assess most response sets (e.g., malingering) among juveniles, and few psychological tests have been studied in the context of juvenile CST evaluations. The field continues to grapple with defining, as well as assessing, critical constructs such as developmental immaturity and psychosocial reasoning. The first comprehensive method for conducting juvenile CST evaluations was only recently offered to the field (Grisso, 2005), and adequate assessment of the utility of its strategies and recommendations has not yet been conducted.

Second, as detailed in Chapter 2, there remain fundamental definitional ambiguities in statutes and case law about critical issues such as the functions, standards, causes, and contextual factors to be considered (Grisso, 1998, 2005; Viljoen & Roesch, 2007). Consequently, it is very difficult for examiners to reach conclusory opinions without making idiosyncratic assumptions about unresolved legal issues. For example, examiners practicing in jurisdictions where there is no law specifying whether or not juveniles adjudicated in juvenile court should be held to a lower CST standard than those adjudicated in criminal court must honor that legal ambiguity even if they have their own personally held opinions on the matter. Embedding one's own definitions in the conclusory opinion can yield inconsistent and potentially unjust court decisions.

Guidance in Offering Ultimate Issue Opinions

Examiners should exhibit significant caution in offering ultimate issue opinions in juvenile CST evaluations. They are probably inappropriate in all but the most extreme cases. When examiners do provide ultimate issue opinions, the rationale for the opinion should be transparent, so that the court is adequately equipped to consider the merits of the examiner's reasoning and reach its own independent determination (Grisso, 2003a; Ryba, Cooper, & Zapf, 2003b; Viljoen & Roesch, 2007). A summary of the functional, causal, and contextual considerations is critical in explaining the reasoning behind ultimate issue opinions for those examiners offering them (Heilbrun, 2001).

But available evidence suggests that judges rely heavily on the opinions of juvenile CST examiners to reach their ultimate CST determinations (e.g., Kruh, Sullivan, Ellis, Lexcen, & McClellan, 2006). So how can examiners best assist the courts? One way for examiners to manage this situation is to refrain from forming judgments about the sufficiency of a youth's abilities until the legal standards have been adequately defined (Grisso, 2005). Examiners can simply offer their functional, causal, and contextual opinions as guidance, stop there, and allow the court to conduct the synthesis required for the ultimate determination.

Alternatively, conclusory opinions can be conceptualized in "if-then" or "stop-short" terms that help the court to identify the relevant legal ambiguities and reach appropriately informed and reasoned decisions. For example, take the case of an 11-year-old evaluated in a jurisdiction where the relevance of immaturity as a cause of incompetence is unclear. If the examiner opines that the youth lacks important CST capacities due to developmental immaturity alone, the examiner may conclude, "It is my opinion that the youth's developmental immaturity causes relevant weaknesses in the youth's abilities to which the competence standard refers, and those weaknesses are as severe as those seen in many other defendants found incompetent. *If developmental immaturity is a legal basis for a finding of incompetence in this court,* then it would be my opinion that the youth is incompetent, using the level of ability that the court typically requires of defendants."

BEST PRACTICE

Be cautious in offering conclusory opinions, leaving it to the court to make the ultimate determination of a juvenile's competence unless the evidence is incontrovertible.

Offering Additional Guidance to the Court

There may be some situations in which it is appropriate for examiners to offer additional guidance during the discussion of their conclusions. For one thing, examiners may have information that can help the court to be sensitive to issues that could threaten a competent defendant's CST functioning as the adjudication proceeds. For example, if a recently stabilized psychotic defendant exhibits lingering symptoms of mild thought disorganization and affective blunting that are not now significantly impairing, the examiner may suggest that the court be sensitive to certain threats to stability (e.g., medication compliance) or signs of deterioration (e.g., increasingly disjointed communications). Similarly, if a defendant is known to respond to family stresses with severe emotion dysregulation that impairs interpersonal relatedness and reasoned thinking for some period after such events, the examiner may warn the court to be aware that such deterioration could occur.

BEST PRACTICE

Even when identified deficits are not so severe as to suggest a finding of IST, inform the court, as appropriate, of issues it should be sensitive to and/or make suggestions for addressing those functional weaknesses.

Another form of guidance could include suggestions for enhancing what Grisso (2000) has called "effectiveness of participation." Even competent defendants may have functional weaknesses that can be addressed as the case proceeds. For example, examiners might have suggestions to help defense attorneys support their client (Barnum, 2000; Melton et al., 2007). In some cases, it might be relevant to suggest that mental health services, albeit not court mandated, could enhance functioning (Barnum, 2000). Sometimes the guidance can be very unique. Grisso (1998), for example, discussed an immature and deaf defendant who better tolerated the stress of trial when using a familiar sign language interpreter rather than a court-appointed interpreter.

6
chapter

Remedial Questions

When a defendant appears to have significant deficits in CST functioning that may yield a determination that he is IST, the examiner must assist the court in determining whether to pursue remediation efforts. The remedial analysis requires consideration of developmental and mental health history, current mental status, information regarding past responses to pharmacological and psychotherapeutic efforts to reduce relevant symptoms, and past responses to educational interventions (Grisso, 2005). The relevant issues are already likely to have been synthesized within responses to the functional, contextual, and, especially, the causal questions (Goldstein et al., 2002; Grisso, 1998, 2003a; Schwartz & Rosado, 2000; Viljoen & Roesch, 2007).

The remedial analysis requires consideration of four main questions, which are taken in turn as follows (Grisso, 1998, 2005; Slobogin et al., 1997; Viljoen & Roesch, 2007). Grisso (2005) has provided examiner forms specific to juvenile CST to facilitate and document this analysis.

Can any of the Deficits Be Remediated?

Courts depend on examiners for guidance on whether the deficits of incompetent defendants can be improved. Even in marginal cases when it is not certain that a youth will be found IST, the likelihood of successful remediation can be considered in if-then terms: "If this defendant is found incompetent, then the likelihood of successful remediation is . . ." (Grisso, 1998).

Unfortunately, there is little research to guide clinicians' opinions about the efficacy of CST remediation with juveniles (Viljoen & Grisso, 2007). The cause of the incompetence is a critical consideration. Most adult defendants found IST due to psychosis can be successfully remediated (Stafford, 2003) and the same may be true for psychotic youth (McGaha, McClaren, Otto, & Petrila, 2001). Less is known about effective remediation with other mental disorders and cognitive deficits. Preliminary research with juveniles suggests that mental retardation reduces the likelihood of successful remediation (McGaha et al., 2001). Clinical judgment suggests that remediation is less likely to be successful when rooted in other problems such as delayed development, normal developmental immaturity, or disorders like language disorders that require long-term interventions (Grisso, 2005; Otto et al., 2006; Schouten, 2003).

In particular, questions have been raised about the likelihood of successful remediation when CST dysfunction is rooted, in whole or in large part, in developmental immaturity (Barnum, 2000; Grisso, 1998). Typical CST remediation services and processes are often a poor fit for such cases, because traditional services target mental illnesses or cognitive deficits. Some jurisdictions allow for the charges to be dismissed with court jurisdiction maintained and interventions implemented through child welfare or child protection mechanisms (Redding & Frost, 2001). Courts sometimes simply allow time for the youth to "grow up" and improve in functioning (Barnum, 2000; Grisso, 1998), which may be the only "intervention" with any likelihood of succeeding. However, mechanisms for remediation through growing up are not likely to be specified in many jurisdictions and they may require much longer trial delays than typical remediation time-lines will allow.

In addition to the causal factor guiding the remediation analysis, the functional analysis may inform whether deficits can be remediated, since some types of deficits will be more remediable than others. For example, Understanding deficits may be more readily improved than Appreciation deficits because repeated exposure to information ("overlearning") can sometimes overcome memory limitations, but overcoming abstraction deficits is much less straightforward. When there are multiple deficits with differential response probabilities, examiners should conceptualize that explicitly (e.g., "Whereas the youth's Understanding deficits may be remediable through education, the Appreciation deficits are unlikely to respond to remediation efforts"). This allows the court to place more or less weight on certain deficits and determine whether or not to pursue remediation, based on the likelihood of success remedying the most critical of those deficits. For example, if a juvenile court judge is applying a basic understanding and communication standard, the difficulties remediating the Appreciation deficits may be less relevant for that judge's analysis. In juvenile court CST evaluations, especially,

BEST PRACTICE

Specify the remediation potential of each deficit so that the court can focus on those efforts that are most likely to restore competence.

providing estimates of success is hampered by these ambiguities about the types and levels of ability required for competent functioning (Evans, 2003; Viljoen & Grisso, 2007).

Examiners are reminded that even a relatively low probability of successful remediation may be considered an adequately *substantial* probability of success by the court (Mossman et al., 2007). Furthermore, that success does not necessarily require the complete remission of relevant symptoms or disorders, but rather an adequate level of relevant CST functioning (Barnum, 2000; Grisso, 1998).

Which Interventions Can Remediate the Relevant Deficits?

When recommending interventions to the court, examiners should consider treatment plans guided by a matching paradigm in which the interventions will be those that most effectively remediate the specific causes of the deficits identified in the evaluation (Barnum, 2000; Davis, 1985; Grisso, 1998; Mossman et al., 2007; Schwartz & Rosado, 2000). For example, if the defendant has particular deficits in Assisting because of language problems, the examiner should consider interventions that would specifically address those language problems. A true "matching paradigm" of deficit to remediation will require an empirically based method for identifying different types of incompetence and determining which interventions work best for each type, but the research for such a paradigm is currently lacking (Zapf, Viljoen, Whittemore, Poythress, & Roesch, 2002). Therefore, the matching must be based on sound clinical judgment.

PSYCHIATRIC INTERVENTION

One of the two main methods for CST remediation is psychiatric intervention. Typically, this involves medications. If psychiatric symptoms cause the relevant interference in CST functioning, the remediation should target the reduction of those symptoms. This is a relatively straightforward process when psychotic symptoms are causing incompetence. When symptoms of disorders such as ADHD,

BEWARE
There is no empirically based method for matching CST deficits with specific remediation interventions.

depression, and anxiety cause incompetence, symptom relief through psychopharmacology and other interventions supported in the child clinical-treatment literature could also yield competent functioning (Grisso, 1998, 2005). However, empirical support for the efficacy of these interventions to remediate CST is lacking (Viljoen & Grisso, 2007). In cases in which medications may be necessary, the possibility of involuntarily administered medication may need to be considered, such as a when there is a past history of poor compliance. There may be special legal procedures for obtaining authorization of involuntary medications (see *Sell v. United States,* 2003).

EDUCATIONAL INTERVENTIONS

Mental retardation may be a relatively common source of incompetence among juveniles (McGaha et al., 2001), and an educational method is more often considered in these cases. Special CST-related education is also considered in cases involving milder intellectual limitations, learning disabilities, and other cognitive weaknesses in communication, memory, and executive function (Viljoen & Grisso, 2007). Developmental immaturity may compound such problems or, on its own, yield significant CST deficits (Viljoen & Grisso, 2007). In these cases, efforts to improve the needed skills are likely to focus on some sort of education.

Educational CST interventions have been used with mentally retarded adult defendants and are modestly effective (Haines, 1983; Anderson & Hewitt, 2002). A number of jurisdictions have developed educational remediation curricula for juveniles

6
chapter

CASE LAW

Sell v. United States (2003)

- The U.S. Supreme Court held that antipsychotic drugs could be administered against the defendant's will for the purpose of restoring competence in serious criminal cases if the treatment is medically appropriate, is substantially unlikely to have side effects that may undermine the trial's fairness, and, taking account of less intrusive alternatives, is necessary to significantly further important governmental trial-related interests.

that cover information similar to that in most functional CST interviews (e.g., Slobogin et al., 1996). When juveniles are IST due to cognitive limitations, a case-by-case analysis of likely success will be necessary. On the one hand, many types of cognitive impairment or immaturity are relatively stable and unlikely to "remit" through interventions. On the other hand, youth with cognitive limitations are capable of improving skills over time, and it is sometimes possible that the specific skills causing incompetence can be remediated through education and continued maturation.

Various CST deficits may require differential educational approaches. When impairments are in Understanding alone, it is reasonable to expect that educational efforts may be effective (Viljoen & Grisso, 2007); however, supportive evidence is lacking. Brief interventions seem to be minimally effective at yielding improved functioning (Cooper, 1997; Viljoen, Odgers, Grisso, & Tillbrook, 2007), and extended curricula for CST education have not been assessed for their efficacy. These curricula tend to focus on rote repetition that supports overlearning of "facts" about the trial process and its participants (Grisso, 2005). But courts (*United States v. Duhon*, 2000) and scholars (Goldstein & Burd, 1990; Levitt & Trollinger, 2002) have noted that the rote and concrete understanding that may result from this overlearning is less adequate than the more meaningful, active participation typically expected for CST. The use of more sophisticated educational techniques, such as multimodal information presentations, active-learning techniques, and systemic and explicit instruction techniques, could potentially provide deeper understanding of basic legal concepts, but these have not yet been studied (Viljoen & Grisso, 2007).

CASE LAW

United States v. Duhon (2000)

- Held that a mentally retarded defendant's memorization of basic legal terms was not sufficient to consider him competent

- Required that the defendant also be able to consult with and assist his attorney and have a rational understanding of the proceedings

As difficult as teaching of adequate Understanding skills to some young defendants may be, effective development of adequate Appreciation, Assisting, and/or Decision-Making skills is likely to be much more difficult (Grisso, 2005; Peterson-Badali & Abramovitch, 1993; Viljoen & Roesch, 2007; Viljoen & Grisso, 2007). Deficits in these domains are often linked with higher-level cognitive processes that are difficult to target. Trying to accelerate abstraction abilities, cause-and-effect thinking, or cognitive processing, suggests Grisso (2005), may be a bit like attempting to force the development of a crawling infant to walk. Nonetheless, Viljoen and Grisso (2007) have suggested exploring possible approaches such as *cognitive acceleration programs* (see Adey & Shayer, 2002) to target Appreciation and/or Decision-Making skills, as well as time-limited communication interventions (e.g., Lamb, Bibby, & Wood, 1997) and social-skills interventions (e.g., Spence, 2003) to target skills for Assisting. Peterson-Badali and Abramovitch (1993) have also discussed methods for teaching defendants cognitive decisional skills. However, there has been no systematic research of these methods, and there is currently no basis for determining which youth will respond to such interventions (Viljoen & Grisso, 2007).

Where and How Can Appropriate Remediation Services Be Accessed?

An outpatient remediation approach is more commonly appropriate with juveniles than the inpatient approach, which is more common with adults (Warren, Aaron, Ryan, Chauhan, & DuVal, 2003). Inpatient psychiatric hospitalization should be reserved for cases involving major mental illnesses, such as psychosis or mania. Sometimes, however, the settings available within a CST remediation system will not match the needs of the juvenile or even preclude successful remediation. Some states have provisions for inpatient and outpatient treatment, while other states allow only for one or the other. Some jurisdictions may restrict certain interventions for certain juveniles; for example, Florida prohibits

BEST PRACTICE
Become familiar with local remediation services available to juvenile defendants to inform your recommendations.

residential placement if the incompetence is based on developmental immaturity. In some jurisdictions, time-limited detention or social-services intervention may also be available for remediation (Katner, 2006; Lexcen, Grisso, & Steinberg, 2004).

Recommending remediation services that are not available is not helpful, so examiners must gain knowledge about the local CST remediation framework. They might consult with clinicians in their jurisdiction who provide these services to better understand which interventions are possible and how successful these interventions have tended to be (Slobogin et al., 1997). Further assistance may be gained from descriptions of model programs, such as those offered by Viljoen and Grisso (2007).

How Long Is Successful Intervention Expected to Take?

Because of the limits placed on competence remediation efforts by *Jackson v. Indiana* (1972) and consequent statutory guidelines, examiners must consider how long successful intervention is expected to take. Given the current status of the empirical literature, gauging the length of time needed for successful remediation can be difficult and rough estimates are often necessary. Legally mandated time intervals for remediation (e.g., 90 days) can provide a useful frame for the estimate. These time parameters for remediation vary across jurisdictions and may differ between juvenile and criminal court within the same jurisdiction (Frost & Volenik, 2004; Redding & Frost, 2001). Alternatively, 3-month periods can be a helpful reference for the court (Grisso, 1998).

Conclusion

Having formulated responses to the functional, casual, contextual, conclusory, and remediation questions, examiners are now prepared to communicate their findings to the parties and/or the court in written reports and, if needed, verbal communication of the findings in testimony. Communication of results and opinions is addressed in the next chapter.

Report Writing and Testimony 7

When an evaluation is court appointed or conducted under statutory mandate, the completion of a written report is often explicitly required. When retained by one of the attorneys, examiners will often provide the attorney with an oral description of the results so that he can assess the need to memorialize the findings in a written report. In many of those cases, too, a written report will be completed. A relatively small percentage of juvenile CST cases will result in a formal CST hearing in which expert testimony is needed.

Much of the process of preparing written reports of forensic evaluations has been described in other literature (e.g., Melton et al., 2007). General principles and guidelines for testimony have also been offered (e.g., Brodsky, 1991). This chapter, therefore, touches only briefly on matters that are general to most forensic reports and testimony, while providing greater detail on matters that pertain especially to reports and testimony in juvenile CST cases.

The Written Report

Purpose of Written Reports

Written juvenile CST reports are intended, first and foremost, to provide useful information to attorneys and the legal decision makers in a manner that can be readily comprehended to reach sound CST decisions. This is not always easy. Examiners may need to effectively describe complex characteristics of defendants, for example, as with a very young defendant who has ADHD, borderline intellectual functioning, and an oppositional interpersonal style.

INFO

The purposes of written reports include the following:

● To provide information to the legal audience to make a CST decision

● To explain the interpretation process and the logic for conclusions

● To document the evaluation process

They may also need to effectively explain intricate issues that often arise in juvenile CST evaluations, such as helping the court to appreciate the unresolved status of the law around the role of deficits caused by developmental immaturity and how that uncertainty was navigated in the evaluation.

Reports serve especially to lay out the interpretation process and offer the examiner's formulation of the logic behind the conclusions of the evaluation. Indeed, for many examiners the interpretation and report-writing processes are simultaneous. A clear description of the examiner's logic can sometimes preclude any need for testimony because the parties are clear about the relevant issues and able to agree on a solution to the matter without a contested hearing (Heilbrun, 2001; Melton et al., 2007).

Finally, the report serves as a professional and sometimes legal record documenting that an evaluation occurred, memorializing the procedures used, the findings obtained, and the limitations (Melton et al., 2007). In doing so, reports can also provide a useful reference for examiners turned expert witnesses as they testify (Heilbrun, 2001).

Effective Report Writing

Because testimony is rare in juvenile CST cases, evaluation reports are often the final communication between examiners and courts. That is, there is rarely opportunity for further elaboration on what is written. Therefore, reports must be readable to meet the goals just reviewed. A readable report helps the court to effectively bridge the

BEST PRACTICE

When writing the report

● Use clear language

● Include only probative and relevant information

● Be objective

● Differentiate between data and opinions

● Be brief

gap between mental health findings and the ultimate legal issues that must be resolved.

CLEAR LANGUAGE

To reduce confusion, report writers should avoid using professional jargon or overly cumbersome language that will be unfamiliar in a legal context. For example, rather than stating, "The youth demonstrated dysarthric speech," it is clearer to explain, "The youth demonstrated severe articulation problems, such as substituting *w* sounds for *r* sounds." When professional jargon cannot be avoided or is important to include, the terms should be defined the first time they are used. Even terms that are common nomenclature for clinicians can confuse court officials.

PROBATIVE AND RELEVANT INFORMATION

Reports must contain only probative and relevant information. Gagliardi and Miller (2007) explain that "[p]robativeness is the degree to which evidence proves or disproves an asserted fact; relevance is whether a particular fact matters to resolving the legal issues in the case" (p. 543). Information that would typically be seen as valuable in other clinical contexts may be inappropriate in a juvenile CST report. For example, discussing the defendant's history of being raped is irrelevant and an invasion of privacy if there is no evidence of sequelae from the incident that impact CST.

OBJECTIVITY

Reports should objectively represent what is known without exaggeration, distortion, or downplaying of contradictory information. Examiners should openly present limitations in the availability, consistency, and quality of data, as well as limitations in the opinions formed due to incomplete support, competing hypotheses that are supported, and limited clarity in science or the law (Conroy, 2006; Gagliardi & Miller, 2007; Heilbrun, 2001; Mossman et al., 2007; Schwartz & Rosado, 2000).

DATA AND OPINIONS

Reports are most helpful to courts when they clearly identify the data (or facts) that were considered, the source(s) of those data, and how they were synthesized into opinions (or inferences). To accomplish this, examiners must be clear about the distinction between data and opinion (Gagliardi & Miller, 2007; Melton et al., 2007). Factual data are directly seen, heard, or read by the examiner, without interpretation (Grisso, 2005). A statement like "The defendant demonstrated immature social skills" is an opinion, whereas the statement, "The defendant frequently interrupted the examiner and offered lengthy stories about irrelevant, autobiographical events," is a fact.

BREVITY

Juvenile CST reports should be as brief as a complete presentation of the evaluation allows, although they will tend to be longer than adult CST reports. Juvenile CST evaluations are likely to have more information sources than adult CST evaluations, more ambiguous diagnostic and legal issues to sort out, and discussions of complex matters pertaining to developmental immaturity that are not relevant for adult CST evaluations.

Organization of the Report

There is no single way to organize juvenile CST reports, but they need to be guided by an explicit organizing framework so that readers can process what is presented and access needed information. Basic organizational guidelines in the literature are appropriate for application in most jurisdictions with little modification. The structure offered in this chapter is presented in Table 7.1, parallels the outline described by Grisso (2005) for juvenile CST evaluation reports, and is supported by discussion of forensic reports in other contexts (e.g., Gagliardi & Miller, 2007). See Grisso (2005) for a juvenile CST sample report.

INTRODUCTORY SECTIONS

Basic identifying information about the evaluation should be obvious to the reader. The name of the defendant who was evaluated, his age or birthdate, and the court case identification number should be clear. The specific charges, the referral reason, and the source or process by which the evaluation referral occurred may also be documented. The date of the evaluation report should be

Table 7.1	Required Report Domains and Suggested Section Headings

IDENTIFYING INFORMATION (or IDENTIFYING INFORMATION AND EVALUATION REFERRAL)

Defendant: *name; date of birth; school grade status; case number; current custody status*

Evaluation: *date interviewed; date of report*

Referral Question: *specific charges; source of referral; reason for CST concerns*

NOTIFICATION (or PREPARATION OF PARTICIPANTS)

Contents of Notification

Understanding of Notification

Signing of Notification

SCOPE AND PROCESS OF THE EVALUATION

Specific Issues of Concern

Adjudicative Competence (or Competence to Stand Trial)

Conceptualization

PROCEDURES (or DATABASE or DATA SOURCES or SOURCES OF INFORMATION)

Interview With Defendant: *date; duration; location; conditions*

Psychological Testing: *full test name; date administered; subject of administration*

Records Reviewed: *type; source; date span*

Interviews Conducted: *type of interview; subject of interview; date of interview; duration of interview*

Validity Concerns: *data source; specific concerns; management of concerns*

Unobtained Records and Interviews: *what was pursued; why pursued; limits caused*

continued

CLINICAL AND DEVELOPMENTAL BACKGROUND (or MENTAL HEALTH BACKGROUND or BACKGROUND)

Relevant Personal History (or Developmental and Clinical History): *family history; early developmental history; trauma history; medical history; academic history; social history (or pastime history); behavioral history; legal history; mental health history*

Mental Status Examination (or Developmental and Clinical Status): *appearance; attitude; motor functioning; speech and communication; cognition; thought process; affect*

Current Symptomatology

Psychological Test Results

COMPETENCE TO STAND TRIAL FUNCTIONING (SEVERAL OPTIONS)

If guided by Dusky

Capacity to Factually Understand

Capacity to Rationally Understand

Capacity to Rationally Assist

OR **if guided by local statute (here, Florida)**

Capacity to Appreciate the Charges or Allegations

Capacity to Appreciate the Range and Nature of Possible Penalties

Capacity to Understand the Adversary Nature of the Legal Process

Capacity to Disclose to Counsel Facts Pertinent to the Proceedings at Issue

Capacity to Manifest Appropriate Courtroom Behavior

Capacity to Testify Relevantly

OR **if guided by a specific juvenile CST assessment tool (here, the JACI)**

The Juvenile Court Trial and Its Consequences

Roles of the Participants

continued

Assisting Counsel and Decision Making

Participating at a Juvenile Court Hearing

OR if guided by a CST model, such as the four capacities

Capacity to Understand the Nature of the Proceedings Against Him: *Understanding; Appreciation*

Capacity to Assist in His Own Defense: *Assisting; Decision Making*

If data were gathered beyond CST interview and observation

Parent's Perceptions of Adjudication

Defense Counsel's Perceptions of Functioning

Past Opinions Regarding Competence to Stand Trial

Other Current Opinions Regarding Competence to Stand Trial

If relevant contextual data were obtained

Demands of the Current Case

OPINIONS (or CONCLUSIONS or INTERPRETATIONS) CONCERNING COMPETENCE TO STAND TRIAL

Summary of CST Functioning

Clinical and Developmental Causes of CST Functioning

Potential Consequences of Deficits

Competence to Stand Trial Opinion

Rationale for Rejecting Alternative Competence Opinions

Potential for Remediation (or Intervention Recommendations, or Remediation Opinions)

7
chapter

clearly noted, which can be especially important to avoid confusion when the same defendant has been evaluated on multiple occasions.

Notification   This section should document the notification provided to examinees about their rights and the limits of confidentiality (Grisso, 1998, 2005; Heilbrun & Collins, 1995; Slobogin et al, 2007). Examiners also typically document the extent to which the notification seemed to be understood and whether a notification form was signed (Gagliardi & Miller, 2007; Grisso, 2005).

Scope and Process   It is helpful to document the manner in which the examiner conceptualized the referral question ("scope"). This section could also be used to explicitly specify the CST conceptualization and definitions being used for the evaluation, including the examiner's management of legal ambiguities. Making these issues explicit helps readers contrast their understanding of the evaluation with that of the examiner. It also reduces the likelihood that the court will inadvertently use the report to address other psycholegal issues, such as applying the term *capacity* from the CST definition to the "capacity" of a young juvenile to commit an offense (also called *the infancy defense*). In addition, attorneys can assess the consistency of their CST conceptualization with that used by the examiner and then offer argument if they disagree with the approach. Examiners also document how information that was obtained regarding the particular concerns about the defendant affected the evaluation strategy. For example, the examiner might explain that a history of ADHD and severe distractibility in court yielded the referral and that since the defendant was also 11 years old, the evaluation focused on potential development-based and ADHD-based impediments to CST.

Procedures and Sources of Information   The report should list each data source relied on by the examiner to reach the conclusions (Grisso, 1998, 2005; Heilbrun, 2001). As shown in Table 7.1, the report should adequately detail the interviews conducted, the documents reviewed, and the testing administered so that readers are not left questioning what occurred. Examiners may have concerns about some of the data in terms of validity (e.g., inaccurate reporting due to faulty memory), completeness (e.g., missing pages from documents), or absence (e.g., refusal to be interviewed; Gagliardi & Miller, 2007). Data concerns should be clearly documented, as should the impact they have on specific opinions offered. For example, missing records from the defendant's early childhood may place limits on the ability to diagnose traumatic stress responses to early childhood experiences, but may place minimal limitations on the CST opinion since it is also clear that the defendant has deficits related to other factors, such as sub-average intelligence. When it is not clear whether missing data are critical, examiners may explain that they will submit a revised opinion if data are obtained later that would change the opinions offered in the report (Mossman et al., 2007).

THREE MODELS FOR THE PRIMARY CONTENT

The heart of the report should present clinical and developmental data and data specific to the issue of CST, as well as clinical and developmental opinions and focused CST opinions. There are three main ways to structure the report of clinical, developmental, and CST data and opinions.

Data Then Opinions Model   One approach might be called the *data then opinions model* (e.g., Grisso, 2005; Mossman et al., 2007). It begins with all relevant data obtained on the clinical and developmental aspects of the case, then all data obtained regarding the youth's specific CST abilities. This discussion is followed by an opinion section that answers and explains the CST referral questions, using the five evaluation analyses as the outline. An advantage of this approach is that it helps examiners and readers remain focused on the issues most relevant to juvenile CST. For example, this approach does not provide a discussion of clinical diagnoses not relevant to CST. Further, this structure supports the report writer's ability to literally walk readers through the analysis that should be considered by the court.

Clinical Then Forensic Model   A second approach could be called the *clinical then forensic model* (e.g., Gagliardi & Miller, 2007; Melton et al., 2007). It begins with a typical description of a child clinical and developmental evaluation, albeit limited to CST-relevant issues. Data on those matters are provided, then interpretations and opinions summarize the important clinical and developmental conclusions. After that, the report moves to forensic data, primarily the data on the youth's CST abilities, followed by interpretations and opinions that focus on the forensic question of CST. The discussion of the forensic opinions uses the five evaluation analyses (functional, causal, contextual, conclusory, and remediation) as the outline. This approach may be particularly useful in jurisdictions that require examiners to first opine about any mental or developmental problems the defendant evidences and, only if there are problems, to proceed to offer data and opinion on CST abilities.

Opinion and Data Model   A third approach could be called the *opinion and data model* (e.g., Meloy, 2000). In this approach, the entire discussion is structured around the five evaluation analyses. For each analysis, the examiner offers her opinion and then offers the data analysis that forms the foundation for that opinion. Traditional report sections, such as history or mental status exam, are not used. Rather, when historical data or data from the mental status exam support or challenge a specific opinion, they are presented during the discussion of how that opinion was formed. This approach supports intense focus on relevant data and helps examiners conduct and communicate the analyses. It can also help limit lengthy narratives and yield briefer reports. However, such narratives can serve to help the court draw an adequate overall picture of the youth.

The data then opinions approach balances assistance in helping the court understand the youth with focused, data-driven opinions. Therefore, this approach is used to structure the ensuing discussion. Even if another organizational approach such as the clinical then forensic or opinion and data approach is used, every report should provide the types of data, opinions, and explanations of those opinions as suggested in this chapter. Each issue may not warrant a separate section, however, depending on the complexity of the case.

THE DATA SECTIONS

Reports must be able to stand alone in providing readers the data used to reach conclusions (Mossman et al., 2007). Both the data and the source(s) of the data should be clearly identified. Most typically, the data

BEST PRACTICE
Be guided by readability in organizing the data for the legal audience.

sources are simply explained in the narrative (e.g., "John's mother reported and school records confirm that John failed all of his classes in the ninth grade"). Another approach is to include superscripts in the narrative that are linked to the data source in a key (e.g., "John failed all of his classes in the ninth grade[2,5]"). Alternatively, the report can include separate sections for each data source. Examiners should focus on data relevant to forming the clinical and developmental opinions, including data supporting counterhypotheses.

Relevant History   To provide a context for any current problems, data from the defendant's history leading up to the evaluation is discussed in a "relevant history" section (Grisso, 2005). Certain historical domains, presented as possible subheadings in Table 7.1, are often suggested (Grisso, 1998, 2005; Schwartz & Rosado, 2000; Slobogin et al., 1997). Use of these domains as subheadings helps structure the report into brief histories of particular issues (e.g., medical history), which can enhance readability and assist readers in locating specific information when it is needed. In some cases, though, the history is best presented in a single integrated chronology that helps the reader to note critical life changes that built up to the current problems (Barnum, 2000; Gagliardi & Miller, 2007).

The history section will typically be constructed on the basis of interviews with the defendant, caregivers, and other third-party informants, and from past records. Consequently, alternate versions of history and pictures of the youth may emerge. In some cases, the source of the discrepancy will be obvious. For example, a defendant who has demonstrated a tendency to portray herself in an overly positive light throughout the interview may provide a self-report that is discrepant from all other data sources, which are otherwise consistent. The report writer can note the discrepancy and explain any adjustments made to how the facts are presented (e.g., the defendant's self-report was opined to be invalid and not used). In other cases, it may be more challenging to determine which set of facts is accurate (e.g., versions of events presented by divorced parents). Then the report should document all competing versions of the facts and the implications of each version for the opinions that are formed, and allow the trier of fact to complete its appropriate function of sorting out those facts (Melton et al., 2007).

Complex social histories or clinical and developmental problems may require detailed discussion of history in some cases (Grisso, 1998). However, to maintain relevance and avoid prejudicial information, some cases will require no more than brief discussions of history. Examiners should be particularly cautious when reporting past behaviors that could result in additional charges, lest the examiner become an unwitting fact witness against the defendant (Melton et al., 2007). When such behaviors are relevant to the evaluation (e.g., to establish a diagnosis of conduct disorder), general descriptions (e.g., "He has engaged in stealing in the past") may be less problematic than more detailed descriptions.

Current Mental and Developmental Status   This section should provide a description of the examiner's observation of the defendant's current presentation to help identify any difficulties. This includes the results on the mental status questioning and behavioral observations made during the interview (Grisso, 1998, 2005; Melton et al., 2007; Schwartz & Rosado, 2000; Slobogin et al., 1997). Report writers may begin to make minor interpretations here to assist the reader in putting what is observed in appropriate context. For example, when concrete thinking is observed in an 11-year-old defendant, the examiner may explain that the defendant "demonstrated age-appropriate concreteness in thought," whereas a 17-year-old with similar abstraction abilities may be described as "demonstrating concrete thinking suggestive of cognitive delays." Still, major interpretations, such as "The youth demonstrated immature cognitive abilities compared to older adolescents," or "The youth is mentally retarded," should be reserved for the opinion sections that will follow. Here, too, data that are relevant in reaching clinical and developmental opinions warrant emphasis. If there have been multiple contacts with the youth, the report should discuss any changes in mental status across the meetings (Gagliardi & Miller, 2007).

Psychological Testing   When psychological testing has been administered in the past or during the current evaluation, this information can be organized in a variety of ways, such as listing test results chronologically or organizing results by the type of domain(s) assessed (e.g., intelligence tests, achievement tests). To help attorneys and judges readily digest the test results, a brief explanation of the nature and purpose of each test administered should be provided. Furthermore, the results should be explained in the most straightforward manner possible. For example, reporting scores as percentiles rather than as T scores or scaled scores may be more appropriate (Gagliardi & Miller, 2007). The presentation of scores should also appropriately reflect that scores are estimates, which can be accomplished by using categorical descriptors of score ranges ("Well Below Average range") or T scores ("Clinically Significant Elevation") that are meaningful to lay audiences. Overly detailed descriptions of the results should also be avoided to aid comprehension (Grisso, 2005). Details about test results not relevant to the issue of CST should be limited if it is appropriate to report the results at all.

CST Abilities   Finally, data about CST abilities should be provided in a separate section, describing what the youth can and cannot do in his role as a defendant. The organization of the CST data is likely to vary across examiners according to their guiding conceptualization of CST and the level of detail they intend to provide. As shown in Table 7.1, subsections may be based on particular functional domains relevant to CST, on the underlying CST conceptualization of a specific assessment tool that was used, or on the CST domains defined by relevant law. Organization of the CST data, to at least some extent, around any concepts specified in local law is recommended, as this best speaks the language of the intended readers.

The data about CST abilities must be specifically relevant to reaching the CST opinions, and data not necessary to reach those opinions must be omitted (Grisso, 1998, 2005). The primary data sources for this section are likely to include the direct observations made during the defendant interview and data obtained during the functional CST interview (Grisso, 2005). If a CST assessment tool was used during the functional interview, a description of the tool, the CST conceptualizations that informed its development, and, perhaps, an explanation of the rationale for using that tool in the instant case can help the reader better understand and judge the evaluation. Information about CST functioning obtained from other sources (e.g., attorneys, caregivers, teachers), and, in some cases, extrapolations from functioning in other contexts (e.g., school records; counseling sessions) should also be discussed.

When describing the CST functional interview, examiners are encouraged to use some quotes or specific examples offered by the defendant or specific behaviors observed, rather than more general descriptions. For example, the report could read, "When asked about his feelings about his attorney, he unexpectedly told a rambling story about a fishing trip with his father," instead of, "He offered off-topic, rambling responses." This kind of specificity helps maintain objectivity and can help the reader better appreciate what occurred during the evaluation interview.

Although examples are helpful in most cases, examiners should be sensitive about including examples that reveal self-incriminating statements. In jurisdictions where *immunity* is specified in law, there is little concern. But when no protections are assured, examiners may be in danger of being called as a fact witness against a youth. Most scholars recommend that any incriminating statements be excluded from the report, although general statements about the quality of the statements in terms of demonstrating communication skills may be appropriate (Barnum, 2000; Grisso, 1998, 2005; Mossman et al., 2007; Oberlander, Goldstein, & Ho, 2001; Viljoen & Roesch, 2007).

Additional Sections   Additional section headings might be added if there are other sources of data relevant to the functional CST analysis, such as parents, defense counsel, older CST evaluations, or another expert's current CST opinion. In addition, examiners are

BEST PRACTICE
Make sure that your opinions are a clearly explained and accurate reflection of what can and cannot be reasonably stated.

encouraged to include a section describing data collected on the contextual demands of the CST case.

THE OPINIONS SECTION

The opinions section clearly identifies the examiner's conclusions that are relevant to the CST referral questions and explains how those conclusions were reached. Stating of conclusions with clarity is important. This is true even if the opinion is not a perfectly precise answer to the question (e.g., "It is my opinion that the defendant's competence limitations are caused by a complex combination of severely impaired social skills, attentional problems, and immature development of cognitive skills that is difficult to specify"). The opinion might even reflect an inability to answer the relevant question (e.g., "Given the complex interplay of developmental issues and mental health symptoms, I am unable to state with any certainty the likelihood that remediation efforts will be successful.")

In addition to stating the opinion, it is absolutely imperative that examiners detail the reasoning behind each opinion they have reached. It is reasonable to assert that one's logic is more important than one's opinion, because the court must have a way to determine the examiner's analysis to form its own opinion on the matter (Conroy, 2006; Mossman et al., 2007; Redding & Frost, 2001; Skeem & Golding, 1998). Therefore, examiners must provide the explicit nexus between the data and their opinions by specifying what data provided in the earlier sections were relied on and explaining the basic underlying logic with which the opinions were reached (Barnum, 2000; Conroy, 2006; Gagliardi & Miller, 2007; Grisso, 1998; 2005; Schwartz & Rosado, 2000; Skeem & Golding, 1998; Slobogin et al., 1997). The explanation should allow the reader to "reason along with" the examiner as the examiner builds the argument (Melton et al., 2007). Omission of an adequate description of the connections between data and opinion is a much too common weakness in forensic evaluation reports (Wettstein, 2005), and

BEWARE
Not providing the reasoning behind opinions is patently substandard practice.

**BEST
PRACTICE**
Cast a wide net that is clearly
marked; that is, include
any potentially relevant
information while also clearly
indicating if its relevance is
an unresolved legal issue.

juvenile CST evaluations appear not to be immune to the problem (Christy, Douglas, Otto, & Petrila, 2004).

As discussed in Chapter 6, when offering juvenile CST opinions, examiners should manage the definitional ambiguity inherent in many jurisdictions by casting a wide net that is clearly marked. Again, this means that examiners should err on the side of expansive views of CST, but they must clearly identify and explain in their reports the ways in which they have done so. For example, if a youth's lack of autonomy is a significant concern in a jurisdiction that has not articulated a clear stance on issues of psychosocial maturity, examiners should document the deficit and point out to the court that the relevance is an unresolved legal issue best left to the court's discretion. Doing so allows the court to include the entirety of the analysis or, as it sees fit, place certain limits on its considerations.

In the approach suggested in this chapter, the opinions section takes one by one the essential questions for addressing CST, from the functional analysis through the remedial question.

Functional Strengths and Weaknesses   The first set of opinions and explanations focuses on the functional strengths and weaknesses in the youth's CST abilities. There are many ways to organize the functional summary, but whatever the organizing principle, it is critical for the examiner to offer an interpretation of the data in ways that can be digested. Readers may be overwhelmed by the details of the CST interview, for instance, and will be aided by summary statements such as, "Although the examinee seemed to understand and appreciate most important legal concepts, his verbal communication abilities are so poor that his ability to assist his attorney or provide relevant testimony should be considered severely impaired."

BEWARE
When the
functional
analysis includes
observation of attorney–
client interactions, report
only on the process of what
was observed and not the
content to avoid violating
attorney–client privilege.

Clinical and/or Developmental Causes Next are opinions and explanations regarding the clinical and/or developmental causes of any deficits in CST ability that were observed. Having identified relevant strengths and weaknesses, examiners must synthesize the historical data, current data, and test data to provide a clear and concise opinion on the clinical and developmental problems that seem most likely to explain CST functioning. In effect, examiners provide two opinions here. First, they offer opinions on the defendant's current clinical and developmental problems. Second, they offer opinions about the specific ways in which these problems are impacting the CST abilities. If it is relevant, the examiner should also consider discussing alternative hypotheses on causes of the problems and the reasons why these hypotheses were ruled out or considered less likely by the examiner.

An illustrative example of a response to the causal question is of use here. An examiner might explain that the defendant's young age placed him at higher risk for immaturely developed abstraction abilities, and that immaturity in these abilities was, in fact, apparent in school records, psychological testing, caregiver reports, and examiner observations during the interview. Therefore, the examiner would offer the opinion that immaturely developed abstraction is a problem for the youth. The examiner might then explain that the specific CST deficits identified in observation and the interview were consistently in domains that require abstraction skills, such as Appreciation and Reasoning, whereas functioning in domains with less demand for abstraction skills, such as Understanding, was adequate. Furthermore, other possible explanations for deficits in Appreciation and Reasoning, such as poor motivation, were considered but judged to be a less likely explanation for the observation, given certain signs or evidence of persistent effort. Therefore, the examiner would offer the opinion that the observed CST deficits were the result of the immaturely developed abstraction skills. Notice that the examiner would explain the data supporting the clinical and developmental problem and draw a direct link between that problem and the CST functional limitations that were identified.

7
chapter

If the report writer uses a clinical then forensic approach to report writing, discussed earlier in this chapter, the first opinion regarding clinical and developmental problems is offered in an earlier section of the report. In that case, the discussion here would focus on the second opinion on how those problems impact CST functioning.

Potential Consequences of the Youth's CST Deficits   The causal analysis is followed by a discussion of the potential consequences of the youth's CST deficits, which addresses the contextual question. This discussion explains to the court why the examiner is or is not (and why the court may or may not) be concerned about the CST deficits identified in the functional analysis. Considerations may include factors like the demands of the instant case and the role of caregivers (Grisso, 2005). For example, if the functional analysis of the youth's autonomy level indicates a dependent, acquiescent style and the contextual data reveal that the youth's caregiver is highly directive and authoritarian, the examiner should explain that the defendant is at risk to form opinions based on the directives of the caregiver, rather than using her own independent preferences.

Just as the examiner may explain here that certain CST deficits are critical to forming a CST opinion, they may also explain that certain deficits are less relevant, based on contextual issues. For example, deficits in verbal expression that impair the defendant's ability to provide testimony may be identified in the functional CST interview and observations, but be explained as minimally relevant given clear evidence from all parties that the defendant is planning to agree to a plea offer from the prosecution. Of course, in explicitly providing the reasoning for viewing any deficits as less important, the court is provided adequate information with which to adjust the analysis if circumstances change, such as if the plea agreement unexpectedly falls through.

Competence to Stand Trial Opinion   Whether the examiner believes the youth is CST or IST is addressed next. In Chapter 6 we explained that each examiner must decide whether to offer an opinion on the ultimate legal question and whether to do this in definitive or "if-then" terms. In fact, however, the issue is actually of minor significance if the examiner has already done what has been described thus far:

- identified relevant CST deficits,
- offered a well-reasoned opinion about the cause(s) of those deficits, and
- explained how those deficits can be expected to impact the defendant's functioning in the actual case.

In doing so, the examiner has provided the court with all it needs to know to form its legal opinion, regardless of whether the examiner uses that as the foundation of a stated conclusory opinion (Grisso, 1998, 2005; Schwartz & Rosado, 2000; Slobogin et al., 1997).

When practicing in jurisdictions that require examiners to form ultimate issue opinions (including some that require opinion boxes to be checked), examiners will need to develop ways to help the court appreciate that reviewing the rationale for the conclusory opinion is critical to resolving the ultimate legal issue. Regardless of whether a specific conclusory opinion is provided, it is good practice to end the conclusory discussion with a statement of the examiner's recognition that the ultimate responsibility for the legal decision belongs to the court (Heilbrun, 2001). In particular, when a conclusory opinion is not specified, such a statement can help make clear to readers that the decision to avoid an ultimate issue opinion does not signal an inferior evaluation.

7
chapter

Potential for Remediation   An estimate of the likelihood of successful remediation is required by law in most jurisdictions when the opinion supports a finding of incompetence (Redding & Frost, 2001). Even when it is not explicitly mandated by law, the remediation opinion is needed because the CST evaluation process inevitably concludes with the court asking, "What is the next step?"

BEST PRACTICE
Include a statement recognizing the court's authority to make the ultimate determination regarding juvenile CST.

As with all of the opinions discussed in this chapter, it is critical that report writers explain exactly how they arrived at their remediation opinions. For example, an examiner might explain that she believes the likelihood for successful remediation is moderate to high because the defendant is older, has relatively mild deficits in intelligence that seem to be causing the CST weaknesses, is described by teachers as able to learn some complex information when motivated to do so, and demonstrated some initial benefit from the minimal education provided during the evaluation interview. The examiner should further explain that the main modality of intervention would be education, as there were no mental health symptoms interfering with CST that would respond to medications; therefore, outpatient services are seen as most appropriate. Further, given the breadth of domains of weakness, it might take as long as several months of weekly to biweekly meetings to provide adequate training.

A remediation opinion should be offered if there is any chance that the youth will be found IST or the court may be left without needed guidance. Because the examiner is often uncertain about how the court will decide the CST question, remediation can be discussed conditionally, such as, "If the defendant is found incompetent, then . . ." (Barnum, 2000).

Testimony

A number of useful books have been written to help examiners cultivate skillful testimony and greater ease on the stand, among them an excellent series of books by Brodsky (1991, 1999, 2004). Experts should remember that their primary goal is to explain their

data and how the opinions were formed in a manner that can be understood by the court regardless of how the court rules. Experts will be more comfortable in this role when they have conducted a well-constructed evaluation that meets practice standards (Brodsky, 1991; Heilbrun, 2001; Heilbrun, Grisso, & Goldstein, 2008).

Testifying About Juvenile CST

Anecdotal evidence suggests that, in general, juvenile cases require expert testimony less often than adult cases. Whether this is true for juvenile CST cases, however, is not clear. Because juvenile CST is a relatively new issue in both juvenile and criminal court (see Chapter 1), parties may be less likely to pursue multiple evaluations and more likely to stipulate to the findings of a single evaluation. On the other hand, the ambiguity of law and practice in this relatively new forensic area might increase the likelihood of testimony in some courts.

Testifying in juvenile court is often a different experience from testifying in criminal court. Despite trends toward a more retributive juvenile court as described in Chapter 1, juvenile court proceedings still tend to be less formal, more collaborative, and attract less public scrutiny than criminal court proceedings. Hearings are more likely to be quiet and orderly (Grisso, 1998). Whether testifying in juvenile or criminal court, experts should consider some unique aspects of testifying about juvenile CST.

OPPORTUNITY FOR LEARNING

Juvenile CST experts should remember that testifying is a precious opportunity to hone their evaluation skills. Through meetings with the attorney(s) before and/or after the testimony, the questions posed during the hearing, and the ultimate decision reached by the court, examiners can better understand what their "consumers" are looking for in their evaluations. This can be critical in a context like juvenile CST, where so much ambiguity exists. For example, Kruh participated in a case that involved thoughtful questioning about childhood oppositionality and a well-reasoned ultimate decision by the court that enhanced his ability to address that issue in future cases.

BEST PRACTICE

When testifying, be aware of potential psychological damage to the youth and use strategies to lessen that damage, if possible, without making the testimony ineffective.

SKILLS AND STRATEGIES

Testifying in juvenile CST cases will require certain skills and strategies that may not be necessary in other contexts. For example, examiners may more often need to assume an educator role. As discussed in Chapter 1, juvenile CST is a relatively new concern in both criminal and juvenile courts. Criminal court attorneys and judges may be unfamiliar with reasons for incompetence that are unique to youth, such as poor psychosocial reasoning, and may not have considered the possibility of developmental immaturity as a potential cause of CST deficits. Juvenile-court attorneys and judges may be unfamiliar with even basic elements of CST and may have never participated in a contested CST hearing. Experts may need to take extra care to explain their terms and concepts on the stand, sometimes even helping the court to be aware of relevant legal issues that remain unresolved.

POTENTIAL FOR PSYCHOLOGICAL DAMAGE TO THE YOUTH

Experts must be sensitive about testifying in front of a youth when the focus is on that youth's problems and weaknesses and in which typically pejorative terms, such as "incompetent," are used. This kind of testimony can yield psychological damage to the youth, especially younger, more cognitively limited, or more mentally ill youth. Testimony can also damage the youth's relationships with caregivers, counselors, or others who have provided information for the evaluation, and/or damage the attorney–client relationship.

For youth who are vulnerable to such damage, juvenile CST experts should consider the benefits of

- testifying in ways that balance negative and positive statements (e.g., "Even though it was clear that my questions were difficult for him, I was very impressed that he did not become angry or upset" or "Her mother explained that even though they love one another very much, the defendant often lashes out at her mother when faced with difficult tasks");

- carefully explaining deficits (e.g., "Verbal expression is more difficult for him than most children his age," instead of, "His verbal expression skills are very poor"); and
- explaining weaknesses in normalizing ways (e.g., "Like most children his age, the defendant has difficulty making well-reasoned decisions about complex issues").

On the other hand, examiners must not soften their presentation to the point that the court does not appreciate the appropriate significance of the problems.

Preparation for Testimony

Taking responsibility for the quality of one's testimony requires preparation beyond one's written report in anticipation of testimony (McCann & Dyer, 1996). It is ill advised for experts to proceed directly from submitting their report to offering testimony. Certain intervening steps are critical, such as preparing for the testimony and consulting with the attorney that has subpoenaed the expert. Other steps should be considered, such as meeting with the defendant. Some preliminary steps common in other contexts, such as depositions (i.e., sworn testimony offered outside of court), are rarely conducted in juvenile CST proceedings.

PREPARING QUESTIONS

Examiners should consider the questions they want to be asked by the attorney calling them, so that they can best explain relevant clinical, psycholegal, and legal aspects of their findings. For example, broad questions like, "In what ways do you see competence to stand trial for juveniles different from competence to stand trial for adults?" or "What evaluation model did you use in this case?" can allow the expert to offer the

BEST PRACTICE

In preparing questions for the attorney, consider the following:

- Child mental health issues
- Juvenile CST evaluation practices
- Relevant law

underlying structure of the testimony that will help the court digest the findings. More focused questions can also be considered on the basis of elements of the evaluation and opinions that are most susceptible to confusion or misunderstanding. For example, an expert may want to be asked, "Doctor, can you explain how a pervasive developmental disorder is different from a developmental disorder?" or "Why did you spend so much time interviewing the defendant's parents?"

MEETING WITH THE ATTORNEY

Experts should then meet with the attorney who is calling them to improve the relevance and effectiveness of the testimony (American Prosecutors Research Institute [APRI], 2006; Brodsky, 1991; Conroy, 2006; Grisso, 1998; Hess, 1999; Melton et al., 2007; Rogers & Shuman, 2005). Arranging of the discussion may require the initiative of the expert, particularly in juvenile court cases, where attorneys may tend to be less formal (Grisso, 1998). Unless retained by one of the attorneys, experts will also typically contact the opposing attorney to alert them to their plan to meet with the attorney calling them and provide the opposing attorney with the opportunity to also discuss matters with them. The meeting with the attorney who has issued the subpoena provides an opportunity for the expert to answer any questions the attorney may have about the evaluation and opinions. The attorney and expert should collaboratively plan the questioning during *direct examination* and discuss challenges to anticipate on *cross-examination*. As mentioned earlier, the newness of juvenile CST issues may increase the likelihood that the examiner will also need to educate the attorney about relevant issues.

REVIEWING OPPOSING EXPERT'S REPORTS

It is not uncommon during these meetings for the attorney to ask the expert to review an evaluation report by an opposing expert to help her prepare for cross-examination of that expert (APRI, 2006; Melton et al., 2007). It is not always clear when the "objective examiner" role begins to bleed into a "partisan consultant" role, and

BEWARE
When reviewing other experts' reports with the attorney, be careful not to cross the line into a consultant role.

experts should proceed cautiously (Diamond, 1992; Heilbrun, 2001). It may be appropriate for experts to offer some guidance to the extent that it is relevant and elicits the reasons for the expert's own conclusions. For example, questioning of the other experts about their use of an adult norms standard can highlight the reason one reached a different opinion using a adolescent norms standard. However, advising the attorney on how to generally impeach an opposing expert may stray too far into the consultant role and compromise the examiner's objectivity or the appearance of neutrality.

MEETING WITH THE DEFENDANT

Experts may be able to reduce any negative impact of the testimony on the youth by meeting with him prior to the hearing to explain what will be said in court and how the youth should understand it (Grisso, 1998). For example, they might explain that "incompetent" is a legal word and does not mean that the examiner is calling the child dumb or bad. When testimony may harm the defendant's relationships with others, such as caregivers or defense attorneys, they also may be invited to the meeting. There has been no research to assess the benefits of such a meeting and there is no clear legal or ethical mandate to conduct them, so examiners should be guided by efforts to reduce the likelihood of harm. So, for example, such meetings may be less warranted with an older adolescent who has a good understanding of the purpose of the evaluation and is less likely to be damaged by what is said. Such a meeting may also help the examiner determine if there have been any substantive changes to the juvenile's functioning since the evaluation interview so that she can provide an addendum to her report if this has occurred.

Procedures During the Hearing

A number of sources have provided helpful discussions of the steps involved in providing testimony (see, for example, Melton et al., 2007; Rogers & Shuman, 2005). In many ways, providing testimony in juvenile CST cases is similar to doing so in other contexts, and this general advice is applicable. The following comments pertain only to those aspects of testimony that may be somewhat different for juvenile court proceedings. Experts are encouraged to obtain a more complete view of the expert testimonial process by consulting the previously cited references.

QUALIFYING THE EXPERT

Testimony will often begin with *qualifying the expert*, in which the court determines if the examiner is qualified to be admitted as an expert witness. The attorney calling the evaluator will seek to establish her credibility as an expert, whereas the opposing attorney will try to downplay it. The qualifying process in juvenile CST cases should document general expertise in forensic assessment and in child and developmental mental health. Experts typically do this by explaining their formal education, practical training and professional experience, professional licensure and certifications, and memberships in professional organizations. They may also discuss publications or professional presentations and prior experiences testifying. Emphasis may be given to experiences relevant to the instant case. The qualifying process can also provide an opportunity to provide evidence of neutrality, such as reporting the percentage of cases in which the expert's findings did not support the side that retained the expert.

DIRECT EXAMINATION

Direct examination is the questioning of the expert by the attorney who called him. The main goals in direct examination are to describe and explain the evaluation methods, the data obtained using those methods, the opinions that were reached on the basis of the data, and the integrated conclusions addressing CST (APRI, 2006). When experts have written a thorough and organized report, they can simply walk through a presentation of the report contents. It is also common for experts to describe competing hypotheses and the reasons they were not retained, as well as any weaknesses or limitations in the evaluation process. These latter steps are honest, ethical, and can strategically "steal the thunder" of attacks during cross-examination.

CROSS-EXAMINATION

Cross-examination is questioning by the opposing attorney and is the point at which the adversarial nature of the proceedings is most apparent. The attorney's goals in cross-examination typically include identifying insufficiencies in the expert's evaluation, pointing out facts the expert was not aware of, highlighting areas of support for and obtaining concessions about issues that are critical to the attorney's case, and establishing any weaknesses or biases of the examiner or her work (APRI, 2006). The questioning may address general issues, such as the formation of opinions from the data, or specific ones, such as questioning the use of a given CST assessment tool or the decision not to administer any psychological tests. Experts should be prepared to discuss their understanding of the relevant legal standards, the empirical support (or lack thereof) for their knowledge and methods, and the reasons for and ways in which they applied both to the current case (Melton et al., 2007; Rogers & Shuman, 2005).

Assistance in navigating the strategies and ploys used by attorneys during cross-examination have been offered in other references, especially the series by Brodsky (1991, 1999, 2004), mentioned earlier in this chapter. Although this guidance is valuable, attorneys are less likely to use more manipulative approaches in the juvenile CST context. CST hearings are typically bench hearings conducted without a jury, and attorneys are less likely to play on emotions, use theatrics, or attempt to impeach the expert in front of judges privy to these tactics. The likelihood of overly aggressive cross-examination is even lower in juvenile court proceedings, unless the stakes are particularly high (e.g., the youth faces possible waiver to criminal court if found competent; Grisso, 1998) or the attorneys are more accustomed to criminal court practice. Whatever strategies may be used, the primary goal of the expert is to remain an educator and to maintain poise rather than becoming angry, defensive, or flustered.

KEY QUESTIONS

Our anecdotal experience is that certain key questions may arise at juvenile CST hearings, either during cross-examination or on direct examination to defuse the effectiveness of the challenge during

Be prepared to respond to key questions regarding the following:

- Age-equivalents of the youth's functioning

- Deficits in only one domain

- Expectations for the assistance of the attorney

- The ultimate opinion

- Remediation

- Future consequences of deciding that the youth is not remediable

cross-examination. Possible responses to a few such questions are offered.

1. Doctor, isn't it true that the defendant functions at the level of a 6-year-old?

Perhaps because courts tend to prefer using clear, straightforward variables when reaching decisions, attorneys may press experts to provide age-equivalents when describing immature or impaired youth. Consistent with the discussion of immaturity in Chapter 2, experts should avoid broad descriptions like, "She functions at the level of a 6-year-old," and keep the discussion to specific abilities, such as decision-making abilities. Age-equivalents with an empirical basis should be emphasized. For example, an expert who administered an intelligence test may be able to state, "Her overall verbal cognitive skills were similar to those of a 6-year-old." Experts should be cautious when presenting age-equivalents estimated by caregivers, teachers, or other collateral informants. They should consider the informant's experience with a broad range of children before offering statements like, "Her teacher says her ability to make decisions is like that of a 6-year-old," and when such statements are reasonable should also remind the court that such estimates are gross. Similar care should be given to the explanation when experts offer their own gross estimates.

2. Doctor, you said that the defendant understands and appreciates most legal terms and can make rational decisions. Doesn't that make him competent?

When a defendant shows adequate skills in most domains but severe deficits in one domain, attorneys may try to use the list of adequate abilities to present the youth as competent. Experts are advised to nondefensively explain that sometimes even a single deficit, such as verbal reception and expression skills, can be so impaired that it alone will be a severe impediment in court. To the extent that it is possible to make such predictions, examples of the types of problems the youth is expected to experience can help the court see this. For example, an expert might say, "Even though my only concern is about his verbal skills, I think it will be an extremely laborious process for his attorney to elicit information and even when she does, it will be difficult for her to know the accuracy of what he says. And I think that he is at very high risk to provide inaccurate statements if he testifies, not out of purposeful manipulation but out of confusion about the intent of the question."

3. *Doctor, you said that with an attorney who provides extra assistance you think the defendant can function adequately. Do you really expect a defense attorney to be able to offer that kind of assistance?*

The level of fully independent functioning required of the defendant is not always clear in law, so defense attorneys may question an expert's expectation that their assistance can adequately manage identified deficits. The extent of assistance that is appropriate may be a legal issue and/or a question of local expectations about what defense attorneys can or should do. For example, substantial assistance may be more typical and reasonable in a jurisdiction with more manageable attorney–client ratios. Therefore, judgments about the appropriateness of defense attorney assistance are best left to the legal decision maker, and experts should limit their testimony to the types of assistance they believe will yield adequate functioning.

7
chapter

4. *Doctor, what is your opinion? Is the defendant competent or not?*

Again, providing CST opinions that speak directly to the ultimate issue are controversial and particularly problematic in juvenile CST contexts because of substantial ambiguity about the legal standards to be applied. Examiners who decide to refrain from such opinions can readily accomplish this in the written report. The matter can become more complicated when one is in court testifying for legal professionals who tend to place high value on such opinions (Poythress, 1981). Experts can consider comparing the specific youth to other defendants (Grisso, 1998). For example, the expert might respond, "Because I found that the defendant's skills for communicating with his attorney or on the stand are poor and because the defendant was easily confused by more complex legal terms, his functioning seems to be consistent with defendants who are typically found IST."

If pressed, experts could modestly assert the limits of mental health expertise and their need to avoid offering opinions on sociomoral issues about which they have no special expertise (Barnum, 2000). In doing so, experts can highlight the unique ambiguities of juvenile CST standards. They might say, for example, "It is very difficult for me to offer a yes/no opinion about her competence when I am not certain of whether we are judging competence in comparison to adult functioning or typical adolescent functioning." Experts who do offer ultimate issue opinions should be clear in their testimony about how they are defining critical legal terms and standards, that the ultimate issue opinion is based on common-sense judgments and moral values rather than science, and that the opinion should be considered advisory.

5. *Doctor, what makes you so certain that remediation won't work with the defendant?*

Because the job of courts is adjudication, prosecutors and judges may be reluctant to dismiss charges without an attempt at CST remediation. Questions about remediation may tend to include a search for a reason that remediation is a reasonable step. When offering opinions about the likelihood that remediation will be successful, experts must be forthcoming about the lack of an empirical basis for their opinions. Still, there are likely to be cases when remediation efforts are clearly futile. A good response is to explain the interventions that will target specific deficits and what is known about the success of such approaches in other contexts. For example, an expert might explain, "The defendant's inattention and distractibility seem to be the result of his posttraumatic stress disorder from his sexual abuse. The optimal duration of treatment is not known, but the treatment of this disorder with children has required as many as 30 weekly sessions" (see Taylor & Chemtob, 2004). "Therefore, it seems unlikely that his inattention will be adequately reduced within the 90 days afforded for remediation in statute." Experts should take care, especially when testifying in criminal court, to explain that the remediation of youth is often a very different endeavor than the typical restoration of psychotic adult defendants. Some judges may need to be broken of the assumptions they have used to reach more traditional restoration decisions.

> 6. *Doctor, if you are telling us that the defendant's functioning is inadequate and the remediation is not likely to be successful, aren't you giving the defendant a free pass to keep committing offenses with no fear of consequences?*

For obvious reasons, courts may become concerned that the issue of CST could render them impotent to prosecute future offenses. It is important to remind courts, when appropriate, that a finding of so-called *permanent incompetence* in the instant case does not necessarily mean that the youth will *never* be competent. Experts should explain that all youth are in a process of development and even severely immature or impaired youth will show improving skills as they age; at least some of those youth will cross the threshold from incompetence to competence. One of the authors has had repeated experience with youth referred for multiple CST evaluations over the course of their adolescence who are severely impaired upon first evaluation but demonstrate much more adequate abilities at a second, fourth, or even sixth evaluation when they are older. Many of these youth were found incompetent initially, but later found competent in subsequent cases.

Conclusion

This volume has discussed the unique context within which juvenile CST evaluations are conducted. It has given recommendations for navigating the legal and clinical ambiguities inherent in such evaluations, as well as for assessing the threats to CST that are unique to juvenile defendants. It is hoped that developments in law, empirical research, and juvenile CST assessment tools will continue to refine the practices of juvenile CST examiners in the future. Until then, the current discussion aims to effectively assist examiners engaging in this challenging practice.

Appendix

A Sample Notification Script

As you know, you have legal charges against you right now. The judge in your case wants you to talk to a doctor because the judge has some questions about you that a doctor can help to answer. I am a doctor and I am going to try to help the judge.

The judge wants to figure out if you understand the charges against you and understand what will happen when you go to court. The judge also wants to figure out if you can work with your lawyer to defend against the charges. So, I'm going to ask you questions about how court works and how to work with a lawyer.

To answer these questions, I also need to get to know you. So, I am going to ask questions about things such as school, your family, and how you've been feeling. Also, I will talk to people who know you, such as your family, teachers, or other doctors. I also will look at your school and medical records. All of these things will help me to get to know you.

Then, I'll use what I learn about you to answer the questions the judge has. When I have my answers I will write a report that I'll send to the judge and lawyers in your case. Also, I might have to go to court so that I can tell the judge and lawyers in person about this interview and explain what I wrote in my report.

I am telling you this because you need to know that this interview and this evaluation are NOT confidential. Do you know what confidential means? [If no, explain: That means I cannot keep anything I learn a secret from the judge and the lawyers.] Most of the time when you talk to a doctor, the only things that aren't a secret are things that you tell them about children or older people who are being abused, or things you tell them about wanting to hurt yourself or other people. Those things aren't a secret when you talk to me either, because doctors have to do what they can to stop people from getting hurt. But I am a special kind of doctor and nothing at all that you tell me will be a secret. I have to tell the judge and lawyers what I find out about you. Some of what I tell them could help you with your case, but some of what I tell them may not be good for your case. My job is just to be honest with them about what I find out.

Because of that, you have some rights that are important for you to understand and remember. Rights are things that you are allowed to do. You have the right not to speak to me. If you do decide to talk to me, you have the right to refuse to answer any questions that you don't want to answer. I will have to write in my report about any questions that you do not answer, but you are still allowed to refuse to answer. You also have the right to have your lawyer here while we talk.

Do you have any questions about what I've just said?

Do you agree to go ahead with the evaluation today?

Please explain to me in your own words what I just told you about why you are here.

[If inadequate: What did I tell you the judge wants to know about you?]

[If still inadequate: Now I will ask you some questions about what I explained. You can answer with a "yes" or "no."

- Did I tell you I will ask questions about what you understand about court and how to work with your attorney?

- Did I tell you that I will be talking to other people who know you and looking at your records?

- Did I tell you that you have to answer all of my questions, even if you don't want to?

- Did I tell you that I will send a copy of my report from this evaluation to the judge and the attorneys?

- Did I tell you that I am here to give you mental health treatment?]

Appendix | B

Suggestions for Questioning Younger or More Limited Juvenile Defendants

(Adapted with permission from Anne Graffam Walker, PhD)[1]

General precepts:

1. Note the processing load that the youth is being asked to carry by questioning. Aim for simplicity and clarity. Questioning is most clear when it matches the simplicity and brevity of speech offered by the youth. Note when this is discrepant from what is typical in court.

2. Be alert for possible miscommunication. If a youth's answer seems inconsistent with prior answers, or doesn't seem to make sense, check out the possibility that there is some problem 1) with the way the question was phrased or ordered, 2) with a literal interpretation on the part of the youth, or 3) with assumptions the question makes about the youth's linguistic/cognitive development or knowledge of the adult world.

Some specifics:

1. Consider breaking long sentences/questions into shorter ones that have one main idea each.

2. Consider choosing easier words over harder ones: use Anglo-Saxon expressions such as "show,"

---

[1]Walker, A.G. (1994). *Handbook on questioning children: A linguistic perspective.* Washington, DC: American Bar Association.

"tell me about," or "said" instead of the Latinate words "depict," "describe," or "indicated."

3. Avoid legal jargon and frozen legalisms such as "What if anything,"or "Did there come a time."

4. It is important that examiner and youth use words to mean the same thing, so run a check now and then on what a word means to each youth. Some youth may not be good at definitions, but can still be asked, "Tell me what you think a _____ is," or "What does a _____ do?" The youth may not provide an adult-like answer, however, even if the word is well-known. The inability to define a word does not mean that the youth does not know what the word means. Definitions require *linguistic* skill.

5. Note when youth are directly asked about abstract concepts and their ability to work with them.

6. Avoid the question of belief (e.g., "Do you believe that the defense attorney will help you?").

7. Avoid using the word "story" (e.g., "Tell me your story in your own words."). "Story" means both "narrative account of a happening" and "fiction." Adults listening to adults take both meanings into consideration. Youth listening to adults, however, might well hear "story" as only the latter. "Story" is not only an ambiguous concept, it can be prejudicial.

8. Redundancy in questions can be useful. Repeat names and places often instead of using strings of (often ambiguous) pronouns. Avoid unanchored "that"s and "there"s. Give verbs all of their appropriate nouns (subjects and objects), as in "Tell *me* what happened when *you* and *your mother* went to the doctor," instead of "Tell what happened."

9. Carefully watch the use of pronouns (including "that"). Be sure they refer either to something you can physically point at, or to something in the

very immediate spoken past, such as in the same sentence or in the last few seconds.

10. In a related caution, be very careful about words whose meanings depend on their relation to the speaker and the immediate situation, such as personal pronouns (I, you, we), locatives (here, there), objects (this, that), and verbs of motions (come/go; bring/take).

11. Consider avoiding tag questions (e.g., "You've started a lot of fights, *haven't you?*"). They are confusing to some youth. Avoid, too, "yes/no" questions that are packed with lots of propositions. (Example of a bad simple-sounding question, with propositions numbered: "[1] Do you remember [2] when I asked you [3] if you know [4] what a defense attorney is, and [5] you said, [6] 'My friend'?" It is unclear what a "yes" or "no" answer would mean to this question.)

12. See that the youth stays firmly grounded in the appropriate questioning situation. If you are asking about the past, be sure the youth understands that. If you shift to the present, make that clear too. If it's necessary to have the youth recall a specific time/date/place in which an event occurred, consider reminding the youth of the context of the questions with statements like, "I want you to think back to . . .," or "I'm going to ask you some questions about . . ."

13. Explain to youth why they are being asked the same questions more than once. Repeated questioning is often interpreted (by adults as well as by children) to mean that the first answer was regarded as a lie, or wasn't the answer that was desired.

14. Be alert to the possibility of very literal and concrete approaches to language. For example, referencing

the defense attorney as "on your side" could be interpreted as a reference to his or her physical location in the courtroom.

15. Don't assume youth can give "reliable" estimates of time, speed, distance, height, weight, color, or to have mastered any relational concept, including kinship. (Even adults' ability to give many of these estimates is vastly overrated.)

Vocabulary:

1. Use words that are short (1–2 syllables) and common (e.g., "house" instead of "residence").

2. Translate difficult words into easier phrases (e.g., "what happened to you" instead of "what you experienced").

3. Use proper names and places instead of pronouns. (e.g., "what did Marcy do?" instead of "what did she do?"; "in the house" instead of "in there").

4. Use concrete, visualizable nouns (e.g., "courtroom") instead of more abstract ones (e.g., "at court").

5. Use verbs that are action oriented (e.g., "tell me about" instead of "describe").

6. Substitute simple, short verb forms for multi-word phrases when possible (e.g., "if you *went*" instead of "if you *were to have gone*").

7. Use active voice for verbs instead of the passive (e.g., "Did you see a doctor?" instead of "Were you seen by a doctor?"). [Note: One exception is the passive "get" (e.g., "Did you get to talk to your lawyer?" is easier to process than "Were you able to talk with your lawyer?").]

Putting words together:

1. Aim for one main idea per question/sentence.

2. When combining ideas, introduce no more than one new idea at a time.

3. Avoid interrupting an idea with a descriptive phrase. Put the phrase (known as a relative clause) at the end of the idea instead (e.g., "Please tell me about *the new school program where your classes are small*" instead of "The *new school program where your classes are small* is what I want you to tell me about.").

4. Avoid difficult-to-process connectives like "while" and "during."

5. Avoid negatives whenever possible.

6. Avoid questions that give the youth only two choices. Add an open-ended choice at the end. (e.g., "Is a murder more serious than an assault, or is it less serious, or is it something else?"

References

Abramovitch, R., Higgins-Bliss, K. L., & Bliss, S. R. (1993). Young person's comprehension of waivers in criminal proceedings. *Canadian Journal of Criminology, 35,* 309–322.

Abramovitch, R., Peterson-Badali, M., & Rohan, M. (1995). Young people's understanding and assertion of their rights to silence and legal counsel. *Canadian Journal of Criminology, 37,* 1–18.

Adey, P., & Shayer, M. (2002). Cognitive acceleration comes of age. In M. Shayer & P. Edy (Eds.), *Learning intelligence: Cognitive acceleration across the curriculum from 5 to 15 years* (pp. 1–17). Buckingham: Open University Press.

Allard, P., & Young, M. (2002). Prosecuting juveniles in adult court: Perspectives for policymakers and practitioners. *Journal of Forensic Psychology Practice, 6,* 65–78.

Alexander, C., Kim, Y., Ensminger, M., Johnson, K., Smith, B., & Dolan, L. (1990). A measure of risk taking for young adolescents: Reliability and validity assessments. *Journal of Youth and Adolescence, 19,* 559–569.

Ambrosini, P.J. (2000). Historical development and present status of the Schedule for Affective Disorders and Schizophrenia for School-Age Children (K-SADS). *Journal of the American Academy of Child and Adolescent Psychiatry, 39,* 49–58.

American Academy of Psychiatry and the Law. (2005). *Ethical guidelines for the practice of forensic psychiatry.* Retrieved June 6, 2007, from https://www.aapl.org/ethics.htm.

American Bar Association Center on Children and the Law. (2006). *Recommendations from the ABA Youth at Risk Initiative Planning Conference.* Washington, DC: Author.

American Bar Association Juvenile Justice Center. (1995a). *A call for justice: An assessment of access to counsel and quality of representation in delinquency proceedings.* Washington, DC: Author.

American Bar Association Juvenile Justice Center. (1995b). *Essentials of law-related education: A guide for practitioners and policy makers.* Washington, DC: Author.

American Prosecutors Research Institute. (2006). *A prosecutor's guide to psychological evaluations and competency challenges in juvenile court.* Alexandria, VA: Author.

American Psychiatric Association. (2000). *Diagnostic and statistical manual of mental disorders.* (4th ed., text revision). Washington, DC: Author.

Anderson, S. D., & Hewitt, J. (2002). The effect of competency restoration training on defendants with mental retardation found not competent to proceed. *Law and Human Behavior, 26,* 343–352.

Andrews, D. A., & Bonta, J. (2007). *The psychology of criminal conduct.* Cincinnati, OH: Anderson Publishing.

Angold, A., Costello, E. J., & Worthman, C. M. (1999). Pubertal changes in hormone levels and depression in girls, *Psychological Medicine, 28,* 51–61.

Arnett, J. (1992). Reckless behavior in adolescence: A developmental perspective. *Developmental Review, 12,* 339–343.

Aro, H., & Taipale, V. (1987). The impact of timing of puberty on psychosomatic symptoms among 14- to 16-year-old Finnish girls. *Child Development, 58,* 261–268.

Associated Press. (2007). Sex abuse case dropped because of delays in search for interpreter. Retrieved February 9, 2008, from http://www.cnn.com/2007/US/07/22/charges.dismissed.ap/index.html

Ausness, C. (1978). The identification of incompetent defendants: Separating those unfit for adversary combat from those who are fit. *Kentucky Law Journal, 66,* 666–706.

Austin, W. G. (2002). Guidelines for utilizing collateral sources of information in child custody evaluations. *Family Court Review, 40,* 177–184.

Baerger, D. R., Griffin, E. F., Lyons, J. S., & Simmons, R. (2003). Competency to stand trial in preadjudicated and petitioned juvenile defendants. *Journal of the American Academy of Psychiatry and the Law, 31,* 314–320.

Baranoski, M. V. (2003). Commentary: Children's minds and adult statutes. *Journal of the American Academy of Psychiatry and the Law, 31,* 321–326.

Barkley, R.A. (1996). Attention-deficit/hyperactivity disorder. In E. J. Mash and R. A. Barkley (Eds.), *Child psychopathology.* New York: Guilford Press.

Barnum, R. (2000). Clinical and forensic evaluation of competence to stand trial in juvenile defendants. In T. Grisso & R. G. Schwartz (eds.) *Youth on trial: A developmental perspective on juvenile justice* (pp. 73–103). Chicago: University of Chicago Press.

Barnum, R., Silverberg, J., & Nied, D. (1987). Patient warnings in court-ordered evaluations of children and families. *Bulletin of the American Academy of Psychiatry and the Law, 15,* 283–300.

Benthin, A., Slovic, P., & Severson, H. (1993). A psychometric study of adolescent risk perception. *Journal of Adolescence, 16,* 153–168.

Berndt, T. J. (1979). Developmental changes in conformity to peers and parents. *Developmental Psychology, 15,* 608–616.

Beyth-Marom, R., Austin, L., Fischoff, B., Palmgren, C., & Quadrel, M. J. (1993). Perceived consequences of risky behaviors: Adults and adolescents. *Developmental Psychology, 29,* 549–563.

Bonnie, R. J. (1992). The competence of criminal defendants: A theoretical reformulation. *Behavioral Sciences and the Law, 10,* 291–316.

Bonnie, R. J. (1993). The competence of criminal defendants: Beyond *Dusky* and *Drope*. *University of Miami Law Review, 47,* 539–601.

Bonnie, R. J., & Grisso, T. (2000). Adjudicative competence and youthful offenders. In T. Grisso & R. Schwartz (Eds.), *Youth on trial: A developmental perspective on juvenile justice* (pp. 73–103). Chicago: University of Chicago Presss.

Bonovitz, J., & Bonovitz, J. (1981) Diversion of the mentally ill into the criminal justice system: The police intervention perspective. *American Journal of Psychiatry, 138,* 973–976.

Booth, A., Johnson, D. R., Granger, D. A., Crouter, A. C., & McHale, S. M. (2003). Testosterone and child and adolescent adjustment: The moderating role of parent–child relationships. *Developmental Psychology, 39,* 85–98.

Borum, R., & Grisso, T. (1996). Establishing standards for criminal forensic reports. *Bulletin of the American Academy of Psychiatry and the Law, 24,* 297–317.

Borum, R., & Grisso, T. (2007). Developmental considerations for forensic assessment in delinquency cases. In A. Goldstein (Ed.), *Forensic psychology: Emerging topics and expanding roles.* Hoboken, NJ: John Wiley & Sons.

Boyd, J. C. (1999). *The competence-related abilities of juveniles prosecuted in criminal court.* Unpublished dissertation, University of South Florida, Tampa.

Brittain, C. V. (1963). Adolescent choices and parent-peer cross-pressures. *American Sociological Review, 28,* 385–391.

Brodsky, S. (1991). *Testifying in court: Guidelines and maxims for the expert witness.* Washington, DC: American Psychological Association.

Brodsky, S. (1999). *The expert expert witness: More maxims and guidelines for testifying in court.* Washington, DC: American Psychological Association.

Brodsky, S. (2004). *Coping with cross-examination and other pathways to effective testimony.* Washington, DC: American Psychological Association.

Brooks-Gunn, J., & Reiter, E. O. (1990). The role of pubertal processes in the early adolescent transition. In S. Feldman & G. Elliott (Eds.), *At the threshold: The developing adolescent* (pp. 16–53). Cambridge, MA: Harvard University Press.

Brown, B. B. (1990). Peer groups and peer cultures. In S. S. Feldman & G. R. Elliott (Eds.), *At the threshold: The developing adolescent.* (pp. 171–196). Cambridge, MA: Harvard University Press.

Bruck, M., & Ceci, S. J. (2004). Forensic developmental psychology: Unveiling four scientific misconceptions. *Current Directions in Psychology, 13,* 229–232.

Bugental, D. B., Shennum, W., Frank, M., & Ekman, P. (2001). "True lies": Children's abuse history and power attributions as influences on deception. In V. Manusov & J. H. Harvey (Eds.), *Attribution, communication behavior, and close relationships: Advances in personal relations* (pp. 248–265). Cambridge, England: Cambridge University Press.

Bukatman, B. A., Foy, J. L., & Degrazia, E. (1971) What is competence to stand trial? *American Journal of Psychiatry, 127,* 1225–1229.

Burnett, D. M., Noblin, C. D., & Prosser, V. (2004). Adjudicative competence in a juvenile population. *Criminal Justice & Behavior, 31,* 438–462.

Buss, E. (1996). "You're my what?" The problem of children's misperceptions of their lawyer's roles. *Fordham Law Review, 64,* 1699.

Buss, E. (2000). The role of lawyers' in promoting juveniles' competence as defendants. In T. Grisso & R. G. Schwartz (Eds.), *Youth on trial: A developmental perspective on juvenile justice* (pp. 243–265). Chicago: University of Chicago Press.

Butts, J. A., & Snyder, H. N. (1997). *The youngest delinquents: Offenders under 15* (Report). Washington, DC: U.S. Department of Justice, Office of Juvenile Justice and Delinquency Prevention.

Casey, B. J., Galvan, A., & Hare, T. A. (2005). Changes in cerebral functional organization during cognitive development. *Current Opinion in Neurobiology, 15,* 239–244.

Cashmore, J., & Bussey, K. (1990). Children's conceptions of the witness role. In J. Spencer, G. Nicholson, R. Flin, and R. Bull (Eds.), *Children's evidence in legal proceedings: An international perspective.* Cambridge, England: University of Cambridge, Faculty of Law.

Cauffman, E., & Steinberg, L. (2000). (Im)maturity of judgment in adolescence: Why adolescents may be less culpable than adults. *Behavioral Sciences and the Law, 18,* 741–760.

Cauffman, E., & Woolard, J. (2005). Crime, competence, and culpability: Adolescent judgment in the justice system. In J. Jacobs & P. A. Klaczynski (Eds.), *The development of judgment and decision-making in children and adolescents* (pp. 279–301). Mahwah, NJ: Lawrence Erlbaum.

Cauffman, E., Woolard, J., & Reppucci, N. D. (1999). Justice for juveniles: New perspectives on adolescents' competence and culpability. *Quinnipiac Law Review, 18,* 403–419.

Centers for Disease Control and Prevention. (2006). Youth behavior surveillance—United States, 2005. *Morbidity and Mortality Weekly Report, 55* (SS-5), 1–108.

Christy, A., Douglas, K. S., Otto, R. K., & Petrila, J. (2004). Juveniles evaluated incompetent to proceed: Characteristics and quality of mental health professionals' evaluations. *Professional Psychology: Research and Practice, 35,* 380–388.

Cicchetti, D. (1984). The emergence of developmental psychopathology. *Child Development, 55,* 1–7.

Cicchetti, D. (1990). A historical perspective on the discipline of developmental psychopathology. In J. Rolf, A. Master, D. Cicchetti, K. Nuechterlien, & S. Wintraub (Eds.), *Risk and protective factors in the development of psychopathology* (pp. 2–28). New York: Cambridge University Press.

Cicchetti, D. (1993). Developmental psychopathology: Reactions, reflections, projections. *Developmental Review, 13,* 471–502.

Cicchetti, D., & Rogosch, F. A. (2002). A developmental psychopathology perspective on adolescence. *Journal of Consulting and Clinical Psychology, 70,* 6–20.

Committee on Ethical Guidelines for Forensic Psychologists (1991). Specialty guidelines for forensic psychologists. *Law and Human Behavior, 15,* 655–665.

Conroy, M. A. (2006). Report writing and testimony. *Applied Psychology in Criminal Justice, 2,* 237–260.

Constantinou, M., & McCaffrey, R. J. (2003). Using the TOMM for evaluating chidlren's effort to perform optimally on neuropsychological measures. *Child Neuropsychology, 9,* 81–90.

Cooper, D. K. (1997). Juveniles' understanding of trial-related information: Are they competent defendants? *Behavioral Sciences and the Law, 15,* 167–180.

Courtney, J. C., Dinkins, J. P., Allen, L. M., & Kuroski, K. (2003). Age related effects in children taking the Computerized Assessment of Response Bias and Word Memory Test. *Child Neuropsychology, 9,* 109–116.

Cowden, V. L., & McKee, G. R. (1995). Competency to stand trial in juvenile delinquency proceedings—Cognitive maturity and the attorney–client relationship. *Journal of Family Law, 33,* 629–660.

Cruise, K. R., & Rogers, R. (1998). An analysis of competency to stand trial: An integration of case law and clinical knowledge. *Behavioral Sciences and the Law, 16,* 35–50.

Dahl, R. (2003). Beyond raging hormones: The tinderbox in the teenage brain. *Cerebrum: The Dana Forum on Brain Science, 5,* 7–22.

Davis, D. L. (1985). Treatment planning for the patient who is IST. *Hospital and Community Psychiatry, 36,* 268–271.

Dawson, D., & Kraus, L. J. (2005). Competency to stand trial. In L. J. Kraus & W. Arroyo (Eds.), *Recommendations for juvenile justice reform* (2nd ed.). Washington, DC: American Academy of Child and Adolescent Psychiatry.

DeThorne, L. S., & Schaefer, B. A. (2004). A guide to nonverbal IQ measures. *American Journal of Speech-Language Pathology, 13,* 275–290.

Diamond, B. L. (1992). The forensic psychiatrist: Consultant versus activist in legal doctrine. *Bulletin of the American Academy of Psychiatry and the Law, 20,* 119–132.

Donders, J. (2005). Performance on the Test of Memory Malingering in a mixed pediatric sample. *Child Neuropsychology, 11,* 221–227.

Drizin, S. A. (2003). Research on juvenile competency: A defender's perspective. *Social Policy Report, 17,* 8–9.

Dulit, E. (1989). Adolescent psychological development. Normal and abnormal. In R. Rosner & H. Schwartz (Eds.), *Juvenile Psychiatry and the Law* (pp. 219–236). New York: Plenum Press.

Duncan, P. D., Ritter, P. L., Dornbusch, S. M., Gross, R. T., & Carlsmith, J. M. (1985). The effects of pubertal timing on body image, school behavior, and deviance. *Journal of Youth and Adolescence, 14,* 227–235.

Epstein, H. T. (1978). Growth spurts during brain development: Implications for educational policy and practice. In J. S. Chall & A. F. Mirsky (Eds.), *Education and the brain: The seventy-seventh yearbook of the national survey for the study of education, Part II* (pp. 343–370). Chicago: University of Chicago Press.

Epstein, H. T. (1986). Stages of human brain development. *Developmental Brain Research, 20,* 114.

Evans, T. M. (2003). Juvenile competency to stand trial: Problems and pitfalls. *American Journal of Forensic Psychology, 21,* 1–12.

Eveleth, P. B., & Tanner, J. M. (1990). *Worldwide variation in human growth.* London: Cambridge University Press.

Farrell, A. D., & White, K. S. (1998). Peer influences and drug use among urban adolescents: Family structure and parent–adolescent relationship as protective factors. *Journal of Consulting and Clinical Psychology, 66,* 248–258.

Faust, D. (1989). Data integration in legal evaluations: Can clinicians deliver on their premises? *Behavioral Sciences and the Law, 7,* 469—483.

Faust, D., Hart, K. J., Guilmette, T. J., & Arkes, H. R. (1988). Neuropsychologists capacity to detect adolescent malingerers. *Professional Psychology: Research and Practice, 19,* 508–515.

Favole, R. J. (1983). Mental disability in the American criminal process: A four-issue survey. In J. Monahan & H. J. Steadman (Eds.), *Mentally disordered offenders: Perspectives from law and social science* (pp. 247–295). New York: Plenum Press.

Federle, K. (1988). Overcoming the adult–child dyad: A methodology for interviewing and counseling the juvenile client in delinquency cases. *Journal of Family Law, 26,* 545–578.

Feld, B. (1999). *Bad kids: Race and transformation of the juvenile court.* Oxford, England: Oxford University Press.

Ferguson, A., & Douglas, A. (1970). A study of juvenile waiver. *San Diego Law Review, 7,* 39–54.

Ficke, S. L., Hart, K. J., & Deardorff, P. A. (2006). The performance of incarcerated juveniles on the MacArthur Competence Assessment Tool—Criminal Adjudication (Mac-CAT-CA). *Journal of the American Academy of Psychiatry and the Law, 34,* 360–373.

Flavell, J. H., Miller, P. H., & Miller, S. A. (2001). *Cognitive development* (4th ed). Englewood Cliffs, NJ: Prentice Hall.

Fletcher, K. E. (1996). Childhood posttraumatic disorder. In E. J. Mash & R. A. Barkley (Eds.), *Child psychopathology.* New York: Guilford Press.

Frost, L. E., & Volenik, A. E. (2004). The ethical perils of representing the juvenile defendant who may be incompetent. *Journal of Law & Policy, 14,* 327–358.

Fulero, S. M., & Finkel, N. J. (1991). Barring ultimate issue testimony: An "insane" rule? *Law & Human Behavior, 15,* 495–504.

Furby, L., & Beyth-Marom, R. (1992). Risk taking in adolescence: A decision-making perspective. *Developmental Review, 12,* 1–2.

Gagliardi, G. J., & Miller, A. K. (2007). Writing forensic psychological reports. In R. Jackson (Ed.), *Learning forensic assessment* (pp. 539–564). New York: Routledge Publishers.

Garb, H. N. (1989). Clinical judgment, clinical training, and professional experience. *Psychological Bulletin, 105,* 387–396.

Gardner, W. (1993). A life-span rational-choice theory of risk taking. In N. Bell & R. Bell (Eds.), *Adolescent risk taking.* Thousand Oaks, CA: Sage Press.

Gardner, W., & Herman, J. (1991). Adolescents' AIDS risk taking: A rational choice perspective. In W. Gardner, S. Millstein, & B. Wilcox (Eds.), *Adolescents in the AIDS epidemic* (pp. 17–34). San Francisco: Jossey-Bass.

Ge, X., Kim, I. J., Brody, G. H., Conger, R. D., Simmons, R. L., Gibbons, F. X., & Cutrona, C. E. (2003). It's about timing and change: Pubertal transition effects on symptoms of major depression among African American youths. *Developmental Psychology, 39,* 430–439.

Gerken, J. L. (2004). A librarian's guide to unpublished judicial opinions. *Law Library Journal, 96,* 475–501.

Giedd, J. N., Blumenthal, C., Jeffries, N. O., Castellanos, F. X., Liu, H., Zijdenbos, A., Paus, T., Evans, A. C., & Rapoport, J. L. (1999). Brain development during childhood and adolescence: A longitudinal MRI study. *Nature Neuroscience, 2,* 861–863.

Golding, S. L., & Roesch, R. (1988). Competency for adjudication: An international analysis. In D. N. Weisstub (Ed.), *Law and mental health: International perspectives* (Vol. 4, pp. 73–109). New York: Pergamon Press.

Golding, S. L., Roesch, R., & Schreiber, J. (1984). Assessment and conceptualization of competency to stand trial: Preliminary data on the Interdisciplinary Fitness Interview. *Law and Human Behavior, 8,* 321–334.

Goldstein, A. M. (2002). *Handbook of psychology: Vol. 11. Forensic psychology.* New York: John Wiley & Sons.

Goldstein, A. M., & Burd, M. (1990). The role of delusions in trial competency evaluations: Case law and implications for forensic practice. *Forensic Reports, 3,* 361–386.

Goldstein, N. E., Thomson, M. R., Osman, D., & Oberlander, L. (2002). Advocating a functional approach to determining adjudicative competency in juveniles. *Journal of Forensic Psychology Practice, 2,* 89–97.

Gotlib, I. H., Lewinsohn, P. M., & Seeley, J. R. (1995). Symptoms versus a diagnosis of depression: Differences in psychsocial functioning. *Journal of Consulting and Clinical Psychology, 63,* 90–100.

Graber, J., Lewinsohn, P., Seeley, J., & Brooks-Gunn, J. (1997). Is psychopathology associated with the timing of pubertal development? *Journal of the American Academy of Child and Adolescent Psychiatry, 36,* 1768–1776.

Green, P., & Flaro, L. (2003). Word Memory Test performance in children. *Child Neuropsychology, 9,* 189–207.

Greenberg, S. A. & Shuman, D. W. (1997). Irreconcilable conflict between therapeutic and forensic roles. *Professional Psychology: Research and Practice, 28,* 50–57.

Greene, A. L. (1986). Future-time perspective in adolescence: The present of things future revisited. *Journal of Youth and Adolescence, 15,* 99–100.

Grisso, T. (1980). Juveniles' capacities to waive *Miranda* rights: An empirical analysis. *California Law Review, 68,* 1134–1166.

Grisso, T. (1981). *Juveniles' waiver of rights: Legal and psychological competence.* New York: Plenum Press.

Grisso, T. (1983). Juveniles consent in delinquency proceedings. In G. Melton, G. Koocher, & M. Saks (Eds.), *Children's competence to consent* (pp. 131–143). New York: Plenum Press.

Grisso, T. (1986). *Evaluating competencies: Forensic assessment and instruments.* New York: Plenum Press.

Grisso, T. (1996). Pretrial clinical evaluations in criminal cases: Past trends and future directions. *Criminal Justice and Behavior, 23,* 90–106.

Grisso, T. (1997). The competence of adolescents as trial defendants. *Psychology, Public Policy, and Law, 3,* 3–32.

Grisso, T. (1998). *Forensic evaluation of juveniles.* Sarasota, FL: Professional Resource.

Grisso, T. (2000). What we know about youth's capacities as trial defendants. In T. Grisso & R. Schwartz (Eds.), *Youth on trial: A developmental perspective on juvenile justice* (pp. 9–31). Chicago: University of Chicago Press.

Grisso, T. (2003a). *Evaluating competencies: Forensic assessments and instruments* (2nd ed.) New York: Kluwer/Plenum.

Grisso, T. (2003b). Forensic evaluation in delinquency cases. In A. M. Goldstein (Ed.), *Handbook of psychology: Vol. 11. Forensic psychology.* Hoboken, NJ: John Wiley & Sons.

Grisso, T. (2005). *Evaluating juveniles' adjudicative competence: A guide for clinical practice.* Sarasota, FL: Professional Resource Press.

Grisso, T., Cocozza, J., Steadman, H., Fisher, W., & Greer, A. (1994). The organization of pretrial forensic evaluation services: A national profile. *Law and Human Behavior, 18,* 377–393.

Grisso, T., Miller, M. O., & Sales, B. (1987). Competency in juvenile court. *International Journal of Law and Psychiatry, 10,* 1–20.

Grisso, T., & Pomiciter, C. (1977). Interrogation of juveniles: An empirical study of procedures, safeguards, and rights waiver. *Law and Human Behavior, 1,* 321–342.

Grisso, T., & Quinlan, J. (2005). Juvenile court clinical services: A national description. *Juvenile and Family Court Journal, 56,* 9–20.

Grisso, T., & Ring, M. (1979). Parents' attitudes toward juveniles' rights in interrogation. *Criminal Justice and Behavior, 6,* 211–226.

Grisso, T., & Schwartz, R. (Eds.). (2000). *Youth on trial: A developmental perspective on juvenile justice.* Chicago: University of Chicago Press.

Grisso, T., & Seigel, S. K. (1986). Assessment of competency to stand criminal trial. In W. J. Curran, A. L. McGarry, & S. A. Shaw (Eds.), *Forensic psychiatry and psychology: Perspectives and standards for interdisciplinary practice* (pp. 145—165). Philadelphia: F. A. Davis.

Grisso, T., Steinberg, L., Woolard, J., Cauffman, E., Scott, E., Graham, S., Lexcen, F., Reppucci, N. D., & Schwartz, R. (2003). Juveniles' competence to stand trial: A comparison of adolescents' and adults' capacities as trial defendants. *Law & Human Behavior, 27,* 333–363.

Group for the Advancement of Psychiatry. (1974). *Misuse of psychology in the criminal courts: Competency to stand trial.* New York: Committee on Psychiatry and Law.

Gudeman, H. (1981). Legal sanctions and the clinician. *The Clinical Psychologist, 34,* 15–17.

Gudjonsson, G. H. (1992). *The psychology of interrogations, confessions, and testimony.* New York: John Wiley & Sons.

Gudjonsson, G. H. (2003). *The science of interrogations and confessions: A handbook.* Chichester, England: John Wiley & Sons.

Gudjonsson, G. H., & Singh, K. (1984). Interrogative suggestibility and delinquent boys: An empirical validation study. *Personality and Individual Differences, 5,* 425–430.

Haines, A. (1983). Legal studies and developmentally disabled persons. *Australia and New Zealand Journal of Developmental Disabilities, 9,* 129–133.

Heilbrun, K. (1992). The role of psychological testing in forensic assessment. *Law and Human Behavior, 16,* 257–272.

Heilbrun, K. (2001). *Principles of forensic mental health assessment.* New York: Kluwer Academic/Plenum.

Heilbrun, K., & Collins, S. (1995). Evaluations of trial competency and mental state at time of offense: Report characteristics. *Professional Psychology: Research and Practice, 26,* 61–67.

Heilbrun, K. S., Goldstein, N. E., & Redding, R. E. (2005). *Juvenile delinquency: Prevention, assessment, and intervention.* New York: Oxford University Press.

Heilbrun, K., Grisso, T., & Goldstein, A. M. (2009). *Foundations of forensic mental health assessment.* New York: Oxford University Press.

Heilbrun, K., Hawk, G., & Tate, D. (1996). Juvenile competence to stand trial: Research issues in practice. *Law and Human Behavior, 20,* 573–578.

Heilbrun, K., Rogers, R., Otto, R. (2002). Forensic assessment: Current status and future directions. In J. R. P. Ogloff (Ed.), *Taking psychology and law into the 21st century.* New York: Kluwer Academic/Plenum Publishers.

Heilbrun, K., Warren, J., & Picarello, K. (2003). Third-party information in forensic assessment. In J. B. Weiner (Ed. in Chief) & A. M. Goldstein (Vol. Ed.), *Handbook of psychology: Vol. 11. Forensic psychology* (pp. 65–87). Hoboken, NJ: John Wiley & Sons.

Hess, A. K. (1999). Serving as an expert witness. In A. K. Hess & I. B. Weiner (Eds.), *The Handbook of Forensic Psychology* (2nd ed., pp. 521–555). New York: John Wiley & Sons.

Institute of Law, Psychiatry, and Public Policy, University of Virginia (1998, January). *Juvenile forensic update training.* Charlottesville, VA: Author.

Jensen, P. S. (2003). Comorbidity and child psychopathology: Recommendations for the next decade. *Journal of Abnormal Child Psychology, 31,* 293–300.

Jessor, R. (1992a). Reply: Risk behavior in adolescence: A psychosocial framework for understanding and action. *Developmental Review, 12,* 374–390.

Jessor, R. (1992b). Risk behavior in adolescence: A psychosocial framework for understanding and action. In D. Rogers & E. Ginzburg (Eds.), *Adolescents at risk: Medical and social perspectives.* Boulder, CO: Westview Press.

Johnson, K. M. (2006). Juvenile competency statutes: A model for state legislation. *Indiana Law Journal, 81,* 1067–1095.

Jones, M. (2004). The varying threshold of competence to proceed in juvenile court: Opinions of judges, attorneys, and forensic examiners. *Dissertation Abstracts International: Section B: The Sciences and Engineering, 64,* (3-B), 1498.

Kamphaus, R. W., & Frick, P. J. (2001). *Clinical assessment of child and adolescent personality and behavior* (2nd ed.). Boston: Allyn and Bacon.

Katner, D. R. (2006). The mental health paradigm and the MacArthur study: Emerging issues challenging the competence of juveniles in delinquency systems. *American Journal of Law, Medicine, & Ethics, 32,* 503–583.

Kazdin, A. E. (2000). Adolescent development, mental disorders, and decision making of delinquent youths. In T. Grisso & R. Schwartz (Eds.), *Youth on trial: A developmental perspective on juvenile justice* (pp. 9–31). Chicago: University of Chicago Press.

Krosnick, J. A., & Judd, C. M. (1982). Transitions in social influence at adolescence: Who induces cigarette smoking? *Developmental Psychology, 18,* 359–368.

Kruh, I. P. (2006, March). *Separating therapeutic from forensic roles in the juvenile justice system.* Paper presented at the Conference of the American Psychology-Law Society, St. Petersburg, FL.

Kruh, I. P., & Brodsky, S. L. (1997). Clinical evaluations for transfer of juveniles to criminal court. *Behavioral Sciences and the Law, 15,* 151–165.

Kruh, I. P., & Lexcen, F. (2007, June). *The Juvenile Adjudicative Competence Interview (JACI): Recommendations for clinical use.* Paper presented at the Conference of the International Association of Forensic Mental Health Services, Montreal, Quebec.

Kruh, I. P., Sullivan, L., Ellis, M., Lexcen, F., & McClellan, J. (2006). Juvenile competence to stand trial: A historical and empirical analysis of a juvenile forensic evaluation service. *International Journal of Forensic Mental Health, 5,* 109–123.

Laboratory of Community Psychiatry, Harvard Medical School (1973). *Competence to stand trial and mental illness* (DHEW Publication No. ADM77–103). Rockville, MD: Department of Health, Education and Welfare.

Lahey, B. B., Applegate, B., Waldman, I. D., Loft, J. D., Hankin, B. L., & Rick, J. (2004). The structure of child and adolescent psychopathology: Generating new hypotheses. *Journal of Abnormal Psychology, 113,* 358–385.

Lamb, S. J., Bibby, P. A., & Wood, D. J. (1997). Promoting the communication skills of children with moderate learning difficulties. *Child Language Teaching and Therapy, 13,* 261–278.

Larson, L. E. (1972). The influence of parents and peers during adolescence: The situation hypothesis revisited. *Journal of Marriage and the Family, 34,* 67–74.

Lawrence, R. (1983). The role of legal counsel in juveniles' understanding of their rights. *Juvenile and Family Court Journal, 34,* 49–58.

Levin, H. S., Culhane, K. A., Hartmann, J., Evankovich, K., Mattson, A. J., Harward, H., Ringholz, G., Ewing-Cobbs, L., & Fletcher, J. M. (1991). Developmental changes in performance on tests of purported frontal lobe functioning. *Developmental Neuropsychology, 7,* 377–395.

Levitt, G., & Trollinger, J. (2002). Juvenile competence to stand trial: Challenges, frustrations and rewards of restoration training. *American Journal of Forensic Psychiatry, 23,* 57–65.

Lewis, C. (1981). How adolescents approach decisions: Changes over grades seven to twelve and policy implications. *Child Development, 52,* 538–544.

Lexcen, F. J., Grisso, T., & Steinberg, L. (2004). Juvenile competence to stand trial. *Children's Legal Rights Journal, 24,* 2–11.

Loeber, R., Slot, N. W., and Stouthamer-Loeber, M. (2007). A three-dimensional, cumulative developmental model of serious delinquency. In P. O. Wikström and R. Sampson (Eds.), *The social contexts of pathways in crime: Contexts and mechanisms* (pp. 153–194). Cambridge, UK: Cambridge University Press.

MacArthur Foundation Research Network on Adolescent Development and Juvenile Justice (2006, September). *Adolescent legal competence in court* (Issue Brief No. 1). Philadelphia: Author.

Manoogian, S. (1978). *Factors affecting juveniles' comprehension of Miranda rights.* Unpublished doctoral dissertation, St. Louis University, Missouri.

Marguilies, P. (1996). The lawyer as caregiver: Child client's competence in context. *Fordham Law Review, 64,* 1473–1504.

Marlowe, D. (1995). A hybrid decision framework for evaluating psychometric evidence. *Behavioral Sciences and the Law, 13,* 207–228.

Mash, E. J., & Barkley, R. A. (2007). *Assessment of childhood disorders* (4th ed.). New York: Guilford Press.

Mash, E. J., & Hunsley, J. (2005). Evidence-based assessment of child and adolescent disorders: Issues and challenges. *Journal of Clinical Child and Adolescent Psychology, 34,* 362–379.

Mattanah, J. J., Becker, D. F., Levy, K. N., Edell, W. S., & McGlashan, T. H. (1995). Diagnostic stability in adolescents followed up two years after hospitalization. *American Journal of Psychiatry, 152,* 889–892.

May, J.C., Delgado, M.R., Dahl, R., Fiez, J.A., Stenger, V.A., Ryan, N., & Carter, C.S. (2004). Event-related fMRI of reward related brain activity in children and adolescents. *Biological Psychiatry, 55,* 359–364.

McCann, J. T. (1998). *Malingering and deception in adolescents: Assessing credibility in clinical and forensic settings.* Washington, DC: American Psychological Association.

McCann, J. T., & Dyer, F. J. (1996). *Forensic assessment with the Millon Inventories.* New York: Guilford Press.

McClellan, J. M., & Werry, J. S. (1999). Schizophrenic psychosis. In H. C. Steinhausen & F. Verhulst (Eds.), *Risks and outcomes in developmental psychopathology.* Oxford, UK: Oxford University Press.

McGaha, A., McClaren, M., Otto, R. K., & Petrila, J. (2001). Juveniles adjudicated incompetent to proceed: A descriptive study of Florida's competence restoration program. *Journal of the American Academy of Psychiatry and Law, 29,* 427–431.

McGarry, A. L., Curran W. J., Lipsitt, P. D., et al. (1973). *Competency to stand trial and mental illness: Final report from the Laboratory of Community Psychiatry, Havard Medical School.* DHEW Publication No. (HSM) 73–9105. Washington, DC: Government Printing Office.

McKee, G. R. (1998). Competency to stand trial in preadjudicatory juveniles and adults. *Journal of the American Academy of Psychiatry and the Law, 26,* 89–99.

McKee, G. R., & Shea, S. J. (1999). Competency to stand trial in family court: Characteristics of competent and incompetent juveniles. *Journal of the American Academy of Psychiatry and the Law, 27,* 65–73.

McMahon, R. J., & Frick, P. J. (2007). Conduct and oppositional disorders. In E.J. Mash and R.A. Barkley (Eds.), *Assessment of childhood disorders* (4th ed., pp. 132–183). New York: Guilford Press.

Meloy, R. (2000). *Violence risk and threat assessment.* San Diego, CA: Specialized Training Services.

Melton, G. B., Petrila, J., Poythress, N., Slobogin, C., Lyons, P., & Otto, R. K. (2007). *Psychological evaluations for the courts: A handbook for mental health professionals and lawyers* (3rd ed.). New York: Guilford Press.

Moffitt, T. (1993). Adolescence-limited and life-course persistent antisocial behavior: A developmental taxonomy. *Psychological Review, 100,* 674–701.

Morse, S. (1978). Law and mental health professionals: The limits of expertise. *Professional Psychology, 9,* 389–399.

Mossman, D., Noffsinger, S. G., Ash, P., Frierson, R. L., Gerbasi, J., Hackett, M., Lewis, C. F., Pinals, D. A., Scott, C. L., Sieg, K. G., Wall, B. W., & Zonana, H. V. (2007). AAPL practice guideline for the forensic psychiatric evaluation of competence to stand trial. *Journal of the American Academy of Psychiatry and the Law, 35,* S3–S72.

Mumley, D., Tillbrook, C., & Grisso, T. (2003). Five year research update (1996–2000): Evaluations for competence to stand trial (adjudicative competence). *Behavioral Sciences and the Law, 21,* 329–350.

Murphy, K. R., & Davidshofer, C. O. (1988). *Psychological testing: Principles and applications.* Englewood Cliffs, NJ: Prentice-Hall.

Nelson, E., Leibenluft, E., McClure, E., & Pine, D. (2005). The social re-orientation of adolescence: A neuroscience perspective on the process and its relation to psychopathology. *Psychological Medicine, 35,* 163–174.

Nicholson, R. A., Barnard, G. W., Robbins, L., & Hankins, G. (1994). Predicting treatment outcome for incompetent defendants. *Bulletin of the American Academy of Psychiatry and Law, 22,* 367–377.

Nicholson, R. A., & Kugler, K. E. (1991). Competent and incompetent criminal defendants: A quantitative review of comparative research. *Psychological Bulletin, 109,* 355–370.

Nurmi, J. (1991). How do adolescents see their future? A review of the development of future orientation and planning. *Developmental Review, 11,* 1–59.

Oberlander, L. B., Goldstein, N. E., & Ho, C. N. (2001). Preadolescent adjudicative competence: Methodological considerations and recommendations for practice standards. *Behavioral Sciences and the Law, 19,* 545–563.

O'Brien, B. S., & Frick, P. J. (1996). Reward dominance: Associations with anxiety, conduct problems, and psychopathy in children. *Journal of Abnormal Child Psychology, 24,* 223–240.

Office of Juvenile Justice and Delinquency Prevention. (1998). *The youngest offenders, 1996,* U.S. Department of Justice OJJDP Fact Sheet No. 87. Washington, DC: Author.

Office of Juvenile Justice and Delinquency Prevention. (1999). *Residential placement of adjudicated youth, 1987–1996*, U.S. Department of Justice OJJDP Fact Sheet No. 117. Washington, DC: Author.

Otto, R. K. (2006). Competency to stand trial. *Applied Psychology in Criminal Justice, 2*, 82–133.

Otto, R. K., Borum, R., & Epstein, M. (2006). Evaluation of children in the juvenile justice system. In D. Faust (Ed.), *Coping with psychiatric and psychological testimony* (6th ed.). New York: Oxford University Press.

Otto, R. K., & Goldstein, A. M. (2005). Juveniles' competence to confess and competence to participate in the juvenile justice process. In K. Heilbrun, N. E. S. Goldstein, & R. E. Redding (Eds.), *Juvenile delinquency: Prevention, assessment, and intervention* (pp. 179–208). New York: Oxford University Press.

Otto, R. K., & Heilbrun, K. (2002). The practice of forensic psychology: A look toward the future in light of the past. *American Psychologist, 57*, 5–18.

Otto, R. K., Slobogin, C., & Greenberg, S. A. (2007). Legal and ethical issues in accessing and utilizing third-party information. In A. Goldstein (Ed.), *Forensic psychology: Emerging topics and expanding roles*. Hoboken, NJ: John Wiley & Sons.

Owen-Kostelnik, J., Reppucci, N. D., & Meyer, J. R. (2006). Testimony and interrogation of minors: Assumptions about maturity and morality. *American Psychologist, 61*, 286–304.

Palav, A. (2004). Performance of children with neurodevelopmental disorders on neuropsychological effort tests. *Dissertation Abstracts International: Section B: The Sciences and Engineering, 64(9-B)*, 4629.

Patterson, G. R., & Forgatch, M. S. (1987). *Parents and adolescents living together: Part 1. The basics*. Eugene, OR: Castalia.

Paus, T., Zijdenbos, A., Worsley, K., Collins, D. L., Blumenthal, J., Giedd, J. N., Rappoport, J. L., & Evans, A. C. (1999). Structural maturation of neural pathways in children and adolescents: In vivo study. *Science, 283*, 1908–1911.

Perlin, M. L. (1996). 'Dignity was the first to leave': *Godinez v. Moran*, Colin Ferguson, and the trial of mentally disabled criminal defendants. *Behavioral Sciences & the Law, 14*, 61–82.

Peterson-Badali, M., & Abramovitch, R. (1992). Children's knowledge of the legal system: Are they competent to instruct legal counsel? *Canadian Journal of Criminology, 34*, 139–160.

Peterson-Badali, M., & Abramovitch, R. (1993). Grade-related changes in young people's reasoning about plea decisions. *Law and Human Behavior, 17*, 537–552.

Peterson-Badali, M., Abramovitch, R., & Duda, J. (1997). Young children's legal knowledge and reasoning ability. *Canadian Journal of Criminology, 39*, 145–170.

Pierce, C. S., & Brodsky, S. L. (2002). Trust and understanding in the attorney–juvenile relationship. *Behavioral Scienes and the Law, 20*, 89–107.

Platt, A. (1969). *The child savers.* Chicago: University of Chicago Press.

Poythress, N. (1981). *Conflicting postures for mental health expert witnesses: Prevailing attitudes of trial court judges.* Unpublished manuscript on file with the Department of Training and Research, Center for Forensic Psychiatry, POB 2060, Ann Arbor, MI 48106.

Poythress, N. G., Bonnie, R. J., Monahan, J., Otto, R., & Hoge, S. K. (2002). *Adjudicative competence: The MacArthur studies.* New York: Kluwer Academic/Plenum Publishers.

Poythress, N., Lexcen, F. J., Grisso, T., & Steinberg, L. (2006). The competence-related abilities of adolescent defendants in criminal court. *Law and Human Behavior 30,* 75–92.

Quadrel, M., Fischoff, B., & Davis, W. (1993). Adolescent (in)vulnerability. *American Psychologist, 48,* 102–116.

Read, A. (1987). *Minor's ability to participate in the adjudication process: A look at their understanding of court proceedings and legal rights.* Unpublished master's thesis, University of Toronto, Ontario, Canada.

Redding, R. E. (2000). Adjudicative competence in juveniles: Legal and clinical issues. *Juvenile Justice Fact Sheet.* Charlottesville, VA: Institute of Law, Psychiatry, & Public Policy, University of Virginia.

Redding, R. E., Floyd, M. Y., & Hawk, G. L. (2001). What judges and lawyers think about the testimony of mental health experts: A survey of the courts and bar. *Behavioral Sciences and the Law, 19,* 583–594.

Redding, R. E., & Frost, L. E. (2001). Adjudicative competence in the modern juvenile court. *The Virginia Journal of Social Policy and the Law, 9,* 353–409.

Redlich, A. D., Silverman, M., & Steiner, H. (2003). Pre-adjudicative and adjudicative competence in juveniles and young adults. *Behavioral Sciences and the Law, 21,* 393–410.

Reppucci, N. D. (1999). Adolescent development and juvenile justice. *American Journal of Community Psychology, 27,* 307–326.

Richardson, G., Gudjonsson, G. H., & Kelly, T. P. (1995). Interrogative suggestibility in an adolescent forensic population. *Journal of Adolescence, 18,* 211–216.

Robey, A. (1965). Criteria for competency to stand trial: A checklist for psychiatrists. *American Journal of of Psychiatry, 122,* 616–623.

Roesch, R., & Golding, S. (1980). *Competency to stand trial.* Urbana-Champaign: University of Illinois Press.

Roesch, R., Zapf, P., Golding, S., & Skeem, J. (1999). Defining and assessing competency to stand trial. In A. K. Hess & I. Weinder (Eds.), *The handbook of forensic psychology* (2nd ed., pp. 327–349). New York: John Wiley & Sons.

Rogers, R. (1997). *Clinical assessment of malingering and deception* (2nd ed.). New York: Guilford Press.

Rogers, R. (2001). *Handbook of diagnostic and structured interviewing.* New York: Guilford Press.

Rogers, R. (2003). Standardizing DSM-IV diagnoses: The clinical applications of structured interviews. *Journal of Personality Assessment, 81,* 220–225.

Rogers, R., Grandjean, N., Tillbrook, C. E., Vitacco, M. J., & Sewell, K. Q. (2001). Recent interview-based measures of competency to stand trial: A critical review augmented with research data. *Behavioral Sciences and the Law, 19,* 503–518.

Rogers, R., Hinds, J. D., & Sewell, K. W. (1996). Feigning psychopathology among adolescent offenders: Validation of the SIRS, MMPI-A, and SIMS. *Journal of Personality Assessment, 67,* 244–257.

Rogers, R., Jackson, R. L., Sewell, K. W., Tillbrook, C. E., & Martin, M. A. (2003). Assessing dimensions of competency to stand trial: Construct validation of the ECST-R. *Assessment, 10,* 344–351.

Rogers, R., & Shuman, D. (2005). *Fundamentals of forensic practice: Mental health and criminal law.* New York: Springer.

Rogers, R., Ulstad, K. L., Sewell, K. W., & Reinhardt, V. (1996). Dimensions of incompetency: A factor analytic study of the Georgia Court Competency Test. *Behavioral Sciences and the Law, 14,* 323–330.

Rohde, P., Lewinsohn, P., & Seeley, J. (1997). Comparability of telephone and face-to-face interviews in assessing Axis I and Axis II disorders. *American Journal of Psychiatry, 154,* 1593–1598.

Rudolph, K., Hammen, C., & Burge, D. (1994). Interpersonal functioning and depressive symptoms in childhood: Addressing the issues of specificity and comorbidity. *Journal of Abnormal Child Psychology, 22,* 355–371.

Ryan, E. P., & Murrie, D. C. (2005). Competence to stand trial and young children: Is the presumption of competence valid? *Journal of Forensic Psychology Practice, 5,* 89–102.

Ryba, N. L., Cooper, V. G., & Zapf, P. A. (2003a). Assessment of maturity in juvenile competency to stand trial evaluations: A survey of practitioners. *Journal of Forensic Psychology Practice, 3,* 23–45.

Ryba, N. L., Cooper, V. G., & Zapf, P. A. (2003b). Juvenile competence to stand trial evaluations: A survey of current practices and test usage among psychologists. *Professional Psychology: Research & Practice, 34,* 499–507.

Sattler, J. M. (2001a). *Assessment of children: Behavioral, social, and clinical foundations* (4th ed.). San Diego, CA: Jerome M. Sattler, Publisher.

Sattler, J. M. (2001b). *Assessment of children: Cognitive application* (4th ed.). La Mesa, CA: Jerome M. Sattler, Publisher.

Sattler, J. M. (2006). *Assessment of children: Behavioral, social, and clinical foundations* (5th ed.). La Mesa, CA: Jerome M. Sattler, Publisher.

Saunders, L.E. (1981). Ignorance of the law among teenagers: Is it a barrier to the exertion of their rights as citizens? *Adolescence, 16,* 711–726.

Savitsky, J. C. & Karras, D. (1984). Competency to stand trial among adolescents. *Adolescence, 19,* 349–358.

Saywitz, K. (1989). Chidlren's conceptions of the legal system: "Court is a place to play basketball." In S. Ceci, D. Ross, & M. Toglia (Eds.), *Perspectives on children's testimony.* Springer-Verlag.

Schachar, R., & Logan, G. D. (1990). Impulsivity and inhibitory control in normal developmental and childhood psychopathology. *Developmental Psychology, 26,* 710–720.

Scherer, D. G. (1991). The capacities of minors to exercise voluntariness in medical treatment decisions. *Law and Human Behavior, 15,* 431–449.

Scherer, D. G., & Reppucci, N. D. (1988). Adolescents' capacities to provide voluntary informed consent: The effect of parental influence and medical dilemmas. *Law and Human Behavior, 12,* 123–141.

Schmidt, M. G., Reppucci, N. D., & Woolard, J. L. (2003). Effectiveness of participation as a defendant: The attorney–juvenile client relationship. *Behavioral Sciences and the Law, 21,* 175–198.

Schouten, R. (2003). Training for competence—Form or substance? *Journal of the American Academy of Psychiatry and the Law, 31,* 202.

Schwartz, R., & Rosado, M. (Eds.) (2000). *Evaluating youth competence in the justice system.* Washington, DC: American Bar Association Juvenile Justice Center, Juvenile Law Center, and Youth Law Center.

Scott, E., & Grisso, T. (2005). Developmental incompetence, due process, and juvenile justice policy. *North Carolina Law Review, 83,* 102–147.

Scott, E., Reppucci, N., & Woolard, J. (1995). Evaluating adolescent decision making in legal contexts. *Law and Human Behavior, 19,* 221–244.

Selman, R. (1980). *The growth of interpersonal understanding: Developmental and clinical analyses.* New York: Academic Press.

Sentencing Project. (2000). *Elements of a defender program providing representation for youths prosecuted in (adult) criminal court.* Washington, DC: Author.

Shaw, P., Greenstein, D., Lerch, J., Klasen, L., Lenroot, R., Gotgay, N., Evans, A., Rapoport, J., & Giedd, J. (2006). Intellectual ability and cortical development in children and adolescents. *Nature, 440,* 676–679.

Shepard, R., & Zaremba, B. (1995). When a disabled juvenile confesses to a crime: Should it be admissible? *Criminal Justice, 9,* 31–32.

Shuman, D. W. (1994). *Psychiatric and psychological evidence* (2nd ed.). New York: McGraw-Hill.

Siassi, I. (1984). Psychiatric interview and mental status examination. In G. Goldstein & H. Hersen (Eds.), *Handbook of psychological assessment* (pp. 259–275). New York: Pergamon Press.

Silverberg, S. (1986). Psychological well-being of parents with early adolescent children. Unpublished doctoral dissertation, University of Wisconsin–Madison.

Skeem, J., & Golding, S. (1998). Community examiners' evaluations of competence to stand trial: Common problems and suggestions for improvements. *Professional Psychology: Research and Practice, 29,* 357–367.

Slobogin, C., Grisso, T., Otto, R., Kuehnle, K., Poythress, N., Kazimour, K., & Boyd, J. (1997). *Juvenile competencies in the justice system: Assessment &*

treatment. Tampa: Department of Mental Health Law and Policy, The Louis de la Parte Florida Mental Health Institute at the University of South Florida.

Sowell, S. J., Trauner, D. A., Gamst, A., & Jernigan, T. L. (2002). Development of cortical and subcortical brain structures in childhood and adolescence: A structural MRI study. *Developmental Medicine and Child Neurology, 44,* 4–16.

Spence, S. H. (2003). Social skills training with children and young people: Theory, evidence and practice. *Child and Adolescent Mental Health, 8,* 84–96.

Stafford, K. P. (2003). Assessment of competence to stand trial. In A. M. Goldstein (Ed.), *Forensic psychology* (pp. 359–380). New York: John Wiley & Sons.

Stahl, A.L., Puzzanchera, C., Livsey, S., Sladky, A., Finnegan, T.A., Tierney, N. and Snyder. H.N. (2007). *Juvenile Court Statistics 2003–2004.* Pittsburgh, PA: National Center for Juvenile Justice.

Steinberg, L. (2002). *Adolescence* (6th ed.). New York: McGraw-Hill.

Steinberg, L. (2007). *Adolescence* (8th ed.). New York: McGraw-Hill.

Steinberg, L., & Cauffman, E. (1996). Maturity of judgment in adolescence: Psychosocial factors in adolescent decision making. *Law and Human Behavior, 20,* 249–272.

Steinberg, L., Grisso, T., Woolard, J., Cauffman, E., Scott, E., Graham, S., Lexcen, F., Reppucci, N. D., & Schwartz, R. (2003). Juveniles' competence to stand trial as adults. *Social Policy Report, 17,* 3–15.

Steinberg, L., & Schwartz, R. (2000). Developmental psychology goes to court. In T. Grisso & R. Schwartz (Eds.), *Youth on trial: A developmental perspective on juvenile justice* (pp. 9–31). Chicago: University of Chicago Press.

Steinberg, L., & Silberberg, S. B. (1986). The vicissitudes of autonomy in early adolescence. *Child Development, 57,* 841–851.

Stice, E., Presnell, K., & Bearman, S. (2001). Relation of early menarche to depression, eating disorders, substance abuse, and comorbid psychopathology among adolescent girls. *Developmental Psychology, 37,* 608–619.

Strauch, B. (2003). *The primal teen.* New York: Anchor Books.

Susman, E. (1997). Modeling developmental complexity in adolescence: Hormones and behavior in context. *Journal of Research on Adolescence, 7,* 283–306.

Susman, E. J., Inoff-Germain, G., Nottelmann, E. D., Loriaux, D. L., Cutler, G. B., & Chrousos, G. P. (1987). Hormones, emotional dispositions and aggressive attributes in young adolescents. *Child Development, 58,* 1114–1134.

Susman, E., & Rogol, A. (2004). Puberty and psychological development. In R. Lerner & L. Steinberg (Eds.), *Handbook of adolescent psychology.* New York: John Wiley & Sons.

Tanner, D. (1972). *Secondary education.* New York: Macmillan.

Taylor, T. L., & Chemtob, C. M. (2004). Efficacy of treatment for child and adolescent traumatic stress. *Archives of Pediatrics and Adolescent Medicine, 158,* 786–791.

Teplin, L. A., Abram, K. M., McClelland, G. M., Dulcan, M. K., & Mericle, A. A. (2002). Psychiatric disorders in youth in juvenile detention. *Archives of General Psychiatry, 59,* 1133–1143.

Tillbrook, C., Mumley, D., & Grisso, T. (2003). Avoiding expert opinions on the ultimate legal question: The case for integrity. *Journal of Forensic Psychology Practice, 3,* 77–87.

Tobey, A., Grisso, T., & Schwartz, R. (2000). Youths' trial participation as seen by youths and their attorneys: An exploration of competence-based issues. In T. Grisso & R. Schwartz (Eds.), *Youth on trial: A developmental perspective on juvenile justice* (pp. 225–242). Chicago: University of Chicago Press.

Ventrell, M. R. (1995). Rights & duties: An overview of the attorney-client relationship. *Loyola University Chicago Law Journal, 26,* 259–284.

Viljoen, J. L., & Grisso, T. (2007). Prospects for remediating juveniles' adjudicative incompetence. *Psychology, Public Policy, and Law, 13,* 87–114.

Viljoen, J. L., Klaver, J., & Roesch, R. (2005). Legal decisions of preadolescent and adolescent defendants: Predictors of confessions, pleas, communication with attorneys, and appeals. *Law and Human Behavior, 29,* 253–277.

Viljoen, J. L., Odgers, C., Grisso, T., & Tillbrook, C. (2007). Teaching adolescents and adults about legal proceedings: A comparison of pre- and post-teaching scores on the Mac-CAT-CA. *Law and Human Behavior, 31,* 419–432.

Viljoen, J. L., & Roesch, R. (2005). Competence to waive interrogation rights and adjudicative competence in adolescent defendants: Cognitive development, attorney contact, and psychological symptoms. *Law and Human Behavior, 29,* 723–742.

Viljoen, J. L., & Roesch, R. (2007). Assessing adolescents' adjudicative competence. In R. Jackson (Ed.), *Learning Forensic Assessment* (pp. 291–312). London: Lawrence Erlbaum.

Viljoen, J. L., Vincent, G. M., & Roesch, R. (2006). Assessing adolescent defendant's adjudicative competence: Interrater reliability and factor structure of the Fitness Interview Test–Revised. *Criminal Justice and Behavior, 33,* 467–487.

Viljoen, J. L., Zapf, P. A., & Roesch, R. (2007). Adjudicative competence and comprehension of Miranda rights in adolescent defendants: A comparison of legal standards. *Behavioral Sciences and the Law, 24,* 1–19.

Walker, A. G. (1994). *Handbook on questioning children: A linguistic perspective.* Washington, DC: American Bar Association.

Wall, S., & Furlong, M. (1985). Comprehension of Miranda rights by urban adolescents with law-related education. *Psychological Reports, 56,* 359–372.

Warren, J. I., Aaron, J., Ryan, E., Chauhan, P., & DuVal, J. (2003). Correlates of adjudicative competence among psychiatrically impaired juveniles. *Journal of the American Academy of Psychiatry and the Law, 31,* 299–309.

Warren, J., Fitch, L., Dietz, P., & Rosenfeld, B. (1991). Criminal offense, psychiatric diagnosis, and psycholegal opinion: An analysis of 894 pretrial referrals. *Bulletin of the American Academy of Psychiatry and the Law, 19,* 63–69.

Warren, J., Rosenfeld, B., Fitch, W. L., & Hawk, G. (1997). Forensic mental health clinical evaluation: An analysis of interstate and intersystemic differences. *Law and Human Behavior, 21,* 377–390.

Warren-Leubecker, A., Tate, C., Hinton, I., & Ozbek, N. (1989). What do children know about the legal system and when do they know it? First steps down a less traveled path in child witness research. In S. Ceci, M. Toglia, & D. Ross (Eds.), *Perspectives on children's testimony* (pp. 158–183). New York: Springer-Verlag.

Wasserman G. A., McReynolds L. S., Lucas C. P., Fisher P., & Santos L. (2002). The voice DISC-IV with incarcerated male youths: Prevalence of disorder. *Journal of the American Academy of Child and Adolescent Psychiatry, 41,* 314–321.

Weider, S., & Greenspan, S. (1992). An integration of developmental–structuralist and mediated learning experience. (MLE) approaches to learning. *International Journal of Cognitive Education and Medicated Learning, 2,* 210–223.

Wenar, C., & Kerig, P. (2000). *Developmental psychopathology: From infancy through adolescence.* Boston: McGraw-Hill.

Wettstein, R. M. (2005). Quality and quality improvement in forensic mental health evaluations. *Journal of the American Academy of Psychiatry and Law, 33,* 158–175.

Wong, C., Crosnoe, R., Laird, J., & Dornbusch, S. (2003). *Relations with parents and teachers susceptibility to friends' negative influences and adolescent deviance.* Unpublished manuscript, Department of Sociology, University of Texas at Austin.

Woolard, J. L. (1998). *Developmental aspects of judgment and competence in legally relevant contexts.* Unpublished doctoral dissertation, University of Virginia.

Woolard, J. L. (2005, March). *Parental involvement and juvenile participation: Comparing parents' and youths' decision making about the juvenile justice process.* Paper presented at the Conference of the American Psychology-Law Society, La Jolla, CA.

Woolard, J. L. (2006, March). *Who's in charge in juvenile court? Family-wide competence, capacity, and authority in juvenile justice decision making.* Paper presented at the Conference of the American Psychology-Law Society, St. Petersburg, FL.

Woolard, J., Fried, C., & Reppucci, N. D. (2001). Toward an expanded definition of adolescent competence in legal situations. In R. Roesch, R. Corrado, & R. Dempster (Eds.), *Psychology in the courts:*

International advances in knowledge (pp. 21–40). London: Routledge.

Woolard, J. L., & Harvell, S. (2005). The MacArthur Competence Assessment Tool—Criminal Adjudication. In T. Grisso & G. Vincent (Eds.), *Handbook of mental health screening and assessment for juvenile justice.* New York: Guilford Press.

Wulach, J. S. (1980). The incompetency plea: Abuses and reforms. *Journal of Psychiatry and Law, 8,* 317–328.

Wynkoop, T. F. (2003). Neuropsychology of juvenile adjudicative competence. *Journal of Forensic Neuropsychology, 3,* 45–65.

Young, H., & Ferguson, L. (1979). Developmental changes through adolescence in the spontaneous nomination of reference groups as a function of decision context. *Journal of Youth and Adolescence, 15,* 407–423.

Youngstrom, E. A., Findling, R. L., & Calabrese, J. R. (2003). Who are the comorbid adolescents? Agreement between psychiatric diagnosis, youth, parent, and teacher report. *Journal of Abnormal Child Psychology, 31,* 231–245.

Zapf, P. A., Hubbard, K. L., Cooper, V. G., Wheeles, M., & Ronan, K. A. (2004). Have the courts abdicated their responsibility for determination of competency to stand trial to clinicians? *Journal of Forensic Psychology Practice, 41,* 27–44.

Zapf, P. A., & Roesch, R. (1998). Fitness to stand trial: Characteristics of remands since the 1992 Criminal Code Amendments. *Canadian Journal of Psychiatry, 43,* 287–293.

Zapf, P. A., & Roesch, R. (2005). An investigation of the construct of competence: A comparison of the FIT, the MacCAT-CA, and the MacCAT-T. *Law and Human Behavior, 29,* 229–252.

Zapf, P. A., & Roesch, R. (2009). *Evaluation of Competence to Stand Trial.* New York: Oxford University Press.

Zapf, P. A., & Viljoen, J. L. (2003). Issues and considerations regarding the use of assessment instruments in the evaluation of competency to stand trial. *Behavioral Sciences and the Law, 21,* 351–367.

Zapf, P. A., Viljoen, J. L., Whittemore, K. E., Poythress, N. G., & Roesch, R. (2002). Competency: Past, present, and future. In J. R. P. Ogloff (Ed.), *Taking psychology and law into the 21st century.* New York: Kluwer Academic/Plenum Publishers.

Zaremba, B. (1992). *Comprehension of Miranda rights by 14–18 year old African-American and Caucasian males with and without learning disabilities.* Unpublished doctoral dissertation, College of William and Mary, School of Education, Williamsburg, Virginia.

Tests and Specialized Tools

ASEBA: Achenbach System of Empirically Based Assessment (Achenbach & Rescorla, 2001)

BASC-2: Behavior Assessment System for Children, Second Edition (Reynolds & Kamphaus, 2004)

BPRS-C: Brief Psychiatric Rating Scale for Children (Hughes, Rintelmann, Emslie, Lopez, & McCabe, 2001)

BRIEF: Behavior Rating Inventory of Executive Function (Gioia, Isquith, Guy, & Kenworthy, 2000)

CAST*MR: Competence Assessment for Standing Trial for Defendants with Mental Retardation (Everington & Luckasson, 1992)

CBCL: Child Behavior Checklist (Achenbach & Rescorla, 2001)

CDI: Children's Depression Inventory (Kovacs, 1992)

CPT: Continuous Performance Test (Riccio, Reynolds & Lowe, 2001)

DISC-IV-P: Diagnostic Interview Schedule for Children, Version IV-Parent (Shaffer, Fisher, Lucas, Dulcan, & Schwab-Stone, 2000)

DISC-IV-Y: Diagnostic Interview Schedule for Children, Version IV-Youth (Shaffer, Fisher, Lucas, Dulcan, & Schwab-Stone, 2000)

ECST-R: Evaluation of competency to stand trial—revised (Rogers, Tillbrook, & Sewell, 2004)

FIT-R: Fitness Interview Test–Revised (Roesch, Zapf, Eaves, & Webster, 1998; Roesch, Zapf, & Eaves, 2006)

J-CAP: Florida juvenile competency assessment procedure (Otto, 1996)

JACI: Juvenile Adjudicative Competence Interview (Grisso, 2005)

K-SNAP: Kaufman Short Neuropsychological Assessment Procedure (Kaufman & Kaufman, 1994)

MacCAT-CA: MacArthur Competence Assessment Tool—Criminal Adjudication (Poythress, Nicholson, Otto, Edens, Bonnie, Monahan, & Hoge, 1999)

MACI: Millon Adolescent Clinical Inventory (Millon, 1993)

MMPI-A: Minnesota Multiphasic Personality Inventory–Adolescent Version (Butcher, Williams, Graham, Archer, Tellegen, Ben-Porath, & Kaemmer, 1992)

OWLS: Oral & Written Language Scales (Carrow-Woolfolk, 1995)

Respondent's Attorney Competence Questionnaire (Kruh, Sullivan, & Dunham, 2001)

RCMAS: Revised Children's Manifest Anxiety Scale (Reynolds & Richmond, 1985)

RST-I: Risk-Sophistication-Treatment Inventory (Salekin, 2004)

SCICA: Semistructured Clinical Interview for Children and Adolescents (McConaughy & Achenbach, 2001)

SIRS: Structured Interview of Reported Symptoms (Rogers, R., Bagby, & Dickens, 1992)

TOMM: Test of Memory Malingering (Tombaugh, 1996)

TSCC: Trauma Symptom Checklist for Children (Briere, 1996)
UNIT: Universal Nonverbal Intelligence Test (Bracken & McCallum, 1998)
Vineland II: Vineland Adaptive Behavior Scales, Second Edition (Sparrow, Cicchetti, & Balla, 2005)
WASI: Wechsler Abbreviated Scale of Intelligence (Psychological Corporation, 1999)
WISC-IV: Wechsler Intelligence Scale for Children, Fourth Edition (Wechsler, 2003)
WJ III COG: Woodcock-Johnson Tests of Cognitive Abilities, III (Woodcock, McGrew, & Mather, 2002)
WMT: Word Memory Test (Green & Astner, 1995; Green, Allen, & Astner, 1996)
WRAT-4: Wide Range Achievement Test, Fourth Edition (Wilkinson & Robertson, 2006)
WRAML-2: Wide Range Assessment of Memory and Learning, Second Edition (Sheslow & Adams, 2003)

References for Tests and Specialized Tools

Achenbach, T. M., & Rescorla, L. A. (2001). *Manual for the ASEBA school-age forms and profiles.* Burlington, VT: University of Vermont, Research Center for Children, Youth, and Families.

Bracken, B. A., & McCallum, R. S. (1998). *Universal Nonverbal Intelligence Test.* Itasca, IL: Riverside Publishing.

Briere, J. (1996). *Trauma Symptom Checklist for Children (TSCC) professional manual.* Odessa, FL: Psychological Assessment Resources.

Butcher, J. N., Williams, C. L., Graham, J. R., Archer, R. P., Tellegen, A., Ben-Porath, Y. S., & Kaemmer, B. (1992). *Minnesota Multiphasic Personality Inventory–Adolescent Version (MMPI-A): Manual for administration and scoring and interpretation.* Minneapolis: University of Minnesota Press.

Carrow-Woolfolk, E. (1995). *Oral & Written Language Scales.* Circle Pines, MN: American Guidance Service.

Everington, C., & Luckasson, R. (1992). *Competence Assessment for Standing Trial for Defendants with Mental Retardation (CAST*MR): Test manual.* Worthington, OH: IDS Publishing Corporation.

Gioia, G. A., Isquith, P. K., Guy, S. C., & Kenworthy, L. (2000). *Behavior Rating Inventory of Executive Function.* Odessa, FL: Psychological Assessment Resources.

Green, P., Allen, L., & Astner, K. (1996). *Manual for computerized Word Memory Test, U.S. version 1.0.* Durham, NC: Cognisyst.

Green, P., & Astner, K. (1995). *The Word Memory Test.* Edmonton: Neurobehavioral Associates.

Grisso, T. (2005). Juvenile Adjudicative Competence Interview. In Grisso, T., *Evaluating juveniles' adjudicative competence: A guide for clinical practice.* Sarasota, FL: Professional Resource Press.

Hughes, C. W., Rintelmann, J., Emslie, G. J., Lopez, M., & McCabe, N. (2001). A revised anchored versions of the BPRS-C for childhood psychiatric disorders. *Journal of Child and Adolescent Psychopharmacology, 11,* 77–93.

Kaufman, A. S., & Kaufman, N. L. (1994) *Kaufman Short Neuropsychological Assessment Procedure.* Circle Pines, MN: American Guidance Service.

Kovacs, M. (1992). *Children's Depression Inventory.* North Tonawanda, NY: Multi-Health Systems.

Kruh, I. P., Sullivan, L., & Dunham, J. (2001). *Respondent's Attorney Competence Questionnaire.* State of Washington Department of Social and Health Services, Child Study & Treatment Center.

McConaughy, S. H., & Achenbach, T. M. (2001). *Manual for the Semistructured Clinical Interview for Children and Adolescents* (2nd ed.). Burlington, VT: University of Vermont, Center for Children, Youth, & Families.

Millon, T. (1993). *Millon Adolescent Clinical Inventory.* Minneapolis: National Computer Systems.

Otto, R. K. (1996). *Florida juvenile competency assessment procedure.* Tampa: Department of Mental Health Law and Policy, the Louis de la Parte Florida Mental Health Institute at the University of South Florida.

Poythress, N. G., Nicholson, R., Otto, R. K., Edens, J. F., Bonnie, R. J., Monahan, J., & Hoge, S. K. (1999). *The MacArthur Competence Assessment Tool—Criminal Adjudication: Professional manual.* Odessa, FL: Psychological Assessment Resources.

Psychological Corporation (1999). *Wechsler Abbreviated Scale of Intelligence.* San Antonio, TX: Author.

Reynolds, C. R., & Kamphaus, R. W. (2004). *BASC-2: Behavior Assessment System for Children* (2nd ed.). Circle Pines, MN: AGS Publishing.

Reynolds, C. R., & Richmond, B. O. (1985). *Revised Children's Manifest Anxiety Scale (RCMAS).* Los Angeles: Western Psychological Services.

Riccio, C. A., Reynolds, C. R., & Lowe, P. A. (2001). *Clinical applications of continuous performance tests: Measuring attention and impulsive responding in children and adults.* New York: John Wiley & Sons.

Roesch, R., Zapf, P., & Eaves, D. (2006). *Fitness Interview Test–Revised: A structured interview for assessing competency to stand trial.* Sarasota, FL: Professional Resource Press.

Roesch, R., Zapf, P., Eaves, D., & Webster, C. D. (1998). *Fitness Interview Test* (rev. ed.). Burnaby, BC: Mental Health, Law and Policy Institute, Simon Fraser University.

Rogers, R., Bagby, R. M., & Dickens, S. E. (1992). *Structured Interview of Reported Symptoms.* Odessa, FL: Psychological Assessment Resources.

Rogers, R, Tillbrook, C. E., & Sewell, K. (2004). *Evaluation of competency to stand trial—revised. Professional manual.* Lutz, FL: Psychological Assessment Resources.

Salekin, R. T. (2004). *Risk-Sophistication-Treatment Inventory.* Lutz, FL: Psychological Assessment Resources.

Shaffer, D., Fisher, P., Lucas, C. P., Dulcan, M. K., & Schwab-Stone, M. E. (2000). NIMH Diagnostic Interview Schedule for Children, Version IV (NIMH DISC-IV): Description, differences from previous versions, and reliability of some common diagnoses. *Journal of the American Academy of Child and Adolescent Psychiatry, 39,* 28–38.

Sheslow, D., & Adams, W. (2003). *Wide Range Assessment of Memory and Learning* (2nd ed.). Los Angeles: Western Psychological Services.

Sparrow, S. S., Cicchetti, D. V., & Balla, D. A. (2005). *Vineland Adaptive Behavior Scales* (2nd ed.). Circle Pines, MN: AGS Publishing.

Tombaugh, T. N. (1996). *TOMM: Test of Memory Malingering.* Toronto, Canada: Multi-Health Systems.

Wechsler, D. (2003). *Wechsler Intelligence Scale for Children* (4th ed.). San Antonio, TX: The Psychological Corporation.

Wilkinson, G. S., & Robertson, G. J. (2006). *The Wide Range Achievement Test* (4th ed.) *(WRAT-4).* Lutz, FL: Psychological Assessment Resources.

Woodcock, R. W., McGrew, K. S., & Mather, N. (2002). *Woodcock-Johnson Tests of Cognitive Abilities, III.* Itasca, IL: Riverside.

Cases and Statutes

Bellotti v. Baird, 443 U.S. 622 (1979).

Buchanan v. Kentucky, 483 U.S. 402 (1987).

Cooper v. Oklahoma, 517 U.S. 348 (1996).

Drope v. Missouri, 420 U.S. 162, 95 S. Ct. 896 (1975).

Dusky v. United States, 362 U.S. 402 (1960).

Estelle v. Smith, 451 U.S. 454 (1981).

Florida Statutes 985.223(2).

Florida Rule of Juvenile Procedure 8.095(d)(1)(B).

G.J.I. v. State of Oklahoma, 778 P.2d 485 (Okla. Crim. 1989).

Godinez v. Moran, 509 U.S. 389 (1993).

Haley v. Ohio, 332 U.S. 597 (1948).

In re Causey, 363 S0.2d 472 (La. 1978).

In re Gault, 387 U.S. 1 (1967).

In re K.G., 808 N.E. 2d 631 (Ind. 2004).

In re Michael Roger Johnson (Ohio 1983), unreported.

In re Paula McWhorter (Ohio 1994), unreported.

In the Interest of S.H., A Child, 469 S.E.2d 810 (Ga. Ct. App. 1996).

In the Matter of Robert Lloyd (Ohio 1997), unreported.

In the Matter of the Welfare of D.D.N., 582 N.W.2d 278, 281 (Minn. Ct. App. 1998).

Jackson v. Indiana, 406 U.S. 715, 92 S. Ct. 1845 (1972).

Kent v. United States, 383 U.S. 541 (1966).

Llamera v. Commonwealth, 243 Va. 262, 264, 414 S.E.2d 597, 598 (1992).

Medina v. California, 112 S. Ct. 2572 (1992).

Ohio v. Settles, No. 13–97–50, 1998 Ohio App. LEXIS 4973, at *8 (Ohio App. 3d. Sept. 30, 1998).

Parham v. J.R., 442 U.S. 584 (1979).

Pate v. Robinson, 383 U.S. 375 (1966).

People v. Carey, 615 N.W.2d 742, 748 (Mich. Ct. App. 2000).

Rees v. Peyton, 384 U.S. 312 (1966).

Regina v. Taylor, 77 C.C.C. (3d) 551 (Ont. C.A.) (1992).

Sell v. United States, 539 U.S. 166 (2003).

State v. Burnett, 2005 Ohio 49 (Ohio Ct. App. 2005).

State v. E.C., 922 P.2d 152 (Wash. Ct. App. 1996).

Tate v. State, 864 S0.2d 44, Fla. 4th DCA (2003).

Texas Criminal Procedures Article 46B.025.

United States v. Duhon, 104 F.Supp.2d 663 (W.D. La. 2000).

United States v. Holmes, 671 F.Supp. 120 (D. Conn. 1987).

United States v. Villegas, 899 F2d 1324 (2nd Cir. 1990), *cert denied* 498 U.S. 991.

Washington v. Swenson-Tucker, 131 Wash. App. 1045, unreported.

Wilson v. United States, 391 F.2d 460 (1968).

W.S.L. v. Florida, 470 So.2d 828, 829 (Fla. Dist. Ct. App. 1985).

Key Terms

adjudicative competence: a newer term used for CST as it more accurately reflects the need of defendants to meaningfully participate in all stages of the adjudication process, not just at trial.

adjusted bar: a standard for the abilities required for juvenile court defendants to be found competent to stand trial that consists of only a subset of the abilities required of adult defendants in criminal court.

adolescent norms standard: a "lower-bar" standard for the abilities required for juvenile court defendants to be found competent to stand trial that consists of the same basic abilities as those required of adult defendants in criminal court, but requires those abilities to be only as well developed as is typical of adolescents.

adult CST: the application of the CST doctrine exclusively to adult criminal court defendants.

adult norms standard: a standard for the abilities required for juvenile court defendants to be found competent to stand trial that is the same standard applied to adult defendants in criminal court.

age-peer norms standard: a "lower-bar" standard for the abilities required for juvenile court defendants to be found competent to stand trial that consists of the same basic abilities as those required of adult defendants in criminal court, but requires those abilities to be only as well developed as is typical of youth of the same age.

Appreciation: one of four capacities typically associated with CST; the ability to manipulate what is factually understood, appropriately contemplate the implications and significance of what is understood, and apply that knowledge in actual case-related situations without distortion or irrationality (e.g., appreciate the reasons for providing an accurate account of the alleged offense to the defense attorney).

Assisting: one of four capacities typically associated with CST; the ability to meaningfully aid the defense attorney in developing a defense during attorney consultations and presenting the defense at trial through testimony and adequately following and comprehending the testimony of other witnesses.

autonomy (also known as conformity and compliance): the extent to which individuals think and behave in ways that are self-reliant, self-governing, and independent so that decisions properly integrate the perspectives of others without inappropriate dependence or rejection.

basic understanding and communication standard: a standard for the abilities required for juvenile court defendants to be found competent to stand trial that consists of only a rudimentary understanding of the court process and fundamental communication abilities, without a requirement for rational appreciation skills or independent decision-making abilities.

Bonnie's model: a model of competence to stand trial based on a proposal of Richard Bonnie (1992) that includes two related constructs, *competence to assist counsel* and *decisional competence*.

civil commitment: legally mandated psychiatric treatment based on specific criteria, usually including imminent risk of harm to self, risk of harm to others, and/or an inability to maintain adequate self-care.

clinical then forensic model: an approach to forensic mental health evaluation report writing in which a typical clinical evaluation is provided first, including clinical data and opinions, followed by the presentation of forensic data and opinions.

cognitive acceleration programs: educational programs aimed at providing the social and environmental circumstances most likely to cause a specific cognitive skill to be attained once maturation has created the foundational capacity for that new skill to emerge.

cognitive complexity model: a model of competence to stand trial based on sophistication of cognitive abilities needed to be competent that includes two prongs: (a) factual understanding and (b) rational abilities (including both rational consultation abilities and rational understanding).

cognitive slowing: evidencing a slowing of information processing compared to typical abilities.

competence remediation: a more accurate term than *competence restoration* when referencing interventions aimed at establishing competence in juvenile defendants, since it is less likely that incompetent juvenile defendants have been competent in the past.

competence restoration: intervention services aimed at establishing competence in a defendant found Incompetent to Stand Trial so that the adjudication process can go forward; based on the notion that psychotic defendants were once competent and can be "restored" to competence if the psychosis is diminished.

competence to assist counsel: a construct in Bonnie's model of competence to stand trial that references a basic understanding of the trial process, as well as the ability to work with and assist counsel by relating relevant facts.

competence to proceed to adjudication: a newer term used for CST, as it more accurately reflects the need of defendants to meaningfully participate in all stages of the adjudication process, not just at trial.

competence to stand trial (CST): a legal doctrine that requires meaningful participation of criminal defendants in their defense at various stages of the proceedings by requiring that defendants possess specific relevant capacities (see Understanding, Appreciation, Assisting, and Decision Making).

competency domains model (also known as semantic analysis model): a model of competence to stand trial based on the wording of the *Dusky* standard that includes two prongs: (a) the rational ability to consult with counsel, and (b) rational and factual understanding of the proceedings.

court-appointed evaluations: evaluations ordered by and "owned by" the court. Therefore, the court controls access to its contents through its own distribution practices or through statutes that direct the examiner on how to make those distributions.

criminal court CST: the application of the CST doctrine to defendants, adult or juvenile, who are being tried in criminal court.

cross-examination: testimony provided in response to questioning by the attorney who did not call the witness; more likely to take on an adversarial tone.

data then opinions model: an approach to forensic mental health evaluation report writing in which relevant clinical and forensic data are presented first, followed by clinical and developmental opinions.

decisional competence: a construct in Bonnie's model of competence to stand trial that references a contextualized capacity to engage in cognitive and psychosocial reasoning processes and make independent decisions with input from counsel.

Decision Making: one of four capacities typically associated with CST; the ability to consider alternatives and make adequately reasoned legal choices, such as when pleading guilty, going to trial, accepting a plea agreement offer, testifying, calling certain witnesses, or considering certain defenses.

delayed development: immaturity that is relative to typically developing age-peers. For example, some children will demonstrate delayed development of abstraction skills compared to those of most children their age.

developmental psychopathology: a model of psychopathology in youth in which disorders are understood as exaggerations of, adaptational compromises in, or failures of normal development that, once developed, continue to interact with the normal developmental process in complex ways.

direct examination: testimony provided in response to questioning by the attorney who called the witness; more likely to be conducted in a supportive tone.

discrete abilities model: a model of competence to stand trial based on a distinction between "thought" and "action," as well as the sophistication of cognitive abilities needed to be competent that includes three prongs: (a) rational ability to consult with counsel, (b) factual understanding of the proceedings, and (c) rational understanding of the proceedings.

distractibility: evidencing a susceptibility to diverting attention from identified tasks due to other stimuli in the environment.

effectiveness of participation: a reference coined by Grisso (2000) to the full range of types and degree of abilities relevant to participating as a defendant in a legal proceeding; extends beyond those types and degree of abilities relevant to CST. Examiners can identify deficits in effectiveness of participation that do not meet the criteria for incompetence to help maximize the participation of the defendant.

ex parte **evaluations:** evaluations conducted on behalf of one of the attorneys within the context of being retained by that attorney. The results of the evaluation are typically shared with that attorney only, to be used at the discretion of the retaining attorney and as specified in law.

flexible assessment battery: an approach to developing an evaluation by selecting assessment methods for purposes relevant to the unique aspects of the examinee and the presenting concerns. This is in contrast to a standardized protocol that comprehensively samples all aspects of the examinee's functioning, regardless of the unique issues that precipitated the evaluation.

flexible bar: a standard for the abilities required for juvenile court defendants to be found competent to stand trial that matches the level of needed protection given the seriousness of sanctions being faced, maintaining traditional CST requirements when serious sanctions are faced but reducing the requirements when less serious sanctions are faced.

forensic assessment instruments (FAIs): structured quantitative interview tools designed for focused assessment of the functional legal abilities of direct relevance to legal questions. Several FAIs have been developed for assessment of CST abilities among adult defendants with potential use in juvenile CST evaluations (e.g., Fitness Interview Test–Revised).

functional CST interview: the most common method for collecting functional data regarding an examinee's CST capacities through direct questioning.

immature: the status of being less than fully developed. A term that should be applied to specific capacities (e.g., emotionally immature) with a clearly defined reference point (e.g., relative to fully developed adults).

immunity: legal protection against the state using self-incriminating statements made during a competence evaluation against the defendant during the case-in-chief.

impulsivity: evidencing difficulty modulating impulses, resulting in behaviors that seek short-term gain without appropriate consideration of longer-term consequences.

inattention: evidencing difficulty maintaining sustained attention and/or adequate attention to detail.

Incompetent to Stand Trial (IST): a legal finding in which a given defendant is identified as lacking in the abilities necessary to meaningfully participate in a relevant stage(s) of the proceedings.

incomplete development: immaturity that is relative to fully developed adults. For example, all young children demonstrate an incomplete development of abstraction skills.

infancy defense: a claim that a juvenile within a statutorily defined age range (e.g., 7–14 years) was unable to understand the nature of the legal act or appreciate its wrongfulness because of developmental limitations. It is used to block an attempt by the state to overcome the presumption that youth within that age range are incapable of committing offenses.

informed consent: an individual's consent for another person to engage in intervention that would otherwise constitute an invasion of the individual's privacy, after the individual has been fully informed of the nature and consequences of the proposed action, is competent to consent, and consents voluntarily. Informed consent is not necessary on court-ordered or statutorily mandated evaluations in criminal or delinquency cases, or when authorized by legal counsel for the individual.

interpersonal perspective: the ability to take the perspective of another person.

judicial transfers: a court hearing–based discretionary decision process through which certain juvenile defendants can be "transferred" to criminal court where they are "tried as an adult."

juvenile court CST: the application of the CST doctrine to juvenile defendants who are being tried in juvenile court.

juvenile CST: the application of the CST doctrine to juvenile defendants regardless of the court jurisdiction within which the case is being adjudicated (i.e., juvenile court or adult criminal court).

juvenile CST in criminal court: the application of the CST doctrine to juvenile defendants who are being tried as an adult in criminal court.

legal-empirical-forensic model: a model described by Rogers and Shuman (2005) in which forensic evaluation opinions reflect understanding of the relevant legal standards and the application of empirically grounded methods and procedures to the specific case.

lower bar: a standard for the abilities required for juvenile court defendants to be found competent to stand trial that consists of the same basic abilities as those required of adult defendants in criminal court, but does not require those abilities to be as well developed.

notification of rights: an explanation to the youth prior to evaluation contacts and, in some cases, her caregivers, about the conditions and limits of confidentiality inherent in the evaluation; the notification is often memorialized in writing.

opinion and data model: an approach to forensic mental health evaluation report writing in which the discussion is structured around relevant evaluation questions, with each opinion presented with the data analyzed to reach that opinion.

parens patriae: a legal philosophy that affords courts the discretion of a benevolent parent and allows decisions to be based on the "best interests of the child."

perceptions and attitudes about risk: the extent to which evaluations of risk involve appropriate consideration of the range and likelihood of possible negative outcomes and a mature value system (e.g., self-preservation is more important than brief experiences of fun).

permanent incompetence: incompetence that cannot be successfully remediated within the time frames mandated by statute.

perspective taking: the extent to which individuals understand the complexity of a situation and are able to place it in a broader perspective (see *interpersonal perspective* and *temporal perspective*).

poor interpersonal relations: evidencing difficulty in social skills due to weaknesses in reading the social demands of situations, remembering appropriate responses to situations, and/or applying appropriate responses.

predicates: conditions that the law recognizes as relevant potential causes for incompetence. Traditional predicates include psychosis and mental retardation. A greater diversity of predicates, including other mental health issues and normal developmental limitations, may be appropriate for juvenile competence to stand trial.

qualifying the expert: the process of expert testimony through which the court determines if an examiner is qualified to be admitted as an expert witness in the case at hand.

response styles: the subtle or overt motivational approach used by an examinee during an evaluation that can significantly impact the data obtained. For example, some examinees may respond with full honesty and full effort, some may distort the results in an effort to appear a certain way, and others may put forth minimal effort in their responses.

temperance: the extent to which individuals are able to maintain emotional and behavioral control without the interference of significant impulsivity.

temporal perspective: the ability to appropriately consider both long- and short-term implications of decisions and actions.

threshold for questioning competence: the point at which questions about defendants competence are significant enough to warrant a competence evaluation; generally a low threshold.

typical development: development at a level commensurate with typical age-peers. For example, a child with an IQ of 100 is demonstrating typical development of overall intellectual abilities.

ultimate issue opinion: an opinion offered by an expert witness directly addressing the legal determination to be made by the court.

Understanding: one of four capacities typically associated with CST; the ability to possess, whether through prior knowledge or instruction, an understanding of the basic facts of the purpose and process of the legal proceedings in which they are participating (e.g., the role of a defense attorney).

without prejudice: a legal term used when charges are dismissed but allowances are made for the same charges to be brought again at a later date; in contrast to charges dismissed "with prejudice" that cannot be brought again.

Index

About the Authors

Ivan Kruh, PhD, is the Director of Forensic Services at the Child Study and Treatment Center (CSTC) in Tacoma, WA. He conducts preadjudication evaluations of juveniles (such as competence to stand trial, mental state at the time of the offense, and future violence risk) and provides competency remediation services to juveniles. He has offered scholarly publications and presentations about empirical findings and practice issues that have emerged from this work. He is also a clinical assistant professor in the Department of Psychiatry and Behavioral Sciences at the University of Washington, where he directs a postdoctoral fellowship in juvenile forensic psychology. In various contexts, he has provided training about the legal, clinical, and psycholegal aspects of conducting juvenile forensic evaluations to clinical trainees, seasoned clinicians, researchers, administrators, attorneys, and judges for almost 10 years.

Thomas Grisso, PhD, is Professor, Director of Psychology, and Director of the Law and Psychiatry Program at the University of Massachusetts Medical School. His research has examined the application of psychological assessment to questions of legal competencies, and application of clinical and developmental psychology to law, policy, and practice in juvenile justice. Among his 10 books are *Evaluating Competencies* (1986, 2003), *Forensic Evaluation of Juveniles* (1998), *Youth on Trial* (2000, edited with R. Schwartz), and *Double Jeopardy: Adolescent Offenders with Mental Disorders* (2004). He has received the American Psychological Association's award for Distinguished Contributions to Research in Public Policy (1994), an honorary Doctor of Laws degree from the John Jay College of Criminal Justice, City University of New York (1998), the American Psychiatric Association's Isaac Ray Award (2005), and the U.K.'s Royal College of Psychiatrists Honorary Fellow Award (2006). He has received the American Board of Professional Psychology's Award for Distinguished Contributions (2002) and currently is Executive Director of the American Board of Forensic Psychology.